NY 20'02			
DE 17 05			

*The Arab Minority in
Israel, 1967–1991*

The Arab Minority
in Israel, 1967–1991

Political Aspects

JACOB M. LANDAU

CLARENDON PRESS · OXFORD

1993

Oxford University Press, Walton Street, Oxford OX2 6DP
Oxford New York Toronto
Delhi Bombay Calcutta Madras Karachi
Kuala Lumpur Singapore Hong Kong Tokyo
Nairobi Dar es Salaam Cape Town
Melbourne Auckland Madrid
and associated companies in
Berlin Ibadan

Oxford is a trade mark of Oxford University Press

Published in the United States
by Oxford University Press Inc., New York

British Library Cataloguing in Publication Data
Data available

Library of Congress Cataloging in Publication Data
Landau, Jacob M.
The Arab minority in Israel, 1967–1991: political aspects/Jacob
M. Landau.
"This book is the successor to The Arabs in Israel, published in
1969 by Oxford University Press"—T.p. verso.
Includes bibliographical references.
1. Palestinian Arabs—Israel. 2. Israel—Ethnic relations.
3. Jewish–Arab relations—1967–1973– 4. Jewish–Arab
relations—1973– 5. a-is—— ma—— I. Landau, Jacob M. Arabs in
Israel. II. Title.
DS113.7.L28 1993 956.94'004927—dc20 92-26238
ISBN 0–19–827712–1

Typeset by Best-set Typesetter Ltd., Hong Kong
Printed in Great Britain
on acid-free paper by
Bookcraft (Bath) Ltd., Midsomer Norton, Avon

For Smadar and Inbal

Preface

Thanks, entailing no responsibility, are due for research grants from the Levi Eshkol Institute, the Harry S Truman Institute, the Central Authority for Research, and the Shaine Centre—all four at the Hebrew University of Jerusalem; to Ms Mira Reich, of Jerusalem, for editorial improvement of the typescript; and to the staff of the Oxford University Press, Oxford, for patiently attending to the publication of this volume.

J.M.L.

Jerusalem
January 1992

Contents

Tables

Abbreviations

DAP	Democratic Arab Party (al-Ḥizb al-Dīmuqrāṭī al-ʿArabī)
ḤADA<u>SH</u>	Ḥazīt Demōqraṭīt lĕ-<u>Sh</u>alōm w-Viṭaḥōn (Democratic Front for Peace and Security)
ICP	Israel Communist Party (ha-Miflaga ha-Qōmūnīsṭīt ha-Isrĕʾelīt)
ILP	Israel Labour Party (Mifleget ha-ʿAvōda)
MAPAI	Mifleget Pōʿaley Israʾel (The Workers' Party of Israel)
MAPAM	Mifleget Pōʿalīm Mĕʾūḥedet (United Workers' Party)
MK	Member of the Knesset
NRP	National Religious Party
PLO	Palestine Liberation Organization
PLP	Progressive List for Peace (al-Qāʾima al-Mutaqaddima li-ʾl-Salām)
RAQAḤ	Rĕ<u>sh</u>īma Qōmūnīsṭīt Ḥada<u>sh</u>a (New Communist List)

Introduction: Defining the Issues

The 'Arab problem', in so far as Israeli Jews are concerned, may be considered under three main headings—in the State of Israel itself, in the Israeli-held territories, and in the Middle East. Only the first will be discussed in this work, as each merits a separate study. The term 'Arab minority' here includes the Muslims, Christians, and Druzes living in Israel (although they are discussed separately, wherever relevant). It is recognized, of course, that some of the Druzes see themselves as Arabs, while others opt for a distinctive identity. Tiny groups without political influence, such as the Circassians,[1] Bahais, or Armenians, are not discussed.

Compared to other contemporary minorities, the Arab minority in Israel finds itself in a disparate situation which has an impact upon its characteristics and behaviour. Rare are the cases in which a numerically large group of Arabs finds itself a minority in a non-Arab state. Even more unusual is the phenomenon by which a two-thirds majority, in 1948, changed almost overnight into a minority of one-sixth within a state in which a sharp conflictual relation with the rest of the population had already developed. Even though most of the pre-1948 Arab political leaders did not remain in the new state, the memory of having been a political force persisted. No less significant is the fact that most of this minority is related ethnically, culturally, and linguistically, and to a great extent also by religion and national sentiments, to its kinsfolk beyond the political frontiers of the state it inhabits.

These particular conditions distinguish the Arab minority in Israel from the Jewish majority, to a large degree determining the complex reciprocal relationships within the state. While the Jewish majority perceives Israel as a Jewish state, the Arab minority relates to the large Arab masses beyond the borders, whose governments continue to consider themselves at war with the Jewish state. The issues consequent upon this situation have become aggravated since the June 1967 Six Day War, following which the Arabs in Israel entered into daily contact with those in the Israeli-held territories; and even more so since the start of the *intifāḍa*, or uprising, in

---

[1] For the Circassians, see Ōrī Sṭendel, *ha-Cherkesīm bě-Israeʾl* (1973).

these territories, in December 1987. The upsurge of nationalism in the territories has presented the Arabs in Israel with a bitter dilemma—whether to support their people or their state. In other words, they were faced with a conflict between a gut feeling and civic sentiments. The issue of identity, persisting for the Arabs since the first days of the State of Israel and intentionally or unintentionally repressed for a time, with more or less success, became unavoidable after 1967, all the more so since many people felt that their socio-economic and political expectations had remained unfulfilled. This phenomenon was strikingly brought to public attention in Israel during the 1991 Gulf War, when a part of the Arabs in Israel openly displayed their support for Ṣaddām Ḥusayn, most probably due to his promises to back Palestinian national hopes.

On the other hand, the Jewish majority has contributed, knowingly or unwittingly, to a growth in the feelings of alienation among the Arab minority. While in several areas such as security and education one notices more or less defined government policies regarding the Arab citizens in Israel, in most other matters they were left to fend for themselves, possibly in the naïve hope that with the years everything would be all right. This optimistic approach of delaying decisions, rarely successful anywhere in modern times, has proved unjustified in the Israeli context as well. At all events, this attitude of non-policy and postponement of problem resolution was forced, in part, on the Jewish majority by political cleavages and increasing tensions within Israeli Jewish society.

Tensions, even more prominent since the 1973 Yom Kippur War and the 1982 Lebanon War, encouraged a policy of *ad hoc* solutions to all problems which could not be relegated to some future date. There was a consistent absence of cogent decision-making concerning relations between the authorities and the Arab citizens, most particularly since political opinion in Israel reflects all possible shades in this matter. At one end of the spectrum, certain circles openly acknowledge that the Arabs in Israel do not enjoy equal opportunities in cultural and economic affairs; these are actively involved in efforts to redress this situation and to speedily achieve complete equality, for the benefit of both sectors. At the other end are those who argue that, since the Arabs do not share in the Israeli consensus on such central themes as security, settlement, and

Jewish immigration, nothing can be done to smooth the friction between the two sectors. These arguments are also partly reflected in the juridical status of the Arabs in Israel, which is equal to that of the Jews except in some matters connected with the Jewish character of the state, on the one hand, and security issues on the other—all of which frequently leads to heated public debate by lawyers and others.[2]

The study presented here is an entirely new work. In 1969, a volume of mine entitled *The Arabs in Israel: A Political Study* was published by the Royal Institute of International Affairs and Oxford University Press. This, however, focused on the first two decades of the State of Israel and ended with the 1967 War. Since then, in the following twenty-four years, much has changed within the Arab milieu in Israel, as already hinted above: the Arab population has increased visibly, its economic situation has improved, traditional social institutions have been weakened, a very large group of literate people has emerged, and a class of well-educated youngsters has grown up to compete with their Jewish counterparts in matters learned from them and from the lessons of politics in the neighbouring Arab states. The feelings of anomie of a part of these young people have prompted some extreme political views and behaviour: modernization has led to politicization and, apparently, to radicalization, in the attitudes of an important segment within the Arab minority in Israel. An attempt to assess this radicalization, chiefly in the last twenty-four years, is the main purpose of this book.

Although this work focuses on political aspects, a fairly broad background will be required, whose evaluation may shed additional light on the radicalization of these circles where political extremism is forcibly expressed. The present study will try to examine various aspects of the process of alienation among a part of the Arab minority, in the two main areas in which their expectations have not been fulfilled, in the radicals' view—achieving full equality in Israel, on the one hand, and promoting nationalist Arab aspirations, on the other. The main difference between these two sets of expectations of the Arab minority lies in the fact that the former is orientated internally towards Israel, while the latter has led, at least partly, to reservations about the Jewish-majority state or, at least,

[2] David Kretzmer, *The Legal Status of the Arabs in Israel* (1987), 1 ff.

about its methods of administering affairs. In other words, the term 'radicalization' will be applied to those political strategies which place less emphasis on the struggle for full equality as a requirement for coexistence between the two sectors in the State of Israel, but focus instead, or in addition, on forming a competing political entity, by separationist or irredentist tactics. Again, these questions are discussed solely with reference to the Arabs living in Israel proper, not to those in Israeli-held territories in the West Bank and the Gaza Strip. The Druzes in Israel are included, in an attempt to examine the delicate mechanisms of their relations with the Jews on the one hand and the Muslims and Christians on the other.

This study is based on close observation of the political behaviour of the Arab minority in Israel, its political organizations, its electoral trends, problems of identity, political struggles, and other domains; on an analysis of its diverse political views and attitudes, as expressed orally and in writing; and on personal discussions with many Arabs active in Israeli politics or intending to join them, mostly intellectuals and politicians. Obviously, the literature and press produced by the Arabs in Israel or about them have been scanned. Owing to limitations of space, the examination of these aspects, as well as others (economic, social, religious, and so on) has chiefly been done from the political perspective. Since the overall strategies which this minority has developed are the book's main concern, it was not possible to dwell on every single detail. An attempt has been made to present a picture focusing on the more significant aspects, in the most objective way that the materials at my disposal permitted. If the result will be to add to our knowledge of the subject, in a more balanced manner, this study may perhaps assist better understanding of the Arab minority in Israel and promote a smoother relationship between the country's ethnic, political, and religious groups.

1
Some Background Data

The rivalry between Jews and Arabs in the State of Israel has its roots in previous generations. It became sharper during British rule in Palestine (1917–48), owing to the inevitable collision course of two national movements over a relatively small piece of land. The Zionist movement, at least in the early years, demonstrated little awareness of the presence of Arabs in Palestine, noting this fact mostly only since the end of the First World War. The Palestinian Arabs never formed a political or administrative unit within the Ottoman Empire and there were very few indications of a national movement among them while under Turkish domination. Only the definition of Palestine as a separate administrative unit with the establishment of the British Mandate, and the suspicions of Palestinian Arab leaders as to the intentions of the Jewish immigration, aroused nationalist sentiments which, at least among Muslims, assumed a definitely religious character.[1]

Bloody riots in 1920 and 1929, and again from 1936 to 1939, not only added an element of physical violence to Arab nationalist activity in Palestine, but also enabled it to assume international dimensions: in a manner paralleling the support of the Jewish diaspora for the Jews in Palestine, the Arab states, mainly the neighbouring ones, assisted the local Arabs with funds, weapons, and diplomatic involvement. The last was expressed, among other ways, in the rejection by the Arab states of the November 1947 United Nations resolution to set up a Jewish and an Arab state in Palestine. The peak of involvement was military intervention by seven Arab states, whose armies invaded Palestine to thwart the carrying out of the UN resolution. These were Egypt, Syria, Lebanon, Jordan, Iraq, Saudi Arabia, and the Yemen. During

---

[1] Among the most useful works about the Arabs in British-ruled Palestine, see: Ya'aqōv Shim'ōnī, *'Arviyyey Eretz-Isra'el* (1947); Yōsef Waschītz, *ha-'Aravīm bĕ-Eretz-Isra'el* (1947); Michael Assaf, *Hit'ōrĕrūt ha-'Aravīm bĕ-Eretz-Isra'el w-vĕrīhatam* (1967); id., *ha-Yĕhasīm beyn 'Aravīm wĕ-Yĕhūdīm bĕ-Eretz-Isra'el (1860–1948)* (1970). Among the sources, particularly interesting is David Ben-Gurion's *Pĕgīshōt 'im manhīgīm 'Araviyyīm* (1967).

1948, the fighting divided Palestine, for all practical purposes, into Jewish and Arab parts—not according to the UN resolution, but rather along the *de facto* lines of the Armistice Agreements of 1949. Most Palestinian Arabs remained on those lands subsequently annexed by Jordan (the West Bank) or ruled by Egypt (the Gaza Strip), while some left for various Arab states (chiefly Lebanon, Syria, and Jordan) or for other countries.

In Israel there remained an Arab minority, mostly in the rural areas, after more than half the Arab population of the territory which formed the new state had left it.[2] Since then, numerous changes have occurred within the Arab population in Israel. Here reference will be made to statistical, demographic, and environmental changes, leaving other matters for the following chapters.[3]

The most obvious shift was in the sizeable numerical growth of the population, from 156,000 upon the establishment of the state (all of whom were granted Israeli citizenship)[4] to 875,000 at the beginning of January 1991.[5] Consequently, from the point of view of numbers, the Arabs in Israel nowadays constitute a critical mass out of the overall population of five million. There are several reasons for this increase:

1. High fertility: about 4 per cent annually in the first years of the state, one of the highest birth-rates in the world, and approximately three times the Jewish; in recent years, about 3.3

[2] The flight of the Arabs, in 1948–9, was larger in urban areas than in rural ones or in the Bedouin tribes. See Charles Qayman, 'Aḥarey ha-asōn: ha-ʿAravīm bimědīnat Isra'el 1948–1950', *Mahbarōt lě-Mehqar w-lě-vikkōret*, 10 (Dec. 1984). For an Arab interpretation of these events, see Mājid al-Ḥāj, 'al-Lājiʾūn al-ʿArab fī Isrāʾīl', *al-Mawākib*, 5/5–6 (May–June 1988), 12–22; D. Bensimon and E. Errera, *Israël et ses populations* (1977), 220 ff.

[3] In addition to the *Statistical Abstracts of Israel*, see also: Erīk Cohen and Hermōna Grūnau, *Seqer ha-mīʿūṭīm bě-Isra'el* (1972); ʿU. Schmelz, 'ha-Těnūʿa haṭivʿīt wě-gíddūl ha-ōkhlūsiyya', in Aharōn Layi̱sh (ed.), *ha-ʿAravīm bě-Isra'el: rětsīfūt w-těmūra* (1981), 11–45; Yechiel Harari, *The Arabs in Israel 1973: Statistics and Facts* (1974).

[4] Saʿīd Zaydānī, 'al-Muwāṭana al-dimuqrāṭiyya fī Isrāʾīl', *Qaḍāyā*, 4 (Aug. 1990), 3–18.

[5] Most of these data and the following ones are based on the publications of the Central Bureau of Statistics, Jerusalem. For an earlier period see Gad Gilbar, 'Měgammōt ba-hitpattěhūt ha-demōgrafīt ṣhel ʿArviyyey Eretz-Isra'el, 1870–1948', *Cathedra*, 45 (Sept. 1987), 43–56. Gilbar's study was also published in an enlarged form, *Měgammōt ba-hitpattěhūt ha-demōgrafīt ṣhel ha Palestīnīm, 1870–1987* (1989). See also ʿU. Schmelz, 'ha-Mivneh ha-demōgrafī ṣhel ha-ʿAravīm wě-ha-Děrūzīm bě-Isra'el', *ha-Mizrah he-Hada̱sh*, 28/III–12 (1979), 244–54. For earlier years, Maurice Krajzman, *La Minorité arabe en Israël* (1968).

per cent, roughly twice the Jewish rate. It is interesting to note that a number of Arab villages have the highest annual birthrate in the world; these are Kisra, Jisr al-Zarqa, Buʿayna and Najdat, all with approximately 5.5 per cent.

2. Considerable decline in disease and mortality, thanks to a continuous growth in health services and preventive medicine, prenatal counselling and postnatal care, and persuading mothers-to-be to give birth in hospital.

3. Officially authorized family reunions, by which about 40,000 Arabs returned to Israel during the 1950s.

4. Annexation of East Jerusalem to the State of Israel immediately after the end of the 1967 War, and the Golan Heights, with its Druze population, in 1981.

5. The low rate of Arab emigration, chiefly confined to Christian families and to university students who choose to remain abroad after concluding their studies.

What seems surprising, at first glance, is that the numerical ratio between Arabs and Jews has hardly changed: it was approximately 1:5 in 1949 and is 1:6 forty years later. The explanation is to be found in the large waves of Jewish immigration during the early 1950s, which continued, on a more modest scale, in subsequent years. Perhaps this ratio will now change, following the renewed Jewish immigration from the Commonwealth of Independent States (the former Soviet Union) and Ethiopia. It should be emphasized that these ratios refer to residents, not to citizens: about 20 per cent of the Arabs, comprising those in East Jerusalem and the Golan Heights, have consistently refused to accept the Israeli citizenship proposed to them (and hence they cannot vote in Israeli parliamentary elections).

Another characteristic of the Arab minority in Israel is its relative youth, again the result of the fairly large average family and the efficiency of public health services. Almost half the Arabs in Israel are aged 14 or less, compared to about a third of the Jews.[6] Life expectancy has also increased, approaching that of the Jews.

Not less interesting is the geographical spread of the Arabs in Israel, which can perhaps help to explain their politicization and radicalization. Their distinctive distribution patterns have altered

---

[6] Cf. ʿAmīhūd Isrěʾelī, ʿIfyūney ha-mīʿūṭīm bě-Israʾel bi-shěnōt ha-80', *Natīv*, 2/3 (May 1989), 17–26.

but little during the state's existence, owing to the limited rate of internal migration (unlike the pattern in many other countries). There were good reasons for people to remain in their villages and rural settlements—despite their reduced incomes, caused by high natural increase, the expropriation or sale of lands,[7] and the mechanization of agriculture. These reasons were as follows: (1) the small size of Israel and the consequent proximity of urban working sites to rural habitats; (2) the good network of speedy roads and the swift movement of traffic; (3) the high cost of living (in particular, rent) in towns and cities, compared to cost-free residence in the village home; (4) the construction of numerous new homes in the rural areas; (5) the desire to live within one's own group, for traditional reasons, and in order to enjoy particular religious and educational services.[8]

Most Arabs live in five areas: Galilee; Haifa and Mount Carmel; the Little Triangle; Jerusalem; and the Negev. Until the 1967 War, about 58 per cent lived in the Northern district and another 20 per cent in the Haifa district. The annexation of East Jerusalem brought about a relative proportional decline to about 47 per cent in the Northern district and some 16 per cent in the Haifa district, Jerusalem taking second place with approximately 18 per cent; since the reunification of Jerusalem, this district has more than a quarter of non-Jews among its inhabitants. Arabs and Druzes represent more than 60 per cent in the Acre sub-district and the Northern district. Most Arabs thus live in Central Galilee, up to the Lebanese frontier; in the Little Triangle, at the erstwhile border with Jordan (now near the West Bank); and to some extent in the Negev, in proximity to Israel's frontiers with Egypt and Jordan. All this has evident economic and security implications as well as possible grounds for future irredentist claims, calling for joining some Arab state, such as that of Palestine, if it is established. Attempts to settle Jews in some of these vulnerable areas have only partly succeeded, but they did not fail to irritate the local Arab inhabitants.

---

[7] Elie Rekhess, *'Arviyyey Isra'el wĕ-hafqaʿat ha-qarqaʿōt ba-Galīl* (1977). For land sales by the Greek Orthodox, see Yeraḥ Ṭal, 'Mōkhĕrīm et ha-kĕnesiyya', *ha-Aretz*, 24 Dec. 1990, B3.

[8] Cf. 'U. Schmelz, 'ha-Tifrōset ha-merhavīt shel ha-ʿAravīm wĕ-ha-Dĕrūzīm bĕ-Isra'el w-mĕ'afyĕney yishshūveyhem', *ha-Mizraḥ he-Ḥadash*, 29/113–16 (1980), 100 ff.

TABLE 1.1. All-Arab towns, 1 January 1991

Town	Inhabitants
Nazareth	53,600
Umm al-Faḥm	25,400
Ṭaiyyba	21,200
Shafā ʿAmr	20,900
Ṭira*	13,700

* In 1991, Ṭira, with its 16,000 inhabitants, became a town, too.

Source: Central Bureau of Statistics, *List of Localities, Their Population and Codes, 31. 12. 1990*, Technical Publications Series, no. 59 (Jerusalem: 1991).

TABLE 1.2. Arabs in mixed towns, 1 January 1991

Town	Arab population	Total population
Jerusalem	146,300	524,500
Haifa	22,300	245,900
Tel-Aviv–Jaffa	12,400	339,400
Acre	9,290	40,300
Lydda	8,990	43,300
Ramleh	7,980	47,900

Source: As Table 1.1.

Arabs reside in all-Arab or mixed towns, in villages, and in Bedouin encampments. Tables 1.1 and 1.2 show how the Arabs constitute a minority in all the mixed cities, albeit proportionally a sizeable one in reunited Jerusalem and somewhat less so in Acre, Lydda, and Ramleh. The rest live in about a hundred villages (half of them small), all of which are pure Arab (or Druze). In almost all of them one religious denomination predominates; thus the entire Little Triangle is inhabited by Muslims. The Bedouin live in both the Negev and Galilee, in their tent-encampments, a part of which

TABLE 1.3. Non-Jewish population in Israel, 1 January 1991

Religion	Population
Muslims (incl. East Jerusalem)	677,700
Christians (incl. East Jerusalem)	114,700
Druzes and others (incl. the Golan Heights)	82,600
TOTAL	875,000

Source: Statistical Abstract of Israel, 1991.

have been changed into sedentary homes; they, too, are exclusively Muslim. Maʿalōt-Tarshīḥa is the only large village made up of Arabs and Jews.

As we shall see, the religious community framework is significant in determining the political attitudes and involvement of the Arabs in Israel. Earlier, during Ottoman rule, the religious community decided not merely the particular areas traditionally allotted to it by the government—such as the administration of religious institutions and all matters of personal status—but social and economic life as well. The British Mandate maintained these arrangements and the State of Israel inherited them. In recent years, new elements have been introduced by the younger population whose obedience to the religious community leaders has somewhat slackened, but religious affiliation still counts. The religious community continues to provide an institutional framework for political activities, frequently tied to economic ones. Table 1.3 divides the minorities by religious affiliation.[9]

[9] Only the major denominations, which have political importance, are listed, without referring to tiny ones, such as the Bahais.

2

Economic Trends and their Implications

INTRODUCTORY

During the first forty years of the State of Israel, the economic situation of most Arabs visibly improved, their income rising sharply thanks to general economic growth. None the less, many Arabs consider themselves discriminated against in their economic advance, compared with the Jews,[1] and these do not necessarily consist only of those whose personal situation is unsatisfactory—of whom there are quite a few as well.[2] From the perspective of political implications, it matters little whether these feelings are statistically provable or merely imaginary; personal and public sentiments often have more political impact than do facts. At all events, the expectations of certain Jewish political leaders, in earlier years, that economic prosperity would strengthen the Arabs' identification with the state remain doubtful, to say the least.

Both Jewish and Arab sectors enjoyed a large measure of economic autarchy under British rule in Palestine, with each striving (for its own reasons) to be independent of the other. In addition, only limited economic relationships existed between the main blocs of Arab settlement in British-governed Palestine, that is, Galilee, the Triangle, and Negev, and so forth. To a lesser degree, this situation continues in Israel, in which the main Arab economic

---

[1] Cf. Aḥmad Saʿd, 'al-Awḍāʿ al-iqtiṣādiyya li-'l-jamāhīr al-ʿArabiyya fī Isrāʾīl', in Khālid Khalīfa (ed.), Filasṭīniyyūn 1948–1988 (1988), 107–25.

[2] For data about Arabs living under the poverty line, see A. Kaspī, 'Mĕgayyrīm et qav ha-ʿōnī', ha-Aretz, 1 Dec. 1989, Suppl., 9. For slums in Acre, N. Kahanā, 'Raq vīlōn mafrīd beyn mishpaḥa lĕ-mishpaḥa', ibid. 16 Oct. 1989, 11. See also ʿAzīz Ḥaydar, 'Maẓāhir al-faqr bayn al-ʿArab fī Isrāʾīl', al-Aswār, 1 (Spring 1988), 39–55. Aḥmad Ḥusayn Saʿdī, 'al-Faqr fī al-wasaṭ al-ʿArabī: al-ʿArab aqalliyya bayn al-sukkān wa-akthariyya bayn al-fuqarāʾ", al-Jadīd, 2 (Mar. 1990), 39–51. In the teeth of the law and court rulings, there have been cases when Arabs have been underpaid, see Ruth Klinov, 'Yĕhūdīm wa-ʿAravīm bĕ-khōaḥ ha-ʿavōda ha-Isrĕʾelī', Rivʿōn lĕ-Khalkala, 145 (Aug. 1990), 130–44.

blocs are East Jerusalem; the Negev Bedouin; the Arabs of Lydda, Ramleh, Tel-Aviv–Jaffa, Haifa, and Acre; the Little Triangle, ceded to Israel in 1949; and Central Galilee.[3]

Upon the establishment of the State of Israel, the general economic situation of the Arabs changed, owing in particular to impoverishment (following the emigration of the wealthy and the flight of their capital) and the break in relations with the Arab states (which had provided support and investments).

The Jewish sector, which, as a majority, dominated the key economic positions in the state it had set up, was naturally responsible for the economy of the Arab sector, and strove to integrate it. This process was a slow one,[4] owing to the need to care for the absorption of the numerous Jewish immigrants in the 1950s, and to instruct them and the local Arabs in new skills in agriculture and other domains. With the acquisition of such skills in agriculture, various urban occupations, and the liberal professions, the Arabs became increasingly integrated into the Israeli economy, in both public and private sectors. Upon the termination of the Military Administration in Arab-populated border areas—imposed, for security reasons, during the 1948 War and maintained until December 1966—the Arabs could move freely to any place in the country; their joining the Histadrut (the Trade Union Organization) improved both their standing and their income. The economic change was better felt in the private than in the public sector.

Economically, the Arab sector is still largely dependent on the Jewish; while there does not seem to have been any deliberate policy to create this situation, neither do the authorities appear to have exerted themselves to prevent it. The incontrovertible fact remains that, some forty years after the establishment of the state, the average personal income of the Arabs remains below that of the Jews. They still do not own economically significant enterprises—whether industrial, financial, or commercial—and this naturally reinforces the disparity. The figures shown in Table 2.1 indicate

---

[3] Avraham Cohen, ʿArviyyey Israʾel: heybeṭim kalkaliyyim (1986), 3–11.

[4] For criticism regarding the economic progress of the Arab minority, Aziz Haidar, *The Arab Population in the Israeli Economy* (1990), 3–14, 129; Elia Zureik, 'Crime, Justice and Underdevelopment: The Palestinians under Israeli Control', *International Journal of Middle East Studies*, 20/4 (Nov. 1988), 411–42.

TABLE 2.1. Urban households in deciles of net overall income of head of household, 1986–1987 (%)

	Deciles									
	Lowest	2	3	4	5	6	7	8	9	Highest
Jews	55.1	78.0	88.3	90.1	92.9	94.6	97.2	98.0	99.0	99.8
Non-Jews	44.9	22.0	11.7	9.9	7.1	5.4	2.8	2.0	1.0	0.2

Note: The *Abstract* defines as 'urban' any settlement of 2,000 people or more; hence the table comprises most of Isreal's inhabitants, Jews and Arabs alike.

Source: *Statistical Abstract of Israel, 1988*, 294–5, table XI/1.

that, as the deciles of income rise, they increasingly comprise more Jews and fewer Arabs, proportionately.

The structure of the Arab labour force has changed perceptibly in the State of Israel. The proportion of working women has slowly risen to 15 per cent. More than a half of this labour force, men and women, are in the age group 18–34; the ratio of still younger workers declines in this context, due to the post-primary schooling which is open to all. The ratio of the over-55 group has declined as well. So has the ratio of those lacking any schooling (as their numbers diminish in the Arab sector), while the ratio of those with post-primary, secondary, and university education has risen visibly. Concomitantly with the rise in the ratio of these and other educated persons, that of the non-trained has dropped.[5] A contributory cause to this process may be found in the entry of inhabitants from the Israeli-held territories into the Israeli labour market, usually in 'lower' categories of work,[6] which has brought about the upgrading of workers from amongst the Arab minority in Israel, part of them willingly renouncing untrained jobs,[7] particularly in the years of economic growth and prosperity. The main economic change was expressed in the Arab sector in agriculture, employment in con-

[5] For statistical details, Avraham Cohen (n. 3 above), 21–34; Yoram Ben-Porat, *The Arab Labor Force in Israel* (1966); 'U. Schmelz, 'Kōaḥ ha-ʿavōda', in A. Layish (ed.), *ha-ʿAravīm bĕ-Israʾel* (1981), 46–75.

[6] See e.g. Mifqedet Ezor Rĕtsūʿat ʿAzza—Statistīqa, *Muʿasaqīm bĕ-Israʾel: metsīʾūt wĕ-pōtentsyal*.

[7] Moshe Semyonov and Noah Lewin-Epstein, *Hewers of Wood and Drawers of Water* (1987).

TABLE 2.2. Factories in the Arab sector of Israel, 1990

Manufacture	No.
Textiles, clothing	227
Wood products	164
Food Products	156
Building	146
Iron and metal products	81
Paper and printing	36
Electronics	8
Chemicals	7
Glass and jewellery	4
TOTAL	829

Source: Data of the Jaffa Research Center, Nazareth, 1990.

struction work in the village, and the penetration of technology.[8]
The limited extent of industrialization is reflected in Table 2.2.

AGRICULTURE

Arab agriculture in Israel has declined in both area and the number
of those employed in it, in no small degree owing to land expropriations in the first years of the state (and later, if less).[9] While in
the 1960s and 1970s, 54 per cent of all Arabs in Israel were still
employed in agriculture, the figure fell to a mere 7.2 per cent in
1989.

Moreover, Arab agriculture has passed from conservative
farming, mainly supplying the needs of the farmer and his family,
to a system specializing in a small number of domains, employing
innovative, mechanized methods. In practice, Arab farmers in
Israel have accepted all the inputs of modern technology; the use of
fertilizers and of means of preventing crop diseases and parasites

---

[8] ʿAzīz Haydar, 'ha-ʿAvōda ha-ʿAravīt', Pōlīṭiqa, 21 (July 1988), 24–7.
[9] Ran Kislev, 'Land Expropriation: History of Oppression', New Outlook, 19/169
(Sept.–Oct. 1976), 23–32.

has become standard practice. Perhaps the most striking innovation is their move to profitable out-of-season crops, especially export-orientated. Their farming has become intensive rather than otherwise, and co-operative organizations[10] for water supply and produce-marketing have become common; indeed Arab agriculture has increasingly come to resemble the Jewish.[11]

EMPLOYMENT

Arab employment has been changing in character and dimensions,[12] but still it seems that the Arabs have fewer opportunities than Jews to get into profitable, well-paid jobs.[13] Investments in Israeli industry have been growing since the 1950s so that expanding, unsophisticated, enterprises have needed an increasing number of workers, including the unskilled. Many of these were recruited from the Arabs, who found jobs in industry while maintaining their ties to their own villages, chiefly in years of full employment, such as 1963–6. Thus an Arab industrial proletariat began to be formed in the villages without, however, showing signs of urbanization.[14] In 1966 an economic recession started, which brought about sizeable unemployment of unskilled Arab workers, who returned to their villages, reintegrating into their extended families.

This, however, was a short-lived phenomenon, since an economic upsurge became evident after the 1967 War, as already mentioned. Nevertheless, even then a serious problem remained—and is felt to this day—namely, the unemployment of the well-educated, chiefly in jobs appropriate to their skills, teaching excepted. According to the estimate of a well-versed Member of the Knesset (further: MK), Ra'anan Cohen, about 40 per cent of the Arabs

[10] Makhōn Isrĕ'elī lĕ-mehqar w-meyda', *ha-Qŏ'ŏperatsiyya ha-'Aravīt: mehqar hevratī-kalkalī* (1972); Gideon Weigert, 'Arab–Jewish Economic Cooperation in Israel', *Die Welt des Islams*, NS 8/4 (1963), 243–51.

[11] For a different view, Ibrāhīm Mālik, 'al-Zirā'a al-'Arabiyya fī Isrā'īl—mu'ālaja awwaliyya', *al-Jadīd*, 3–4 (Mar.–Apr. 1976), 100–11.

[12] For details, Joseph Ginat, *Ta'asūqa kĕ-gōrem lĕ-shinnuy hevratī ba-kĕfar ha-'Aravī* (1980).

[13] Vered Kraus, 'The Opportunity Structure of Young Israeli Arabs', in John Hofman *et al.*, *Arab–Jewish Relations in Israel* (1988), 67–91.

[14] Nejwa Makhul, 'Changes in the Employment Structure of Arabs in Israel', *Journal of Palestine Studies*, 11/3 (Spring 1982), 77–102, esp. 81.

TABLE 2.3. Employment of minorities in eight governmental departments, 1987

Ministry/Department	Total employees (nos.)	Members of minorities (nos.)	% Minorities in Total
Treasury:			
Customs and VAT	1,747	35	2.0
Income Tax &			
Property Tax	3,598	213	5.9
Health	19,624	1,148	5.9
Religious	80	1	1.3
Education and Culture (Inspectors and teachers excepted)	1,667	21	1.3
Agriculture	2,420	75	3.1
Justice	922	7	0.8
Interior	774	29	3.7
TOTAL	30,832	1,529	5.0

who have earned degrees in Israeli institutions of higher education are unemployed.[15] This situation is also reflected in the report of a public committee of experts appointed on 27 June 1986 by the Prime Minister and the Minister of Finance, to carry out a far-reaching investigation into the civil service. The committee, in turn, appointed on 8 September 1987 a subcommittee made up of Jews, Arabs, and Druzes to ascertain the status of the minorites in the civil service. The data which the subcommittee collected from the various ministries, updated to 31 March 1987, are given in Table 2.3, which shows that the share of minority members in the civil service is considerably lower than their proportionate number in the population as a whole. It is, in this sample, between 0.8 per cent and 5.9 per cent, averaging 5 per cent.[16] Moreover, the data do not comprise the State President's office, the Knesset admin-

---

[15] Ra'anan Cohen, 'Ma shelō' na'aseh ha-yōm yiqsheh lĕtaqqen maḥar', *Davar*, 16 Nov. 1989, 5.

[16] See 'Amōs Gilbō'a, 'Ta'asūqa la-'Aravīm', *Ma'arīv*, 1 June 1990, E4.

istration, the employees of the State Comptroller's office, soldiers and civilians in Israel's Defence Forces, the Ministry of Defence, teachers, policemen, and gaolers. Amongst all these, teachers excepted, the number of Arabs is very small and, had these bodies been included in the above sample, the ratio of Arab employees would have been much less than the given 5 per cent. Even more noticeable was their tiny number among senior civil service officials; in 1987, in the Ministries of Interior, Education, and Culture, 0; Justice, 1; Department of Customs, 4; Income Tax, 1—and only in the Ministry of Health, 31. Even when one takes into consideration the limitations regarding employment in Israel's Defence Forces and the Ministry of Defence, as well as the fact that the large majority of the inhabitants of East Jerusalem refuse to accept Israeli citizenship (and are consequently barred from a permanent job in the civil service), the employment problems besetting the Arabs are clear, mainly with regard to senior positions, which the better-educated would like to fill.

BUILDING HOMES

Continued residence in the villages, and returning to them in times of urban unemployment, along with population increase and growth in economic prosperity, have caused an urgent need for new dwellings. In Israel, the proceedings for obtaining building permits are long-drawn-out, equally so in the Arab and Jewish sectors. However, some Arabs believe that the responsible authorities are particularly unresponsive and create difficulties in granting them such permits, especially since zoning plans are still incomplete in many of their localities.[17] These assumptions have encouraged a wave of speedy home-construction, partly without bothering at all with permits. At least some of these houses were built on public land. All this has resulted in frequent quarrels and arguments with the authorities, who obtain demolition orders from the courts.[18] The large wave of Jewish immigration in 1990 perforce simplified the bureaucratic procedures affecting building-permits, and this

[17] For examples, Ran Kislev, *Hem wĕ-anaḥnū: 'Aravīm bĕ-Isra'el* (1987), 16–17.
[18] Mĕdīnat Isra'el—Misrad ha-Pĕnīm, *Dīn wĕ-ḥeshbōn ha-vĕ'ada ha-beynmisradīt li-vĕniyya biltī-ḥuqqīt ba-migzar ha-'Aravī* (1986); Yosef Goell, 'Demolition Disorders', *Jerusalem Post*, 20 Dec. 1985, 5–6.

brought some relief to the Arab population as well.[19] Most recently, many Arab villages have been sporting new suburbs, more modern and inhabited by younger groups, less dependent on the extended family or on religious ties in mixed villages. The architectural styles and public services, which imitate the Jewish ones, indicate a rise in standards of living.[20] In earlier years Arab villages had lagged considerably behind Jewish localities in terms of road network, electricity, sewage, and telephones. None the less, the industrialization of Arab villages, which could introduce economic prosperity and reduce unemployment, is only in its infancy,[21] despite various expectations expressed from time to time.[22]

ECONOMICS AND POLITICS

One can distinguish, on the economic level, between the main religious communities—Christian, Muslim, and Druze.

The Christians, despite their being divided among different denominations, and their isolation from their Jerusalem centres until 1967, have been economic leaders among the minority group, thanks to their better education, prominence in the liberal professions, and relative wealth. Many are townspeople, and only a few are farmers. While these factors assisted them economically, they also brought about political awareness and activity—nationalist or Marxist.

The Muslims generally—at least, until recently—lagged behind the Christians, educationally and economically; they comprise proportionately more farmers than the Christians and, besides, they include the nomadic Bedouin. The Muslims are divided, ideologically and politically, among fundamentalists, nationalists, and leftists. Their power derives from their forming the largest group among Israel's minorities and in their perception that

[19] 'Aṭallāh Manṣūr, 'ha-Taqqanōt ha-ḥadashōt yaqellū 'al rishshūm mivnīm bamigzar ha-'Aravī', *ha-Aretz*, 2 Jan. 1991, A5.

[20] A. Enden and A. Soffer, *Degem shĕkhūnōt ḥadashōt bi-kĕfarīm 'Araviyyīm bitsĕfōn Isra'el* (1986).

[21] Rāsim Khamāyisī, 'al-Mubādara al-dhātiyya wa-taṣnī' al-qarya al-'Arabiyya', *al-Mawākib*, 2/9–10 (Sept.–Oct. 1985), 16–24; N. Fabian, 'Ḥevley tey'ūs ba-kĕfar ha-'Aravī', *ha-Aretz*, 19 Aug. 1970, 5.

[22] e.g. Ōrī Sṭendel and Emmanūel ha-Rĕ'ūvenī, *ha-Mī'ūṭīm bĕ-Isra'el* (1973), 67–70.

they have great numbers of potential allies, especially since the annexation of East Jerusalem and the disappearance, for most practical purposes, of the 'Green Line' which until 1967 denoted the frontiers between Israel and the neighbouring states.

The Druzes are the smallest group among the minorities. Most of them are villagers; their education, under British rule, was usually no more than rudimentary. Although the state authorities have repeatedly moved to assist them, many of them maintain that their villages suffer from underdevelopment, lack of industrialization, and unemployment. Further, working away from their villages contributes to the disintegration of their traditional institutions, and leads to a rise in their political awareness.

As mentioned above, the relative decline of agriculture affecting all minority groups in Israel was caused not only by the preference of many for other occupations (some of which are urban-orientated), but also by land expropriation. This has been a sensitive subject, both economically and politically. Jewish-owned lands have been expropriated as well, for public purposes, but the relation of Arab villagers to their land was apparently stronger—and it must have been galling to them that the expropriation was ordered by foreigners, the Jewish authorities of the state. Adroit speakers described this as a dark plot, fanning politicization. On 30 March 1976, a 'Land Day' was organized, repeated annually on the same date, in mass strikes and demonstrations with radical ingredients, with slogans against discrimination and for nationalism vying with one another.

The expropriation of land has remained a conflictual area in the relations between the Israeli government and the Arab minority throughout,[23] even at times when no expropriation was being carried out. Various laws and moves were interpreted—sometimes justifiably—as schemes aimed at the expropriation of Arab lands, unrelated to public needs. There is no doubt, indeed, that in certain instances Arab lands were confiscated in order to establish Jewish settlements, as in Galilee in the cases of Upper Nazareth and Carmiel. This was widely interpreted by the Arabs as a political, no less than an economic move—to strengthen the Jewish presence in Galilee. Hence reactions, also, were political. The compensation paid by the state was considered inadequate by its recipients; even when adequate, most proprietors would have preferred to keep their lands rather than get the financial equivalent. Alternative land was not always easily available, and the land–population ratio worsened in the Arab sector, largely owing to its high rate of demographic growth.

At the same time population increase was probably the main factor for Arabs seeking jobs outside the villages, chiefly in Jewish and mixed towns, exploiting proximity to these towns and the availability of speedy transportation. A reciprocal dependence has been fashioned between the Arab and Jewish sectors, with the former worried about the durability of this dependence, well aware that it would be the first to suffer financially in any unemployment-producing economic crisis. Such worries, and the need, in external work, of fending for oneself (not, as formerly, within a village collective), have brought about the individualization of these workers, sharpening their political awareness.

A frequently heard complaint is that industrial enterprises in the Arab villages are few and small, perhaps some 410 in all, employing only about 8,000 workers,[24] a number representing no more than 6 per cent of the Arab labour force in the state. When, in recent years, both the government and the Histadrut began to acknowledge the need for developing Arab villages industrially, they lacked sufficient funds to achieve this.[25] Recent studies indicate that many of the existing enterprises are family-operated: the capital is provided from within the family and increased by small short-term loans (there is a general aversion to mortgaging one's property for long-term loans); the entrepreneur and workers, too, are often members of the same family. A resulting phenomenon is the lack of professionalism: while there is readiness to absorb new information, sufficient funds and appropriate specialization are wanting, along with a proper grasp of the importance of advertising. The general feeling in the villages that little, if anything, is going to change in the situation breeds additional politicization based on

[24] Other data refer to 600 enterprises, but even this calculation attributed to them only 6% of the Arab labour force in Israel. See Yeraḥ Tal, 'ha-Paʿar yigdal, ha-tsĕfīfūt tigbar', *ha-Aretz*, 2 Jan. 1991, B3.

[25] M. M. Brōdnītz and Daniel Chemansky, 'Teyʿūs ha-kĕfar ha-ʿAravī bĕ-Israʾel', *Rivʿōn lĕ-Khalkala*, 128 (Apr. 1986), 533–46; eid., *Piqqūaḥ kalkalī ba-migzar ha-ʿAravī bĕ-Israʾel* (1986), App. 2.

discontent. The same is true of the relatively numerous graduates of secondary schools and universities who, unemployed (except in teaching), continue to reside in their own villages.

As already indicated, Land Day of 30 March 1976 was a watershed in the relations between Jews and Arabs in the State of Israel. Land expropriations in Galilee were interpreted as aimed at creating Jewish security belts in sensitive areas, as part of a general plan to ensure a Jewish majority in every single region—at the expense of Arab landed property.[26] Government moves, whether so intended or not, were exploited by the more extreme Arab political elements to unite moderates and radicals. Among these elements were the Israeli Communist Party, groups of intellectuals, religious figures, heads of municipalities and local authorities, and others. The strikes and demonstrations assumed a violent character and were carried out via clashes with the police and the border guards. Six Arabs were shot dead and there were many wounded on both sides. Although moderation later prevailed, expressed in more conciliatory relations between the branches of the government and the leaders of the Arab minority, every 30 March, in subsequent years, was again a rallying-point, albeit a less violent one. Several administrative organs, spontaneously set up on the eve of 30 March 1976 to co-ordinate attitudes and activities, continued to function as semi-official bodies (although not recognized as such by the government). Moreover, the state authorities allotted lands (out of state properties) to the Arab sector, for farming and building, which brought about a cooling-off of tempers. Still, one should remember that of all the economic grievances of the Arabs in Israel, land expropriation was that which propelled them from political passivity and quiet protest to political activism and organized confrontation with the representatives of the authorities, on a wider national scale—in both Galilee and the Little Triangle—for what was called 'Defence of the Lands'.

Interestingly enough, in the last few years this process has taken on a new shape, in an inverted direction. A number of Jewish *moshavim*, or co-operative settlements, unable to pay back the large bank loans they had taken, and in a state of economic collapse, rent

---

[26] Interpretations concerning land expropriation as government policy vary. See e.g. Aḥmad Saʿd, ʿal-Awdaʿ al-iqtiṣādiyyaʾ (n. 1 above), in K̲h̲ālid K̲h̲alīfa (ed.), *Filasṭīniyyūn 1948–1988* (1988), 107 ff. Cf. Rāsim Ḥamāyisī, *Tik̲h̲nūn wĕ-shikkūn bĕ-qerev ha-ʿAravīm bĕ-Israʾel* (1990).

their lands to Arabs, who thus become *de facto* owners. The process
was defined by Hillel Adīrī, Assistant to the Minister of Agriculture, as follows: 'The class of the Arab *Efendi*, owner of capital and
head of a large family which assists him in farming, has risen
anew . . . he provides the Jewish farmer with easy-term financing,
rents the land from him or its produce, and takes care of all the
rest: ploughing, sowing, irrigating, harvesting, and marketing.'[27]

In recent months, parts of the Arab sector have reasserted
their feelings of economic inferiority versus the Jewish sector by
expressing the anxiety that the large Jewish immigration since 1990
will redirect increased resources to the absorption of the newcomers
at the expense of the Arab minority—in allocating lands for
building, constructing new housing developments with the required infrastructure, setting up enterprises, and creating additional jobs.[28] Militant Arab groups, such as the Sons of the Village
and several Islamic Movement spokesmen (to be discussed later)
have openly proclaimed their opposition to mass Jewish immigration, basing themselves on economic reasons and consequently
on political ones—all the while ignoring the fact that most of the
direct financial burden for absorbing the new immigrants will be
borne by the Jewish, rather than the Arab, sector.

Nevertheless, there is some basis for the apprehensions of certain
groups among the liberal professions. For example, a survey
carried out by the Israel Institute of Technology in Haifa and Koor
Industries, concerning employment in some of those groups, found
that in 1984–6 439 Arab engineers were looking for jobs and that
their chances of finding employment in Arab enterprises then were
slim.[29] It is easy to understand those anxious about the arrival since
1990 of thousands of Jewish engineers from the Commonwealth of
Independent States. Worries about the effect of this Jewish mass
immigration are felt among other circles as well within the Arab
sector, which blame the immigrants for their unemployment (not
always justifiably, since the new immigrants, too, are jobless).[30]
There were even a few instances when Arab physicians and others

[27] Alūf Ben, 'ha-ʿAravīm ḥōzrīm el ha-qarqaʿ', *ha-Aretz*, 31 Aug. 1990, B5.
[28] Avīva Shābī, 'Me-ʿōleh lĕ-ʿoleh asōnenū ʿōleh', *Yĕdīʿōt Aharōnōt*, 23 Nov.
1990, 6–7.
[29] Brōdnītz and Chemansky, *Piqqūaḥ kalkalī* (n. 25 above), App. 5, esp. 118.
[30] Sufyān Kabhā, 'Ma yeytse la-ʿAravīm me-ha-ʿaliyya?', *ha-Aretz*, 7 Dec. 1990,
B3.

were dismissed from their jobs, apparently in order to allocate them to Jewish immigrants.[31] Even if these cases are isolated and certainly do not reflect general trends, it is none the less true that, since the 1980s, relative unemployment has risen in the Arab sector, whose economic level is undoubtedly better than in the Israeli-held territories, but has not reached that of the Jewish population.[32] The core of the matter remains that, in the absence of economic growth and under the impact of increasing unemployment, the weaker groups among the Arabs and parts of the Jewish population are suffering.

---

[31] A. Dayyan, 'ha-Mĕnahel qara᾽ lo wĕ-amar, mitsṭaʿer, illūts taqtsīvī', *ha-Aretz*, 21 Dec. 1990, Suppl., 9, 11.
[32] For details, Y. Algazī, 'Pōʿalīm kaḥōl-lavan', ibid. 28 Mar. 1991, B1.

3

Religious Communities and Politics

INTRODUCTORY

For many generations, religion has had a decisive impact on the life
of Palestine's inhabitants; it is still very significant in many domains,
including the political. As already remarked, every religious
community to a large degree enjoyed autonomous administration
and lawcourts; this situation persists in the State of Israel. Even
though changes in social life, state economics, and education
have brought about a measure of modernization which has to
some extent eroded its former exclusive domination, religion has
maintained itself as a powerful factor. This particularly applies
to the religious communities institutionalized in a pyramidal
hierarchy, such as the Christian, but it holds true, *grosso modo*, for
the Muslims and Druzes as well.[1]

The modernizing facts of life of Israeli society have somewhat damaged the authoritative status of religion among Israel's
minorities no less than among the Jews; more so in the towns,
where secondary and higher education have had an impact on this
process. Structural change in the extended family, or *hamula*,
affected the standing of the religious leaders in every community,
in varying degrees. In more than one way, the religious tolerance
demonstrated by the Israeli authorities, the jealous preservation of
all holy places, the continued respect shown to the heads of all
denominations and their spiritual leaders, as well as fostering a
pluralistic society as far as possible in an era of protracted warfare,
mitigated the decline in the social and political status of religion.
However, increasing contacts between Arab youngsters and Jewish
society (decisively secular), the changes in the structure of the
Arab labour force (reducing financial dependence on heads of
families), the presence of the media (reaching every single home,
both Arab and Jewish) and the service of the Druzes in Israel's

---

[1] Z. Vīlnāy, *ha-Mi'ūṭīm bĕ-Isra'el* (1959); Krajzman, *La Minorité arabe* (Ch. 1 n. 5
above), 30–9.

Defence Forces—all these could not but influence the trend towards secularization and the concurrent decline in the status of institutionalized religion as a leadership factor. The fact that an important share of political activity moved away from traditional structures, such as *hamula* heads and religious leaders, to modern structures, such as political parties and social and economic organizations, brought about the rise of elements competing with the religious leadership, even causing a certain devaluation in religious power as a unifying factor.

Paradoxically, perhaps, owing to the tolerant attitude of the Israeli authorities and of the public, there have been cases of religion clashing with the state laws, as also in several of the Arab states. For example, one may mention the progressive laws relating to women's rights, including monogamy. Other instances refer to religious criticism of the ban on under-age marriages or of public education, overwhelmingly secular. Under Israeli law, it is generally the laws of the state which determine the issue. Hence, it is perhaps no accident that religion is again becoming a uniting nationalist force for the minorities, since it serves as a consolidating element within each denomination, distinguishing it from the Jewish majority in the State of Israel.

THE MUSLIMS

The Muslims have been and still are the largest group within the Arab minority in Israel.[2] According to the 1961 census, their number was 170,830, constituting 7.8 per cent of the entire population and 69.1 per cent of the non-Jews. Since then, thanks to their relatively high natural increase and the 1967 annexation of East Jerusalem, their number has reached (all data correct for 1 January 1991) 677,700, that is, 14 per cent of the entire population and 77.5 per cent of the non-Jews. Since this is a homogeneous population denominationally—almost without exception Sunnite—it demonstrates considerable solidarity in matters bearing on religion. This seems more significant, in the long run, than eco-

---

[2] A useful summary by J. Yĕhōshūʿa, *ha-ʿEda ha-Mŭslĕmīt bĕ-Israʾel* (1973). On their denominational organization, see A. Layish, 'ha-Irgūn haʿadatī shel ha-Mŭslĕmīm', in Layish (ed.), *ha-ʿAravim bĕ-Israʾel* (1981), 104–22.

logical or occupational differences (farmers, townspeople, Bedouin). The Israeli authorities have striven to define and consolidate the administrative structures of the Muslim community and to endow its religious courts with clear-cut powers (chiefly in the *Qadis'* Law, of providing for Muslim religious judges), so that they could continue to deal with all matters already under their jurisdiction during the British Mandate era. This had to be done in view of the desire of the authorities to guarantee a full religious life to all the state's inhabitants, despite the departure in 1948 of many religious officials. As early as 1949, advisory committees, made up of Muslims, were set up in Jaffa, Ramleh, Lydda, Haifa, and Acre, to counsel the state authorities in all matters pertaining to the religious life of their community. None the less, many Muslims expressed dissatisfaction with this procedure by which (so they argued) a non-Muslim institution (the Ministry of Religions in Israel) and a non-Muslim parliament (the Knesset) determine their religious organs. Muslims have demanded, time and again, the right to administer their own religious and spiritual affairs.[3] The feelings of solidarity particular to Muslims in Israel are also due to Islam's being a definitely political religion (without any separation between religion and state); to their residing in fairly monolithic units (in the Negev, the Little Triangle, and their own quarters in Galilee towns and villages); and to the fact that large masses of Muslims live in the surrounding countries, their brothers in religion (and sometimes even blood-kinsmen). Otherwise said, more than other components of the Arab population, Muslims feel that, although a minority in the State of Israel, they constitute a majority in the Middle East as a whole. These feelings have been strengthened further by the fact that in the Middle East Arab nationalist movements have often been inspired by Islam, expressing themselves at times in Islamic terms. Although it seemed in the first three decades of the state that the attachment of Muslims to their religion had been somewhat weakened in Israel, owing to the inroads of modernization, in the fourth decade and the beginning of the fifth, religious awakening became pronounced, expressed in a return to Islam and in the permeation by political Islam of public and private life, as will be described later in the present chapter.

[3] 'Aṭallāh Manṣūr, 'Eyn hakkara memshaltīt ba-'eda ha-Mūslēmīt', *ha-Aretz*, 8 Sept. 1985, 9.

The Muslim community may provide a good illustration of the overall situation of the Arab minority in the State of Israel. As already mentioned, the patterns of self-administration were inherited by Israeli rule from the British Mandate, but with some altered emphases. Politically, special significance attaches to *shar'ī* law, the canonical law (or *sharī'a*) of Islam. This is implemented by a network of religious courts, presided over by the *qadis*, the highest Muslim officials recognized by Israel. They decide on matters of the *waqf* (inalienable religious endowments) and of personal status. Concerning the special standing of the *qadis*, a debate has arisen, presenting arguments reflecting dissatisfaction with the *Qadis'* Law, passed in 1961, which prescribed the rules for appointing these judges by the State President, acting on the recommendations of a nominating committee partly made up of non-Muslims. Other Muslim officials, such as imams (prayer leaders), *khatibs* (preachers), muezzins, registrars, and clerks in mosques, have been appointed by the Ministry of Religions since shortly after the state's establishment—at first perhaps in a somewhat hurried manner and with no careful planning. In addition, Islamic committees have been nominated by the Israeli authorities in mixed towns to safeguard the interests of the Arabs (not only those of the Muslims) in dealings with the authorities in all the localities where they constitute a minority with no representation in the elected municipal or local council. One of the most important powers granted to these committees is to intervene in the disbursement of the revenues of the *waqfs*, again in the interest of their co-religionists. In general, the Israeli authorities used to transfer these funds to educational, religious, and medical institutions in the Islamic sector; since 1965, the responsibility of caring for all this was transmitted to the various Islamic committees themselves.

Following the 1967 War, during their meetings with relatives and friends in Jerusalem and in the Israeli-held territories, the Arabs in Israel discovered that those who had been ruled by Jordan in the West Bank—and, to a lesser extent by Egypt in the Gaza Strip—had developed a well-organized and powerful network of religious organs, excelling in Islamic and Arabic culture. Mutual visits became more and more frequent, and the Israeli authorities, advised by Muslim religious officials in Israel, searched for and found in the territories experts in religion and canonical law, to serve in Israel in various capacities as Muslim officials. Israel and subsequently several Arab states permitted Israeli Muslims to perform the pilgrimage to Mecca and Medina; after peace had been agreed on by Israel and Egypt, Muslims went from Israel to Cairo to study at the religious academy of al-Azhar.

Following these intensive contacts, the Palestinian Muslim identity of the Muslims in Israel was strengthened, thanks to the officials imported from the territories or to those Muslims from Israel who had studied in the territories or in Egypt: these brought back to Israel not only Islamic expertise, but Palestinian Arab nationalism, often anti-governmental or even anti-Israeli. The militancy of the more radical Muslim officials in Israel swept along some of the more moderate, who wished to resemble the others. Both groups found a common language in criticizing the status of Islam in the State of Israel. One of the most articulate among the extremists seems to be Aḥmad Nāṭūr, a graduate of the Hebrew University of Jerusalem, associate-director of the Department for Muslim Affairs in the Ministry of Religions and, since 1984, a *qadi*. Nāṭūr has frequently spoken against the intervention of the state and its organs in matters of *waqf*, of the holy places in Jerusalem, and others, and has urged the restoration of the mosque in Be'er-Sheba, which was turned into a museum, to serve again as a place of prayer.

THE CHRISTIAN COMMUNITIES

The Christians may be considered, in some ways, 'doubly a minority': Arabs in the State of Israel and Christians in the Muslim Middle East. In Israel, they constitute a minority within a minority. Most of them are concentrated in Jerusalem and its vicinity (about 17 per cent of the inhabitants) and the Northern district (mostly Galilee), where about 80 per cent of the Christians live, forming almost half the population in various places. Compared to other minorities in Israel, the ratio of townspeople is high among the Christians. Early in 1991 they numbered about 114,700 (mainly Arabs), that is, only 2.4 per cent of Israel's total population and some 13 per cent of the non-Jewish population—while in 1961 they had numbered 50,543 or approximately 20 per cent of the non-Jews. The relative decline was caused, apparently, both by a birthrate lower than the Muslim (perhaps due to a higher marriage age)[4] and by the annexation of East Jerusalem, a majority of whose inhabitants are Muslims. There was also some Christian emigration, chiefly from Jerusalem.[5] One of their characteristics is that, in contrast to other religious denominations, the Christians have been divided among themselves for generations into various groups, the more important of which are the Greek Catholics (about 33 per cent of all the Christians in Israel), the Greek Orthodox (about 30 per cent) and the Romans or Latins (about 16 per cent); these are the figures within the Green Line boundaries, but not including Jerusalem, where the data are not certain. The other Christian denominations are too small to be involved in any significant political activity. Compared to the Muslims and Druzes, the Christians have a higher ratio of well-educated and affluent townspeople. They are proud of their past services to the Arab nationalist movement. Some of the more prominent Christians adopt an extreme nationalist stand in Arab politics in Israel, because of both a more developed political awareness and a policy of 'taking out insurance' against other groups within the Arab minority. For example, at the end of April 1989, the Christian churches in East Jerusalem forswore their permanent rivalries and issued a strongly worded joint declaration condemning the Israeli government's policies towards the Muslims—without referring at all to terrorist activities against the Jews or even to the killing of their own Christian brothers in Lebanon by Muslims.[6]

Other Christians, however, are in conflict with one another concerning the definition of their identity, both as to their religion, which ties them closely to their co-religionists abroad, and as to their nationality, emphasizing either Arabism or their connection to the State of Israel in which they live, preserving their particular spiritual values and taking care of their own holy places. It seems that at least a part of the Christians in Israel fear an increase in the political-military zealotry of contemporary Islam. It is no accident that, during the 1991 Persian Gulf War, Archimandrite Nethanel (Jamāl) S̲h̲aḥāda, the leader of the Greek Catholic community

---

[4] Alain Franchon, 'La Mort lente des chrétiens de Jérusalem', *Le Monde*, 25 Dec. 1990, 1, 4.
[5] N. Kahanā, 'S̲h̲ĕlīs̲h̲ mi-bĕney ha-ʿeda ha-Yĕvanīt hīggĕrū min ha-aretz me-az pĕrōts ha-intifāda', *ha-Aretz*, 26 Dec. 1990, A5.
[6] Avītal ʿInbar, "Im ha-gav la-qīr', *Dĕvar ha-S̲h̲avūʿa*, 32 (11 Aug. 1989), 9–12.

in Nazareth, gave an interview in which he noted that, had the Christians in Israel volunteered to serve in the Defence Forces, their status would have been stronger, just like that of the Druzes.[7] This and other signs indicate that the Christians are trying to maintain open lines to the State of Israel,[8] no less than to Arab nationalism. In the 1950s, indeed, the Christians carried more weight than the Muslims in country-wide politics, through their alliances with various political parties and with the Histadrut. This was due to their resolute leadership (while the Muslim élites had left in 1948), institutionalized community organization, level of education, and relative modernization—all assisting their integration into the Israeli political system which in itself was patterned on West European models. During those years, they constituted a majority among the minorities' MKs, their reduced ratio in that population notwithstanding. The first Justice of the Peace from amongst the minorities was a Christian. Later, however, the relative political weight of the Christians declined, owing to the numerical increase of the Muslims, the rivalry between the denominations (which prevented the establishment of a common representative body), and the rise of a well-educated political leadership among the Muslims (competing with that of the Christians).

The general policy of Israel's government seems to have been and still is, on the one hand, to let the Christians keep all the privileges which they had possessed in the years of Ottoman and British rule concerning their personal status and community organization; and, on the other, to bring them closer to the Jewish majority—without assimilating them in any way—as an ally and counterweight to the Muslim minority in Israel and the Muslim majority in the Middle East, perceived as a threat to both the Jews and the Christians. The Christians, for their part, reacted somewhat the same way as the Jews had done to their social and political emancipation in nineteenth-century Europe. Some of them assimilated amongst the Muslims, even adopting Muslim names to assist integration into the surrounding society. Others fulfilled a central role in an attempt to modernize Middle Eastern society on Western models, via their intensive activity in Arab national

---

[7] D. Rubinstein, 'Jihād lĕ-ḥillōnīm', *ha-Aretz*, 4 Mar. 1991, B3.
[8] Ecumenical Theological Research Fraternity in Israel, *Christians in Israel and the Yom Kippur War* [1974].

movements. Yet others preferred self-segregation and religious-cultural particularism. Relatively few chose to integrate into the State of Israel and the Jewish consensus, while a majority—among the better-educated, at least—tends to political extremism. These seem to aim for the best of both worlds: maintaining the privileges of their religious denominations and even attempting to broaden their scope; and simultaneously to present themselves as an integral part of the Arab minority in Israel (or even of the Arab people in the Middle East). It is also possible, although not ascertainable, that a part of the Christian Establishment in the State of Israel is still nourished by age-old anti-Jewish sentiment. It seems obvious, anyway, that the Eastern churches were among the groups which applied pressure on the Second Vatican Council in the early 1960s, while it was reconsidering the Jewish role in the crucifixion of Jesus. The original decision proposed to absolve the Jews from the blame for Jesus' death, while the final version declared that not all Jews could be held responsible for it.

Of the two largest Christian denominations in Israel, the Greek Catholics and the Greek Orthodox, the latter are more extreme in their political attitudes. Many of the children of this community are educated in Protestant schools, which usually emphasize Arab tradition and nationalism more than do the Greek Catholic educational establishments. For generations, the Orthodox leaders were Greeks, while most members of the Church were local Arabs. In recent years, Arabs have succeeded in entering the top ranks, and their struggle for the Arabization of their community is well integrated with the trends of Arab nationalism. Perhaps because the Greek Orthodox are the largest Christian group in the Middle East, yet do not enjoy the support of any great power, the Arabs among them feel that they have to demonstrate political extremism, in order to maintain relations with the Muslims, together with a struggle for Arabization (or even Palestinization) of their community. In contrast, the leadership of the Greek Catholics, made up entirely of Arabs, presents a more moderate national stand, characterized in the first twenty years of the State of Israel as ready to co-operate with the state authorities. However, since Archbishop Yūsuf Rāya took up the office vacated by George al-Ḥakīm in 1967, a political change has occurred, perhaps in co-ordination with other Arab groups, with al-Ḥakīm, appointed Patriarch in Damascus, encouraging this trend of a rapprochement to Arab nationalism.

32   *Religious Communities and Politics*

THE DRUZES

The Druzes, fewer in number than either the Muslims or the Christians, are the smallest political minority in Israel (other small minorities, as already said, are devoid of any real political influence).[9] Since 1948, they have been cut off from the larger population centres of their religious communities in Syria and Lebanon. This minority has always distinguished itself by solidarity.[10] This does not necessarily mean that there is a general consensus in every matter. Indeed, there is an ongoing debate on many subjects, one of the most significant being whether the Druzes are a part of the Arabs or a separate people, an issue which will be discussed below (in Chapter 9) in some detail. Here the Druzes will be considered as an element in the mosaic of the political minorities in the State of Israel. According to the 1961 census, 24,282 Druzes were then living in Israel, constituting 1 per cent of the entire population and about 10 per cent of all the non-Jews. On 1 January 1991, they numbered about 82,600, or 9.4 per cent of all the non-Jews, as well as approximately a sixth of all Druzes in the Middle East. One of the causes for their numerical increase, since the 1961 census, was the annexation of the Golan Heights in 1981, inhabited by more than 10,000 Druzes. The Druzes in Israel live in seventeen villages, two of them on the slopes of Mount Carmel and the others in Galilee; nine of these are exclusively Druze, while the others are shared with Christians. Besides farming and handicrafts, most of these villagers depend for their livelihood on external work, generally in Jewish localities. Their occupational patterns resemble those of other villagers among the minorities, with one notable exception—the alternative of serving in Israel's Defence Forces (obligatory since 1956, by law), the police, or the prison service. Even after the completion of their

---

[9] Muṣbāḥ Ḥalabī, *ha-Dĕrūzīm bĕ-Isra'el: tōlĕdōt, massōret wĕ-ōrhōt ḥayyīm* (1973); Salmān Fallāḥ, *Tōlĕdōt ha-Dĕrūzīm bĕ-Isra'el* (1974); Nissīm Dana, *ha-Dĕrūzīm 'eda w-massōret* (1974); Shakīb Ṣāliḥ, *Tōlĕdōt ha-Dĕrūzīm* (1989); Gabriel Ben-Dor, *The Druzes in Israel: A Political Study* (1979).

[10] Thus e.g. the Druzes protested *en masse* against the suspension of Rafīq Ḥalabī, a Druze, from his senior job at the state television. Their protests were among the factors which brought about his reinstatement. See 'Irīt Rōsenblūm, 'Kenes herūm shel ha-'eda ha-Dĕrūzīt hitrī'a neged ha-kavvana lĕhash'ōt et Rafīq Ḥalabī', *ha-Aretz*, 9 Dec. 1990, A4; 'Aṭallāh Manṣūr, 'Me'ōt Dĕrūzīm hit'assĕfū bĕ-Kafr Yāṣīf bĕ-meha'a 'al hadaḥat Rafīq Ḥalabī mi-"mebbaṭ"', ibid. 6 Jan. 1991, A7.

military service, the Druzes sometimes re-enlist, especially in times of economic recession and unemployment. A certain industrial start was made with the inauguration of a factory for stockings and related products, Gibbōr Sabrīna, in the village of Yarka, which was also officially recognized as a preferential industrial area, to lead eventually to the industrialization of the Druze sector. None the less, the Druzes are still awaiting the implementation of a government decision, dating from April 1987, to equate the status of their villages with that of approved developing towns in Israel. There are some indications of late that this is being carried out, but in part only.

Both Ottoman and British rule dispayed little interest in the cultural situation of the Druzes. In Israel, however, compulsory and free education has equated the Druzes with other citizens in this respect as well. It is noteworthy that the first non-Jew to be elected by his peers as president of a students' organization was a Druze, Masʿad Qaddūr, from the village of Dāliyat al-Karmil, who in August 1991 was elected to this position by the students of Tel-Aviv University.[11] Within the Druze community itself, it seems that a sort of dual administration makes most of the public decisions. On the one hand are the Elders, wise in the secret Druze religion (founded by a sect which broke away from Islam some nine hundred year ago); and, on the other, the heads of the *hamulas*— with the Elders generally determining policy. However, modernization, expressed in education, external work, and military service, has brought about a weakening in, although not a breakdown of this system. The standing of the religious leadership of the Druzes was strengthened (with political implications, also) by a series of laws passed in the Knesset during 1957–64, acknowledging them as a 'recognized community', like larger religious groups in Israel, with their autonomous religious administration and special lawcourts, at all legal instances.[12] Increasing the power of the Elders, these laws seem to have further encouraged the Druzes to rally around their religious leadership, as demonstrated in the case of Muṣbāḥ Ḥalabī, son of one of the respected families in the

[11] Avīva Lōrī, 'Mas ʿad Kaddūr, eḥad mi-shellanū', *Maʿarīv*, 30 Aug. 1991, B13; Neḥama Druck, 'Ba-paʿam ha-riʾshōna Dĕrūzī', *Yedīʿōt Aḥarōnōt*, 30 Aug. 1991, Suppl., 31, 90.
[12] For their religious organization, A. Layish and Salmān Fallāḥ, 'ha-Irgūn ha-ʿadatī shel ha-Dĕrūzīm', in Layish (ed.), *ha-ʿAravīm bĕ-Israʾel* (1981), 123–9.

community. Ḥalabī (born in 1942), a writer and journalist, in 1990 published a novel in Arabic, whose title may be translated as *The Diary of a Druze Girl*. In this work, he described Druze life as seen by a young woman, spicing the story with a number of imaginary erotic scenes. Although Ḥalabī openly apologized to the community Elders and publicly burnt all the copies of his book, they nevertheless excommunicated him, and other Druzes shun his company.[13] Only later, in March 1992, was he forgiven. Other Druze writers have published in the community's Arabic-language more conformist organ, *al-Hudà* (The Right Path), issued during the early 1970s, and elsewhere.

The Druzes in Israel are caught, more than the Christians and Muslims, in a dilemma of loyalties. They participated, side by side with the Jews, in the 1948 War, without leaving the country, and they have served in Israel's Defence Forces, in the early years as volunteers, and now as conscripts. All this has forged strong ties between the Druzes and the State of Israel and its Jews,[14] without affecting their powerful historical feelings regarding Druze particularism. In general, they have scant affection for the Muslims, well remembering the authoritarian—even tyrannical—domination of the latter, in Palestine and elsewhere. On a different level, the Druzes in Israel have religious and historical connections with their brothers in Syria and Lebanon. The problem of their peculiar situation was highlighted by Israel's annexation in 1981 of the Golan Heights, with its Druzes (most of whom still declare loyalty to Syria), and then by the 1982 Lebanon War (in which the Lebanese Druzes were directly involved, generally assuming an anti-Israeli stand). Many of the Druzes in Israel are torn between various identities (Israeli, Druze, and Arab) and hence between conflicting loyalties, to their state, their religion, and their people. Many strive for complete equality of opportunities in political, social, and economic life. Against those who are pleased with their overall situation, there are others who complain of what they consider to be discrimination,[15] for example in the opportunities

---

[13] Li'at Rōn, 'Mūkhan lalekhet 'al arba', raq těnū lī liḥyōt', *Ma'arīv*, 28 Aug. 1991, C3.

[14] Gabriel Ben-Dor, 'The Military in the Politics of Integration and Innovation: The Case of the Druze Minority in Israel', *Asian and African Studies*, 9/3 (1973), 339–69.

[15] Yeraḥ Ṭal, 'ha-Děrūzīm mūflīm lamrōt ha-sherūt ha-tsěva'ī', *ha-Aretz*, 26 Dec. 1990, A2.

available to them in housing and jobs, especially after their military service, when they feel that they would like to catch up with other young people, both Muslim and Christian, who, exempted from military service, had used the time to further themselves economically or educationally. As will be indicated later, these attitudes have been reflected in both Druze writing and electoral voting. In so far as this is ascertainable, many Druzes on Mount Carmel, who reside mostly among or near Jews, tend towards Israelism; while some of those in Galilee, neighbours of the Arabs, voice their pro-Arabism, particularly since the annexation of the Golan Heights by Israel has brought them into more direct contact with Syrian and Lebanese Druzes.

In brief, it seems that varying and antagonistic forces affect the political identification of the Druzes in Israel. On the one hand, they are attracted to the state by co-operation with the Jews and common perceptions of the Arabs as the enemy, by social mobility, and by military service. More than 200 Druzes have fallen in the state's wars and many others have been wounded; many have distinguished themselves and been promoted—one Druze is a brigadier-general, there are eighteen colonels, and not a few have seen service in élite, prestigious units.[16] Others, however, tend to identify with the Arabs in Israel, and sometimes in the territories as well, owing to several significant factors, such as an identical language, cultural propinquity, and a feeling of commonality with other minorities against the majority in the State of Israel. Such views are occasionally expressed by the younger Druzes, some of whom are against service in Israel's Defence Forces. Not a few of these also protest against what they see as preferential treatment of Jewish localities over their own villages, which still suffer from underdevelopment in roads, drainage, and other aspects.[17]

A decision adopted at a Cabinet session in April 1987 to grant the Druzes equality in all matters was only partially implemented, and on 1 May 1991 a general protest, demanding full independence, was held in all the Druze villages in Galilee, with a well-co-ordinated stoppage of all municipal services. Two weeks later, an answer was

---

[16] This was the subject of a book by Muṣbāḥ Ḥalabī, published in 1970, and entitled *Bĕrīt damīm*, reviewed by Zě'ev Schiff, 'Dĕrūzīm she-nafĕlū bĕ-shŭrōt TSAHAL', *ha-Aretz*, 28 May 1970, 15.

[17] For their complaints, see 'Rōsh mō'etset Jūlis: 'al ha-sar Magen lĕhitpaṭṭer me-ha-ṭīppūl ba-'eda ha-Dĕrūzīt', ibid. 12 Apr. 1991, A4.

proposed to their demands: a budgetary advance was made to the
Druze local authorities, along with an undertaking, signed by the
Ministers of the Treasury and Interior, for full equalization with
the Jewish local authorities by a given date. One of the more
striking phenomena of this protest strike was the special trip to
Jerusalem of the aged spiritual leader of the Druzes, Sheikh Amīn
Ṭarīf himself, to identify with the strikers—very probably an
attempt by the community's religious leadership to become more
actively involved in the political moves of the Druzes in Israel.

RELIGION AND POLITICS

Religion can reach a state of radical alienation in a certain political
situation and then start to demolish its stability. When a minority's
religion is involved, it can develop a self-defensive ideology through
solidarity and the employment of a protest strategy. In the State of
Israel, the progress and widening of the scope of education, the
feelings of discrimination and inequality, and a rise in politicization,
bordering on radicalization, have led to an increase in the political
activity of the minorities, partly in a religious context. Obvious
signs of this process may be found in all three of Israel's largest
minorities—each in its own peculiar manner—following their
intensive contacts with their brothers in the faith since 1967,
especially in the Israeli-held territories, but also in Egypt and
Lebanon. These contacts had an outcome different from those
expected by the Israeli government, when the religious element
joined the nationalists, in particular among a part of the Muslims,
whose religion is very political; it should be noted that Islam had
already served as a vehicle of nationalist expression in various areas,
including Palestine.[18] In the State of Israel, some of the Muslims
seem to have felt that, at least in the religious and judicial domains,
it was difficult to expect them to constitute a sub-system, sub-
ordinate to the non-Muslim one. As several of their spokesmen
phrased it, this was a delegitimization of Islamic power. East
Jerusalem experts in Islamic law influenced their own circles and
other Arabs in Israel by their spoken and written propaganda,

---

[18] W. L. Ochsenwald, 'Arab Muslims and the Palestine Problem', *Muslim World*,
56/4 (1976), 287–96.

which proved to be a combination of two ideologies—Palestinian nationalism and Muslim revivalism. One result of this process was the increased number of requests by the Muslims in Israel for Islamic guidance, directed to the legal experts in East Jerusalem and the territories. Christians and Druzes showed no dissimilar trends; however, in this context, the advance of politicization and radicalization may be better grasped if discussed by religious denomination.

The Muslims

The Muslims inclined towards radicalization,[19] largely as an extreme expression of the growth of religious fundamentalism among a part of them. An Israeli-Arab writer, Dr Fārūq Muwāsī, refers to this process in an interesting article published in the summer of 1980.[20] As he sees it, the younger Muslims drew away from religion in the 1950s and 1960s. However, in the 1970s and 1980s, this same group returned to Islam, even in its most orthodox fundamentalist expression, as part of a wider movement of return to religion. A central reason was the success of the Ayatollah Khomeynī's Islamic revolution in Iran, which was interpreted as proof that Islam was suitable to govern, providing an alternative to any capitalist or socialist regime, and that the Koran was the one and only constitution that could save the entire world. For some, the return to Islam looked like a way to share in a society where sentiments of brotherhood prevail. The beginnings of this process can be recognized earlier, in the years of British rule in Palestine; signs of it were evident in the first two decades of the state, but it has accelerated since 1967. A significant impact was made by the preachers from the Israeli-held territories, who strove to attract the Muslims in Israel to Islam, also distributing religious pamphlets, many imported from Egypt—so that nowadays up to two-thirds of many village libraries are earmarked for Islam or matters related to it. Almost everywhere, the mosques are full; in numerous villages circles have been set up for Islamic and Koranic studies, in a spirit close to that of the Muslim Brethren; the streets are replete with women and girls in traditional dress, and bearded men sometimes

---

[19] Avner Regev, 'Israeli Arabs and Islam', *Israeli Democracy*, Spring 1991, 30–1.
[20] Fārūq Muwāsī, 'Zāhirat al-tadayyun fī al-shabāb al-ʿArabī', *Āfāq*, 1/1 (July 1980), 65–6.

also in traditional garb. Young fundamentalists who challenge the state-appointed religious establishment have increased their influence in their villages. For instance, in Bāqa al-Gharbiyya they have demanded separation between boys and girls in the schools; in another village, they have constructed a mosque with a special place for themselves and reserved certain hours for their own prayers; in yet other villages they have established groups for the study of Islam and its laws, and for practising religious ceremonies. Since their activity is a reaction to Westernization and atheism, it attracts additional groups based particularly among the lower and poorer strata to whom religion promises the next world in recompense for suffering in this one.

Rising fundamentalism has spread from the all-Muslim Little Triangle to Galilee, frequently accompanied by signs of politicization or even radicalization. Its physical expression consists of constructing mosques, for mass prayers, religious studies, and social activities. Towns and villages which fail to collect dues from their inhabitants for roads and sanitation succeed none the less in mobilizing substantial sums, sometimes even huge amounts, for building mosques. These have become familiar landmarks in places which previously had none or very few, such as Nazareth and Umm al-Fahm. In the latter, for example, a magnificent mosque, comprising altogether several hundred square metres on five floors, with marble panels and windows framed in gilded aluminum, has been constructed. Besides halls for prayer, for men and women separately, there are a huge sport gymnasium, a library, and a reading room. The assumption most probably is that those who come for physical training or library facilities will perforce take part in prayers as well. Much of town life consequently revolves round the mosques, as in many villages, in some of which the medical dispensary or the social club is also located in the same building.[21] In various Muslim villages, fundamentalist circles invest time and funds in developing local education, thus putting many families in a debt of gratitude to them.[22] In summary, such Muslim groups promise a great deal for both this world and the next.

---

[21] The most serious study of this phenomenon, in its Israeli context, is Thomas Mayer's *Hit'ōrērūt ha-Mūslēmīm bĕ-Isra'el* (1988). See also A. Ringel-Hofman, 'ha-Islām kĕvar kān', *Yĕdī'ōt Aharōnōt*, 2 Mar. 1990, Suppl., 18–20.

[22] N. Mendler, 'Doah lĕ-sar ha-hinnūkh: ha-Ahīm ha-Mūslēmiyyīm mishtallĕṭīm 'al mōsēdōt hinnūkh ba-migzar ha-'Aravī wĕ-gōrĕmīm lĕ-haqtsana', *ha-Aretz*, 28 Dec. 1990, 1.

These and others are external signs of a deeper process, evident since the 1970s. Young men who had studied in West Bank colleges, chiefly in Hebron and Nablus, brought the religious message upon returning to their villages in Israel. Quite naturally, they would come together for discussion and common activities; in certain cases this informal type of organization was channelled into a militant, sometimes violent anti-Israeli direction. An example is Usrat al-Jihād (the Family of the Holy War), a clandestine religious and military grouping. This was uncovered in the Little Triangle in 1981, and its members were brought to court and accused of illegal possession of firearms, setting fire to forests and orchards, and the like.[23] The members of this group, numbering about sixty or seventy, trained in the use of weapons in Umm al-Faḥm, Kafr Qāsim, and Bāqa al-Gharbiyya (with some activity in Qalansuwa, too, apparently). All these are in the Little Triangle. Most of the members were young, generally under 25. Their leader, Farīd Abū Mukh, was somewhat older. Born in Bāqa al-Gharbiyya in 1937, he returned to the faith at the age of 40, met Sheikh ʿAbd Allāh Nimr Darwīsh (of whom more later), and under his instruction started studying Islamic literature, mainly the writings of the Muslim Brethren in Syria. The conclusion he reached was that he should set out on an uncompromising struggle against Western colonialism and Zionism. The court before which the members of Usrat al-Jihād were brought sentenced Sheikh Darwīsh to three years (of which he served two), Abū Mukh to ten years (of which he served four), and many others to shorter terms. Most of them used their time in gaol to spread the ideas of their organization, which helped to expand their ranks after their release. Sheikh Darwīsh returned to Kafr Qāsim, to lead the 'Young Muslims' (for whom see below), however keeping within the law. Indeed, those released from prison and their peers were wary, at least for a while, of confrontation with the state authorities or secular elements in the population. In general, their revived organization preferred to act politically rather than militarily, as for instance in Lydda, where a group of young fundamentalists is attempting not only to bring fellow Muslims back to religion, but also to take over political control of the Arab quarters in this mixed town. It has succeeded,

---

[23] Yaʿaqōv Havaqqūq, 'Mishpahat ha-jihād—ha-mahteret ba-Mĕshūllash', ibid. 3 June 1981, Suppl.; ʿAṭallāh Manṣūr, 'Mahteret Mūslĕmīt ba-Mĕshūllash', ibid. 27 Feb. 1981, 15; Mayer (n. 21 above), 42–52.

anyway, in demoting the imam (or prayer leader) of the local mosque,[24] apparently employing threats of violence.

The above are merely a few highlights in the development of a large and growing movement in various Arab localities, at various levels of politicization, frequently displaying verbal radicalism. This is evident both in the content of spoken and written statements in relating to the State of Israel and in the particularly aggressive style, passionately supporting the establishment of an Islamic state in its stead. According to the fundamentalist Islamic view, Palestine was ruled by Muslims since the seventh century AD, granting Jews and Christians merely the status of 'protected people'. Nowadays this has been overturned, with Jews dominating a land sacred to Muslims who, in their perceptions, now feel like 'protected people'—an intolerable reversal of the earlier situation.

No less significant is the organizing of a movement calling itself al-Shabāb al-Muslim, or 'the Young Muslims', which seems generally careful to keep within the limits of the law, following the failure of Usrat al-Jihād.[25] According to a 1981 estimate, about 20 per cent of all youths in Muslim villages then belonged to this movement and other fundamentalist groups.[26] Their power became obvious in the February–March 1989 elections to municipalities and local authorities. The Young Muslims obtained the chairmanship in five places, including Umm al-Faḥm, the second largest all-Arab town in Israel. In addition, some of its adherents were elected as members of local councils (as will be detailed below, in Chapter 8). The most prominent figure in the movement is Sheikh ʿAbd Allāh Nimr Darwīsh, born in 1948, a graduate of the Islamic College in Nablus in 1972, and a retired teacher who had led Usrat al-Jihād. Sentenced to three years and released in 1984, Darwīsh enjoyed an aura of leadership thanks to his trial and term in prison. Although physically handicapped, he seems to be brimming over with energy. A capable organizer and, according to his admirers, a charismatic speaker, he enjoys a special standing among Muslims

---

[24] Details in Ben Kaspīt, 'Khōmeynīzm, ʿeser daqqōt mi-Tel-Avīv', *Maʿarīv*, 14 Sept. 1990, Suppl., 6–10.

[25] For the Young Muslims, see Thomas Mayer (n. 21 above), 56 ff, and his paper 'ha-Tsĕʿīrīm ha-Mūslĕmiyyīm bĕ-Israʾel', *ha-Mizraḥ he-Ḥadash*, 32/125–8 (1989), 10–20.

[26] Ōrlī Azūlay, 'Ṭerōr bĕ-shem Allāh,' *Yĕdiʿōt Aharōnōt*, 6 Mar. 1981, Suppl., 5–7.

in Israel as one of their respected leaders. Although the book he wrote in 1975, *Ilà al-Islām* (Towards Islam), is not political, his subsequent writings and speeches indicate an intention to become the leader of all the Arabs in Israel. He has defined his movement as three-dimensional, Islamic–Arab–Palestinian, reflecting the spirit–blood–flesh of Islamic unity. As Darwīsh perceives it, this framework has become particularly relevant since 1967, when Palestinian Arabs again became united into one people, though under Israeli domination.[27] His platform is a well-thought-out combination of demands for complete civic and economic equality as well as for the achieving of political rights by all Palestinians in Israel, including the right of return for all the refugees, parallel to the Law of Return for the Jews.

Along with Darwīsh, several younger politicians are active together, forming an influential group, for the time being in local politics but aspiring to future country-wide activity. One of these is Ibrāhīm Nimr Ḥusayn, mayor of Shafā ʿAmr. His declared involvement is in the local administration of his town as well as the spread of religion; he perceives fundamentalist Islam as chiefly directed against secularism.[28] An example of his attitude is the dismissal of a local teacher suspected of irreligiousness in the interpretation of a poem in class.[29] Another person, no less active in Islamic politics, is Sheikh Ibrāhīm Ṣarṣūr, head of the Kafr Qāsim local council, and a member of the secretariat and the spokesman of the Young Muslims—a role which he took over from Darwīsh (who is twelve years Ṣarṣūr's senior). Ṣarṣūr is a graduate of Bar-Ilan University, a Jewish religious institution, where he was able to observe the importance of religious organization and to ponder on its use for political objectives. He knows Hebrew and English well and is versed in Israeli politics. While Darwīsh seems to incline towards involving the movement in country-wide politics, Ṣarṣūr prefers, for the time being, local politics in his village and other places. In some ways, relations have been established

---

[27] 'al-Usbūʿ al-jadīd tuḥāwir zaʿīm al-ḥaraka al-Islāmiyya dākhil al-khaṭṭ al-ahdar', *al-Usbūʿ al-Jadīd*, 8 (15 Apr. 1989), 8–11.

[28] Jamīl Dahlān, 'al-Sayyid Ibrāhīm Nimr Husayn raʾīs al-majlis al-baladī Shafā ʿAmr fī ḥadīth ṣarīḥ wa-muthīr', *al-Qasam*, 22 Mar. 1989. See also *al-Ṣirāṭ*, 23 June 1989, 10.

[29] Avīva Shābī, 'Puṭṭar bi-gēlal shīr', *Yĕdīʿōt Aharōnōt*, 8 June 1990, Suppl., 49–50.

between the Islamic movement in Israel and Muslim and Arab organizations in the United States, to get funds for investment in developing Arab towns and villages and promoting Islam. While Ṣarṣūr is generally cautious in his messages, basing them on religious arguments as far as possible, they frequently take on a demanding and sometimes rash tone.[30]

The Islamic movement, combining religion with politics, is maximalist in its political ambitions and aspires to unite and lead all Arabs in Israel, not only the Muslims. In an article in al-Ṣirāṭ (The Right Path), the movement's weekly, this aim is expressed as follows: 'Let us reach true union, in which Islam would be its spirit, original Arabism its blood, noble nationalism its body, peace and just equality its objective, brotherhood its relation, and mutual assistance its custom.'[31] This, indeed, seems to be the slogan of the Islamic movement in Israel, and these motifs frequently recur in its organs, especially al-Ṣirāṭ, issued in Umm al-Faḥm, and al-Qasam, published in Jaffa.

Despite reservations by secular Muslims in Israel, particularly secular intellectuals, afraid that the fundamentalists may take control, socially and politically (on the Iranian model), it seems that the Islamic movement in Israel keeps on growing, numerically, thanks to its success in combining Islamic aspirations with a political appeal, sometimes extreme, for both equality and nationalism. Its power lies in its strategy which, while keeping to Israel's rules of the game, does not hesitate to suggest radical solutions. On the one hand, in its activities, speeches, and writings it is careful not to break the law, lest it be brought to court. Indeed, it actively participated in the local authority elections and may join the parliamentary ones as well, as the Muslim Brethren in Egypt and Jordan have done in recent years. On the other hand, it suggests an Islamic solution to the nationalist claims of the Arabs in Israel (and abroad), arguing that solely in this manner would the expectations of the Palestinians be fully achieved, within the parameters of a much larger Islamic state.[32] Hence the support of the Islamic

[30] See e.g. A. Dayyan, 'ha-Sahar he-ḥadash', Kol ha-ʿIr, 19 Jan. 1990, 29–31.

[31] al-Ṣirāṭ, 23 June 1989, 15: 'Fihā illā waḥda ṣādiqa yakūn al-Islām rūḥuhā wa-al-ʿUrūba al-aṣīla damuhā wa-al-waṭaniyya al-sharīfa laḥmuhā wa-al-Islām wa-al-musāwāh al-ʿādila ghāyatuhā wa-al-ikhāʾ ribāṭuhā wa-al-taʿāwun ʿalā al-birr wa-al-taqwā nahjuhā.'

[32] For recently increasing Pan-Islamic propaganda, Jacob M. Landau, The Politics of Pan-Islam: Ideology and Organization (1990).

Movement in Israel for like-minded groups abroad, such as the Islamic Salvation Front in Algeria. When the latter won the parliamentary elections, the organ of the Islamic Movement in Israel, *Ṣawt al-Ḥaqq wa-'l-Ḥurriya*, congratulated its Algerian counterpart in an enthusiastic editorial of 10 January 1992.

The Christians

The Christians, or at least some of them, have become concerned about the growth and power of the Islamic movement in Israel. This anxiety has had a double consequence. One result was identification by many in the larger denominations, and some in the smaller ones, with Arab, and even Muslim, nationalism, expressing militant anti-Israeli views. Another was taking care to leave the door open to a dialogue with the state and identification with it and its Jewish majority. Again, this attitude was expressed mostly by the smaller denominations. Either way, one notes an apparent tendency among the Christians to maintain a lower profile than the Muslims, both in their pronouncements and in their activities.

As already said, the Christians had been involved in politics as early as the days of the British Mandate in Palestine, in a ratio beyond their numbers. This continued in the first years of the State of Israel, but later the effectiveness of their involvement declined owing to the absolute and relative increase of the Muslims and particularly of their well-educated members. Thus, as mentioned, in the early decades of the state the Christians sent more members than the Muslims to the Knesset, despite their ratio within the minorities; only recently has this changed, another sign of the declining political power of the Christians. This was true of the Histadrut and other workers' organizations as well, at least in the first twelve years after 1948. Soon after 1948, the Histadrut set up a Union of Arab Workers (active until 1960), whose secretary-general was the Greek Orthodox George Saʿd. A competing association was the Congress of Arab Workers, set up by the Israeli Communist Party, which was led by Ṣalībā Khamīs, an Episcopalian. A third organization, the League of the Workers of Nazareth, was created to struggle against Communist influence; it was headed by Nadīm Baṭḥīsh, member of a well-known Roman

44   *Religious Communities and Politics*

Catholic family.[33] In subsequent years, Christians continued to work actively in similar and other political groupings, usually in greater numbers than their population ratio warranted.[34] The special standing of the Christians and their political success are attributable not merely to their important connections with their co-religionists abroad and their privileges as autonomous denominational organizations,[35] but also to the political talents of their leadership. Particularly prominent in this respect was Archbishop George al-Ḥakīm, for many years head of the Greek Catholics. Born in Egypt in 1908, al-Ḥakīm was nominated as Archbishop of Acre, Haifa, Nazareth, and all of Galilee in 1943, serving in this capacity for twenty-four years (until his appointment as Greek Catholic Patriarch in Syria in 1967). Al-Ḥakīm managed to present himself as the leader of all the Christians and even attempted to speak for all Arabs in the State of Israel. He thus appeared not only as a Christian leader but as an experienced politician, basing his activity on his relations with the Vatican and on his own prestige, his economic standing (he developed various enterprises and provided employment for his flock), and his ability to persuade and organize. Al-Ḥakīm was quite popular among the minorities in Israel thanks to his activity on their behalf and his image as a protector of their rights versus the state authorities. He published, in Arabic, *al-Rābiṭa* (The Bond), a periodical focusing on demands for the abolition of the Military Administration or the reduction of its powers; opposition to discrimination and to land expropriation; and calls for providing employment and granting concessions in income tax, municipal taxes, and customs.

In 1981, some Christians attempted to run for the Knesset, on an independent slate headed by Ḥannā Ḥaddād, a retired police officer, but only gathered 8,300 votes. Political power was maintained by Christians solely in the Israeli Communist Party (as will be described in Chapter 7 below), but even there they are in retreat—at least, in the decision-making bodies—owing to the rise in the power of the Muslims in the party. This may have impelled some

---

[33] Daphne Tsimhoni, 'ha-Ma'arakh ha-pōlīṭī shel ha-Nōtsrīm bĕ-Isra'el', *ha-Mizrah he-Hadash*, 32/125–8 (1989), 142.
[34] Examples ibid. 149–59.
[35] Daphne Tsimhoni, 'Continuity and Change in Communal Autonomy: The Christian Communal Organization in Jerusalem 1948–80', *Middle Eastern Studies*, 22/3 (July 1986), 398–417.

of the Christians to intensify their political extremism by increasing their criticism of the State of Israel and their praise for the Palestine Liberation Organization (further: PLO), more particularly since the beginning of the uprising in the territories in December 1987. Still, even if the politicization of a part of the Christian population in Israel has shown signs of radicalization, not all Arab Christians are politically homogeneous. One example, dating from the first half of 1991, is that of some 300 Christian youths who volunteered for service in Israel's Defence Forces—indeed an innovation. In October 1991, a Greek Catholic from the village of 'Usfiyya, named Mīlād Talaḥmī, completed an officers' course with distinction, for the first time in the military service of Christians in Israel. All this shows that friction and conflict between the denominations—and, sometimes, within them—along with their numerical decline, are weakening the Christians' political power in Israel, so that they are pronouncedly becoming a minority within the Arab minority.

The Druzes

Although most elderly and middle-aged Druzes have repeatedly declared their loyalty to the state and commitment to a common destiny with the Jews, the younger Druzes are not all of one mind. Some, indeed, have openly been adopting a hostile attitude, maintaining that they are discriminated against, economically and socially, chiefly in employment, housing, and education—which, they argue, is inappropriate for a community whose sons serve in Israel's Defence Forces. Every such complaint, even if exaggerated, has loud reverberations. The core of the controversy, so it seems, relates to an examination of Druze identity, whether it is separate, Arab,[36] or Israeli (a topic we shall revert to below, in Chapter 9). Taking a stand in the matter determines political behaviour in no little degree. Among the elements with reservations about the close Druze relations with the State of Israel is a circle set up in 1972, entitled the Druze Initiative Committee. The avowed objective of its members, chiefly young men, has been 'to prevent the separation of the Druzes from their Arab brethren', on the one hand, and, on the other, to struggle against conscription. An opposing

---

[36] Yōnatan Oppenheimer, 'ha-Dĕrūzīm bĕ-Isra'el ka-'Aravīm w-khĕ-lo' 'Aravīm', *Maḥabarōt lĕ-Meḥqar w-lĕ-Viqqōret*, 3 (Dec. 1979), 41–58.

group was established, two years later, entitled the Zionist Druze Circle, whose aim is to encourage the Druzes to support the State of Israel fully and unreservedly. These two groupings reflect many of the political trends among the Druzes. The anti-Israeli trend has also been expressed in several small Druze spy rings, which were uncovered and their members brought to trial.[37] More recently, there have been isolated cases of Druzes refusing conscription, such as Hishām Naffāʿ, the son of the Communist MK Muḥammad Naffāʿ, who had also refused to serve, in his time.[38] Samīḥ al-Qāsim, a Druze poet writing in Arabic and an active member of the Israeli Communist Party, has consistently advocated such anti-state attitudes. Nevertheless, many other Druzes refrain from supporting such drastic steps as rejecting military service, and content themselves with verbal and written protest, as in matters relating to education[39] and unemployment. For instance, they have protested that Druzes are not being promoted to jobs at decision-making levels and, in a specific case, that a senior Druze news editor in state television, Rafīq Ḥalabī, had been suspended (he later returned to his job and was promoted).[40] In a mass rally against his suspension, held at Kafr Yāṣīf, in early January 1991, several Druze speakers called for joining with the Arabs in Israel in order to redress their joint grievances. It is even more evident that the nationalist attitudes of the Druzes in the Golan Heights, annexed to Israel in 1981, are equally political, but much more militantly so. Many of them, perhaps most, see themselves as Syrians rather than Israelis, and refuse to accept Israeli identity cards. In various ways, such as demonstrations and strikes, they express their non-adherence to Israel and support for Syria, which they would like to rejoin. To a certain extent, their views and attitudes have influenced the Druzes in the State of Israel. Because of these processes, the Druze community—and, in particular, its youth—is increasingly trying to obtain its economic and social demands

---

[37] R. B. Betts, *The Druze* (1988), esp. 103.

[38] Hayyīm Shībī, 'Sarbanīm bĕ-dam', *Yĕdīʿōt Aharōnōt*, 18 May 1990, Suppl., 18.

[39] Ṣ. Rimāl, 'La-Dĕrūzīm dĕrūshīm merkĕzey ḥinnūkh tīkhōn', *ha-Aretz*, 4 Sept. 1970, 17. The author is a Druze intellectual from the village Yarka.

[40] See a letter by Zakī Kamāl, "Od ʿelbōn la-Dĕrūzīm', ibid. 3 Jan. 1991. The author is the head of a so-called Ideological Circle of Druze University Graduates, in Haifa. For an interview with him, 'The Other Israelis: A MOMENT Interview', *Moment*, 7/4 (Apr. 1982), 11–17.

by political means, similar in many respects to those of other minorities in Israel. The leadership is generally supportive of the state and its authorities; it is not unlikely, therefore, that some of the Druze youth who have reservations about their own religious leadership almost naturally adopt anti-Israeli views as well.

4

Social Change: Village, Town, Tribe

INTRODUCTORY

The process of social change became evident among the Arabs in Palestine during the years of the British Mandate, for instance in the proletarianization of the village and the transformation of the town. In the State of Israel, such changes became more pronounced—in villages, towns, and among Bedouin tribes—owing to the spread of education and literacy, the pervasiveness of mass communication, and constant contact with the neighbouring Jewish society. The process was hastened by the expropriation of Arab agricultural lands[1] and occupational shifts, via the increased mobility of workers in various channels.[2] One may perhaps best describe and assess these changes by focusing on the three categories of habitation, and devoting a separate discussion to the change in the role and status of women.

THE VILLAGE

Most Arab settlements in Israel are rural, in the hilly and mountainous parts of the state (differing in this from the Jewish settlements). The villages have become markedly transformed since 1948,[3] albeit in various ways, depending on the region, the size of the village, and its proximity to main roads or Jewish localities,

---

[1] There were some instances in which Arabs who had left their villages, during the 1948 Arab–Israeli War, were not allowed to return. See 'Taḥrīk qaḍiyyat Iqrit wa-Kafr Barʿam', al-Rābiṭa, 40 (Mar. 1986), 32–5.

[2] Zureik, The Palestinians in Israel (1979), ch. 5. Several articles may be consulted in ʿAzīz Ḥaydar, Henry Rosenfeld, and Reuven Kahana (eds.), ha-Ḥevra ha-ʿAravīt bě-Israʾel: miqraʾa (1983), part i.

[3] A. Shmūʾelī et al., Gilgūlō shel ezōr: ha-Měshullash ha-Qaṭan (1985); Arnon Soffer, 'Geographical Aspects of Change within the Arab Communities in Northern Israel', Middle Eastern Studies, 19/2 (Apr. 1983), 213–43.

and its economic standing.[4] The changes are largely reflected in the modification of the *hamula*, or extended family, pattern, comprising several families (interconnected by blood-ties, factual or imaginary). The role played by the *hamula* is no longer quite what it once was. Various research projects[5] have demonstrated that the *hamula* still constitutes a behavioural centre for the villagers, who usually associate, for business or pleasure, within its framework. It also serves as an important political mechanism in local authority elections and even in elections for the Knesset. However, there are increasing signs that the young, both men and women, especially those who have completed secondary school or studied at the university, are critical of the behavioural rigidity dictated by the village Elders and the traditional circles; they, on the contrary, favour social change in education, dress, dwellings, and the like.[6] The economic significance of the *hamula* has also declined; even the loyalty of its members has been affected, perhaps due to the fact that they are not financially dependent on it, as before—particularly those employed outside their villages.

The 'migrant' Arab worker, as Professor Henry Rosenfeld of Haifa University calls him,[7] became a common phenomenon in the village as early as the first years of the state (indeed even formerly to some extent), and more so since the abolition of the Military Administration in December 1966. The move to salaried labour in the Jewish towns has intensified, starting with the economic growth the country began to enjoy after the 1967 War and the decline in the need for fieldwork in the Arab agricultural sector, due to land expropriation and mechanization. If in 1947 60 to 65 per cent of all employed Arabs were working in agriculture, this ratio declined to 58.2 per cent as early as 1958, 14.5 per cent in 1974,

---

[4] Cf. B. Shīdlōwsky, 'Těmūrōt bě-fīttuaḥ ha-kěfar ha-ʿAravī bě-Israʾel', *ha-Mizrah he-Ḥadash*, 15/57–8 (1965), 25–37; Joseph Ginat, *Těmūrōt bě-mivneh ha-mishpaḥa ba-kěfar ha-ʿAravī*; Arnon Soffer, "ʿArviyyey Israʾel, mi-kěfar lě-metrōpōlīn w-ma halʾa?', *ha-Mizrah he-Ḥadash*, 32/125–8 (1989), 97–105; Henry Rosenfeld, *Hem hayū fallahīm* (1964); id., 'Shīnnūy, maḥasōmīm lě-shīnnūy wě-nīggūdīm ba-mishpaḥa ha-kafrīt', in Layish (ed.), *ha-ʿAravīm bě-Israʾel* (1981), 76–103; Abner Cohen, *Arab Border-Villages in Israel* (1965).

[5] e.g. Mājid al-Ḥaj, 'ha-Hamūla ha-ʿAravīt bě-Israʾel', *Migvan*, 54 (Dec. 1980), 33–6.

[6] Examples in Elī Eyal's 'ha-Mered ha-shaqeṭ shel ha-tsěʿīrīm ha-ʿAraviyyīm', *Maʿarīv*, 22 Jan. 1971, Suppl., 19–21.

[7] Henry Rosenfeld, 'ha-Pōʿel ha-ʿAravī ha-navvad', *Dū-Shavūʿōn ha-Ūnīversīṭa*, 8 (1970), 1, 4.

and a mere 7.2 per cent in 1989. Since, as noted above, industry has been introduced into Arab villages on only a very limited scale, agriculture has remained the basis of livelihood without, however, sufficing for all the inhabitants.

More than half the men working in the Arab sector in Israel were, and are, employed in jobs outside their villages or towns. These are mostly in building and in the services, generally quite well paid; few, however, achieve permanence in their jobs. Arabs have usually been among the first to feel the pinch of recession; consequently they take care to maintain their close continuing relations with *hamula* and village. Most consider themselves as residing in their own villages, returning there every evening, or at least quite often, and reverting to live there altogether in times of unemployment. Thus they serve as agents of modernization in their villages. Arab women employed outside their own villages tend even more to return home every evening. Some of the villagers working in the towns become self-employed, for example as owners of a car, a machine, a shop, a workshop, or the like, thus acquiring special economic and social status. Most others undergo a process of proletarianization; a village proletariat has arisen, somewhat similar to that in the more advanced industrialized societies of the United States and Western Europe.[8]

Change in traditional Arab village society has had political effects as well. The head of the *hamula* has continued, indeed, to enjoy the respect appropriate to an older person, but his political influence has diminished to a greater or lesser extent, as the case may be; this has paralleled the declining status of the family heads, whose sons live at home but gain their livelihood in salaried work. Further, supra-*hamula* groups or cliques emerge, often comprising those who have ceased to be financially dependent on the traditional head. Moreover, the villagers working externally have sizeable sums of ready money in hand, a fact which enhances their prestige and feeling of non-dependence on the village elders.

This process goes together with another, in which democratic institutions—such as the local councils in most villages—compete politically with traditional bodies. Many villages have witnessed, indeed, a new division of power focuses. Nevertheless, it should be

---

[8] E. T. Zureik, 'Transformation of Clan Structure among the Arabs in Israel: From Peasantry to Proletariat', *Journal of Palestine Studies*, 6/1 (Autumn 1976), esp. 47 ff.

emphasized again, the *hamulas* have preserved a considerable amount of power, chiefly in the village's social and economic affairs, so that coalitions and conflicts in no small degree influence political activites, both internal and external. Indeed, groups organized on a supra-*hamula* basis have to take into consideration the existence and power of the *hamulas*. The function and *modus operandi* of the *hamulas*, too, have changed visibly, so that nowadays their struggle for power takes place within the above-mentioned democratic institutions—the local councils and all sorts of committees. Empirical research has demonstrated that, although much *hamula* power is still preserved within the local administration in Israel, it is in continuous decline, to the advantage of rival elements, more modern and characterized by a no less acute political awareness.

This competition, along with the dynamic tempo of life in the State of Israel, has greatly contributed to the changes in the inner structure of the Arab village, its functions, and its physical appearance. Although the detailed processes of change in these and other respects differ from one village to another, the quiet revolution (as well as the not so quiet one) occurring in them has left few Arab villages in their traditional format,[9] while in most of them modernization has made visible inroads—in buildings, road networks, introduction of electricity and running water, even football teams.[10] Numerous houses have been constructed outside the village core, frequently close to the roads and occasionally in Israeli-Jewish style (including multi-storey apartments), ignoring the *hamula* elements. Sometimes, indeed, building activities have not conformed to zoning plans (which in many cases did not exist at all), a fact which has often caused friction with the authorities and the issuing of demolition orders,[11] many of which, however, have not been carried out.

Moreover, in many villages, a modern infrastructure has been substituted for the old one. Wide roads have been constructed, suitable for motor traffic. The introduction of running water made the wells obsolete and freed the women for other work. Almost

---

[9] Cf. Tsvī Lavī', *ha-Mahpekha ha-shēqeta ba-rēhōv ha-ʿAravī* (1970). This is a collection of articles in *Maʿarīv*, 12, 15, and 16 June 1970.

[10] For these changes, Yōram Bar-Gal and Arnon Soffer, *Tĕmūrōt bi-khĕfarey ha-mīʿūtīm* (1976).

[11] Details are occasionally published in the daily press, as well as in an Arab periodical, *Ṣawt al-Qurà* (Voice of the Villages), issued in Haifa since 1990.

ubiquitous electricity encouraged the buying of various home appliances and opened up possibilities of developing mechanized labour. Telephone lines have enabled people to stay in direct touch with friends in other places as well as to establish new connections and pursue the search for business. This transformation brought about further important changes, especially in the larger villages, such as the opening of shops, bank branches, petrol stations, labour exchanges, clinics, as well as an expansion of and improvement in education. When such developments are centred in certain villages, they—together with their added new quarters—assume the character of small towns. In these, an obvious process of urbanization is to be noted, not in the sense of immigration into the towns, but rather in that of a transformation of the rural character into the urban, even though the village inhabitants do not move into towns. Urbanization has reached various stages in different places, with the larger villages gradually acquiring the status of townships.[12]

THE TOWN

As a sort of mirror image to the urbanization of the village, several of the Arab towns look like large villages—certainly those which, until recently, were in fact large villages granted municipal status thanks to the increase in their population. None the less, Arab townspeople are an important focus for social and economic change,[13] and it is among them that politicization is mostly to be observed. Several recently published studies on specific towns seem mainly interested in social conditions and less in political trends, but one can learn from them about these as well.

There are six mixed towns in Israel, inhabited by both Jews and Arabs: Jerusalem, Ramleh, Lydda, Tel-Aviv–Jaffa, Haifa, and Acre. There are five entirely Arab towns: Nazareth, Shafā ʿAmr, Umm al-Faḥm, Ṭaiyyba, and Ṭīra. Because Nazareth borders on Upper Nazareth, a Jewish town, they are sometimes perceived together as a mixed town. Out of the five, Nazareth is closest to the

---

[12] Ibrāhīm Malik, ʿal-Bunya al-ijtimāʿiyya al-ṭabaqiyya li-ʾl-jamāhīr al-ʿArabiyya fī Isrāʾīlʾ, *al-Jadīd*, 2 (Mar. 1990), 4–7.

[13] R. J. Simon, *Continuity and Change: A Study of Two Ethnic Communities in Israel* (1978).

usual concept of a town, on all levels; Shafā ʿAmr (which already had municipal status under the British Mandate) still looks like a large village, as do Umm al-Faḥm, Ṭaiyyba and Ṭīra (which have obtained municipal status only in the last few years; the last-named in May 1991).

To take an example: Shafā ʿAmr and the processes of change in it have been investigated by a sociologist at Haifa University, Dr Majid al-Haj, who published his results in 1987.[14] The fact that Dr al-Haj is both a scholar and a Muslim Arab with good contacts in Shafā ʿAmr favoured his undertaking, and several of his conclusions will be mentioned here, as they are relevant to the urban Arab sector in general. According to his findings, in Shafā ʿAmr with its 20,900 inhabitants the *hamula* has not broken down, but rather modified its functions, taking into consideration new social relations among family cells. For instance, the *hamula*'s role in Shafā ʿAmr is most significant in the municipal elections; this is particularly important, since in Israel these elections are often considered not merely local, but also political. The processes of modernization have altered the basis of local political competition in Shafā ʿAmr from a closed system, anchored in socio-economic stratification, to a more open one, based on the size of the group and its solidarity. As a result, formerly peripheral groups have moved nearer to the centre of the arena where the struggle for political power is waged, basing themselves on common interests. Obviously, practical expressions of these changes have differed from one town to another. I have already alluded to the significance of the Muslim factor in the municipal politics of Umm al-Faḥm, which had 25,400 inhabitants in early 1991. Below (in Chapter 8), in discussion of local administration and elections, some illustrations are given of political competition within the Arab localities in the State of Israel.

As far as mixed towns are concerned, it seems that the processes of social change and subsequent politicization have been accelerated owing to frequent, even continuous contacts with the Jewish population, a part of which, at least, is more modernized. Even though published research on this subject is as yet scarce and often lacking in a comparative dimension, we have at least some relevant information about it.

[14] Majid al-Haj, *Social Change and Family Processes: Arab Communities in Shefar-A'm* (1987).

1. Jerusalem has the largest Arab urban concentration. Few Arabs live in West Jerusalem, most of them (146,300 in early 1991) continuing to inhabit East Jerusalem, annexed to Israel following the 1967 War (the city's combined population, in early 1991, was 524,500). Several features are characteristic of the Arabs in East Jerusalem, distinguishing them from others in Israeli mixed towns: a great majority have refused to accept Israeli citizenship, remaining citizens of Jordan, that is, of a state which since 1948 has considered itself at war with the State of Israel; the population comprises varied elements, ethnically (such as Armenians) and religiously (numerous denominations); owing to the Jordanian connection and the heterogeneity of the population, numerous pre-1967 institutions, both denominational and administrative, continue to function, as well as a wide educational network based on Jordanian curricula. None the less, many East Jerusalem inhabitants have opted, economically, to benefit from Israeli rule, for instance, to get jobs with the Jewish majority (as in the municipality), to obtain subsidies from the National Insurance Institute,[15] and the like. Owing to their considerable number, foreign citizenship, proximity to the Israeli-held territories, and their Jordanian past (in 1948–67), East Jerusalem's inhabitants are the most radical among the Arabs in Israel and the most prone to express themselves politically in an anti-Israeli direction. This has been particularly evident since the start of the *intifāda* in December 1987, their identification with the Arabs in the Israeli-held territories becoming increasingly pronounced.

2. Nazareth, with the second largest urban concentration (53,600 Arab inhabitants in early 1991), is a town with numerous social and economic problems, such as comparatively high unemployment, dense overcrowding, and ideological struggles, both in Upper Nazareth, mostly Jewish, where the Arabs feel discriminated against in housing;[16] and among themselves. There are for example struggles of Christians versus Muslims (previously approximately equal in number, now with a Muslim majority); Communists versus those favouring the state administration;

---

[15] Hishām Nāshif, 'Hishtallĕvūt ha-okhlūsiyya bĕ-Mizraḥ-Yĕrūshalayim bĕ-misgeret ha-bīttūaḥ ha-lĕʾūmī', *Bittūaḥ Lĕʾūmī*, 2 (Dec. 1971), 95–9.

[16] 'al-Iʿtidā' ʿalà ʿAwnī Ḥannā Rūk min al-Nāṣira', *al-Rābiṭa*, 39 (Feb. 1985), 27–30.

and more recently Communists versus extremist Muslims, chiefly fundamentalists. It is not surprising that politicization is rampant in Nazareth, where spokesmen of different groups find frequent opportunities to express themselves in bitterly radical terms regarding their demands for complete equality with the Jews, support for Arabs in territories, and Arab nationalism in general. Their arguments penetrate, both in content and in style, many Galilee villages, to whom Nazareth is a model of political behaviour and expression.

3. Acre, where less than a quarter of the inhabitants are Arabs (9,290 out of 40,300 in early 1991), has experimented with joint housing for Arabs and Jews, with limited success.[17] Tension usually increases economic and political rivalry. In Acre's Arab quarters, political tension exists among the Arabs themselves, rather than with the Jews, since fundamentalist Muslims have succeeded in getting the upper hand in certain matters and lay down the law to their neighbours.[18]

4. Haifa's Arab inhabitants, so it seems, do not have particularly pressing complaints, but in Tel-Aviv–Jaffa they have, mostly as regards housing, and have consequently set up an organization to watch over their interests, entitled Rābiṭat shu'ūn 'Arab Yāfā (Association for the Affairs of the Jaffa Arabs).

According to an editorial in the Communist daily *al-Ittiḥād*,[19] the most common problem facing Arabs in mixed towns is housing, which, the paper claims, causes socio-economic strangulation. The political implications vary, naturally, from one town to another, but find expression mainly in the greater urban centres, inhabited by larger Arab populations. In these, the Arabs are politically articulate not merely in local issues, but in nationalist support for the demands of the Arabs in the territories and those in Israel proper.

---

[17] Details in 'Abd al-Ḥakīm Aghbariyya's "Akkā taḥt al-anqāḍ', *al-Maydān*, 8 (13 Jan. 1990), 7, 15. Cf. Èrik Cohen, *Integration vs. Separation in the planning of a Mixed Jewish–Arab City in Israel* (1973).
[18] See above, Ch. 3.
[19] "Arab al-mudun al-mukhtalaṭa yarfuḍūn al-iqtilā' wa-yurīdūn al-musāwāh', *al-Ittiḥād*, 21 Nov. 1990, 2.

THE BEDOUIN TRIBES

The Bedouin nomads, along with their tribal organization, particularist traditions, and inner divisions,[20] have been an integral part of life in the Negev—and somewhat less so in Galilee—under Ottoman, British, and Israeli rule.[21] The State of Israel provided welfare, education, and health services,[22] and the Bedouin responded loyally, even volunteering to serve in the Defence Forces as scouts. However, the Bedouin were not too happy with the close supervision of Israeli military and other security services, who blocked the cross-frontier movement they had known until 1948. They were also angered by the actions of the so-called Green Patrols, reconaissance units which limited their migration, along with their flocks, to water sources and pastures which they did not own. The tension thus caused has persisted until today and has contributed to a measure of politicization amongst the Bedouin, expressed in increased involvement in Israeli party politics, as will be discussed below.

In recent years, however, other no less far-reaching changes have occurred among the Bedouin, chiefly expressed in a process of sedentarization. Originating during the British Mandate in Palestine,[23] this became official policy in the State of Israel.[24] Wishing to improve their own status and that of their families as regards education, health, and employment, many Bedouin accepted generous offers from the Israeli authorities and willingly moved, after 1960, to permanent homes in Galilee, chiefly in Bosmat Ṭivʿōn. There their occupations are identical with those of others in the same area and, in time, their homes have become

---

[20] Haim Blanc, *The Arabic Dialect of the Negev Bedouin* (1970).
[21] Among various works on the Bedouin in Israel, Emanuel Marx's *Bedouin of the Negev* (1967) deserves special mention.
[22] H. Ben-Adi, 'Doctors to the Bedouin', *Jerusalem Post Magazine*, 17 July 1970, 5.
[23] Joseph Ben-David, 'The Negev Bedouin: From Nomadism to Agriculture', in Ruth Kark (ed.), *The Land that Became Israel: Studies in Historical Geography* (1989), 181–95.
[24] Ghāzī Fallāḥ, 'al-Awja al-jughrāfiyya li-inmāṭ istiqrār al-Badw fī Isrāʾīl', in Khālid Khalīfa (ed.), *Filasṭīniyyūn 1944–1988* (1988), 177–95; G. Kressel, *Praṭiyyūt lĕ-ʿummat shivṭiyyūt: Dīnamīqa shel qĕhīllat Bedwīm bĕ-tahalīkh hitʿaiyyrūt* (n.p.: ha-Kibbūtz ha-Mĕʾuhad, 1976); id., 'ha-Histaggĕlūt ha-eqōlōgīt wĕ-ha-tarbūtīt shel Bedwīm mitʿaiyyrīm bĕ-merkaz ha-aretz', in Layish (ed.), *ha-ʿAravīm bĕ-Israʾel* (1981), 140–67.

conventional, with furniture and electrical appliances.[25] Other Bedouin sedentary settlements are being established following those in Bosmat Ṭivʿōn. The Bedouin who agreed to sell their lands in the Negev obtained good prices—despite certain attempts to persuade them not to sell, with the argument that the whole affair was intended to dispossess and evict them.[26] Perhaps because of such arguments or the influence of Arab teachers from other parts of Israel who came to instruct their children, the Bedouin started to be more aware of their particular problems,[27] and of affairs in Israel, the territories, and the Arab states. All the Bedouin are Muslim, a fact which increases their solidarity; among them, too, there is a trend towards a return to fundamentalist Islam. This process, when combined with arguments relating to economic discrimination, strengthens politicization, perhaps even incipient radicalization, among them.[28] Their politicization is expressed, for instance, by their setting up an association for the defence of Bedouin rights, centred in Beʾer Sheba. Its founder and leader is Nūrī al-ʿUqbī, an erstwhile Bedouin and now a resident of Lydda. He has co-opted Jews, too, into this association.

WOMEN

Throughout the period since the State of Israel was established and most especially in the last two decades, Arab women have taken large strides towards modernization, thanks to compulsory and free education, employment outside their homes, the Jewish social model, and encouragement by various factors, such as the Histadrut. As to education, while 85 per cent of all Arab women had not been to school and were illiterate upon the establishment of the State of Israel, in 1988 this ratio had declined to 24 per cent (mostly the elderly). In that year, 32.4 per cent of Arab women had completed primary schooling; 10 per cent had attended intermediate schools,

---

[25] Tsvī Lavī', 'ha-Bedwīm baʾīm ha-ʿīra: naṯshū ōhel lĕ-maʿan ḥavīla', *Maʿarīv*, 16 June 1970, 16.

[26] Ramzī Ḥakīm, 'Anẓimat al-ṭawārī' fī dawlat al-ṭawāri'', *al-Ittiḥād*, 6 July 1970, 6.

[27] For their complaints, Yĕhūdīt Knöller, 'Tsarōt ḥadashōt bĕ-mivney qevaʿ', *ha-Aretz*, 3 Dec. 1990, B3.

[28] ʿAṭallāh Manṣūr, 'Kĕvar lō' kavōd gadōl', ibid. 4 Mar. 1991, B3.

and 27.7 per cent secondary schools; 6.3 per cent had reached higher education.[29] Women's integration into Israeli society is more pronounced in the Christian denominations, and in the towns rather than the villages or among the Bedouin. None the less, more women— particularly graduates of secondary schools and universities— are increasingly active in rural areas, and also (chiefly in Muslim villages), in local politics, such as elections.[30] This trend notwithstanding, the activity of Arab and Druze women[31] in economic life and in society outside their own localities, and to some extent in politics, is still circumscribed by the bonds of tradition and custom imposed by their religious and social framework.[32] It seems, however, that the days when David Ben-Gurion aroused criticism by shaking hands with Druze women during a visit to Dāliyat al-Karmil in 1970 are past.[33] Nowadays, one can find women of all denominations demanding from themselves and from others greater involvement in politics.[34]

[29] Id., 'Mi-bě'ad la-rě'ala', ibid. 19 Aug. 1990, B3.

[30] Blanche Qamā, *Ma'amad ha-ishsha ha-'Araviyya bě-Isra'el* (1984); Bensimon and Errera, *Israël et ses populations* (1977), 273–9.

[31] For the involvement of Druze women, 'Atallāh Mansūr, 'Hayyīm 'al ha-tsava", *ha-Aretz*, 26 Nov. 1990, B3.

[32] For complaints, Najwà Makhūl, 'al-Mar'a al-Filasṭīniyya fī Isrā'īl bayn wāqi' al-ikhdā' wa-imkānāt al-taḥarrur', *al-Jadīd*, 3 (Mar. 1982), 26–31; Hināf Jad'ūn, 'al-Mar'a al-'āmila mustaghalla min sāḥib al-'amal wa-min al-zawj', *al-Sināra*, 20 Apr. 1990; Amīra Habashī, 'al-Ra'y matà tu'addī al-mar'a al-Filasṭīniyya dawrahā al-thaqāfī wa-'l-ijtimā'ī fī Isrā'īl wa-Filasṭīn al-muḥtalla', *al-Mujtama'*, 18/5 (May 1990), 38–46; Joseph Ginat, *Women in Muslim Rural Society: Status and Role in Family and Community* (1982).

[33] *Yědī'ōt Aḥarōnōt*, 29 Nov. 1970, quoted by Ben-Dor, *The Druzes in Israel* (1979), 122.

[34] e.g. Maryam Mar'ī, 'al-Harakāt al-nisā'iyya fī al-wasaṭ al-'Arabī aydan rukkizat 'alà al-bu'd al-siyāsī awwalan', *al-Sināra*, 9 Aug. 1991, 25; Majdī Halabī, 'Jafrā', *Kull al-'Arab*, 3 May 1991.

5

Education

INTRODUCTORY

Perhaps more than any other aspect of the life of minority groups in the State of Israel, education reflects the struggle they are undergoing: modernism versus tradition, Israelism versus Arabism and Palestinianism. In this context, an Arab educator has defined Arab education in Israel as a battlefield between the Jewish authority and the Arab community.[1] Education not only acts as a focus of coexistence and conflict between majority and minority in Israel but contributes to their moderation or exacerbation.[2] There is total separation in formal education between Jews and Arabs from kindergarten through secondary school, in all forms and grades. However, institutions of higher learning often provide a meeting-point for new—and conflictual—interaction between students of both groups.[3]

If one considers the structures determining common ground and separation, it is clear that little has changed since the thirty years of British rule in Palestine.[4] During the Mandate, there were two disparate sets of education; the British authorities were basically responsible for the Arab, while the Jewish population administered its own schools almost autonomously. One of the results of that situation was that only a part of Arab boys (and still fewer girls) received primary education and fewer (generally the sons of the wealthy) reached secondary schooling.[5] One of the most urgent

---

[1] Sami Marʿi, 'Policy and Counter-Policy: The Status of Arab Education in Israel', in *Relations between Ethnic Majority and Minority* (1987), 38.

[2] See the PLO's attack on Arab education in Israel, without referring at all to its progress, Fayez A. Sayegh, *Discrimination in Education against the Arabs in Israel* (1966).

[3] For conflicts within Arab schools, cf. Yehuda Bien, *Beyt ha-sefer ha-ʿAravī: ʿIyyūn bĕ-veʿayōtav ha-enōshiyyōt* (1976).

[4] Much has been written regarding Arab education in Palestine and Israel. See e.g. S. Kh. Marʿi, *Arab Education in Israel* (1978); S. N. Eisenstadt and Y. Peres, *Some Problems of Educating A National Minority* (1968).

[5] ʿAzīz Haydar, 'al-Taʿlīm al-ʿArabī fī Isrāʾil wa-atharuh ʿalà waḍʿ al-ʿArab fī sūq al-ʿamal', *Qaḍāyā*, 2 (Feb. 1990), 25.

TABLE 5.1. The Increase in Arab schoolchildren in Israel, by type of school (in pupil nos.)

	1948/9	1958/9	1968/9	1978/9	1988/9
Kindergartens	1,124	7,274	14,211	17,368	22,200
Primary schools	9,991	36,903	85,449	124,518	139,600
Intermediate schools	—	—	2,457	14,801	28,928
Secondary schools	14	1,956	8,050	20,275	38,888
Teachers' colleges	—	121	370	485	576
TOTAL	11,129	46,254	110,537	177,447	230,192

Note: The table excludes pupils in non-governmental institutions (17,352 in 1989/90). Also, no distinction is made between Muslims, Christians, and Druzes.
Source: *Statistical Abstract of Israel*, 1990, 613.

tasks of the State of Israel, soon after its establishment, was to expand the network of Arab schools, in order to provide compulsory and free education (one year of pre-schooling and ten school grades), according to the laws passed in 1949 and 1953 for the entire school population, both Jewish and Arab.[6] Later, two more grades (eleventh and twelfth) were made free, but not compulsory, in all schools. This objective was diligently pursued in the Arab sector no less than in the Jewish, although in the early 1950s mass Jewish immigration strained the capabilities of the young state for providing universal education in those years when its investment in education increased disproportionately.

From the very start, the state authorities campaigned to persuade the Arab population of the importance of education (a matter not always taken for granted in some villages and among the Bedouin). Separate classes were opened for boys and girls with women teachers for the latter, whenever parents insisted on such a separation.[7] The main tasks, in both Jewish and Arab sectors, were simultaneously pedagogical and practical: determining the objectives of education,

[6] On the juridical situation of education in Israel, and Arab education particularly, Muḥammad Miʿārī, in *al-Jadīd*, 5 (May 1973), 19–23, 34.

[7] Michael Winter, 'Beʿayōt yĕsōd bĕ-maʿarekhet ha-ḥinnūkh', in Layish (ed.), *ha-ʿAravīm bĕ-Israʾel* (1981), 170.

drawing up curricula, writing textbooks, preparing teachers, building schools, and so forth. As far as Arab schools are concerned, in 1990 their number had reached 420 (330 primary and 90 secondary), comprising 6,695 classes and 6,657 teaching posts, of which 3,260 (or 49 per cent) were filled by women. It is no mean achievement that 96 per cent of the Jews and 87 per cent of the Arabs in Israel can read and write (the others are mostly elderly people, born before the establishment of the state and not enjoying any education). The ratio of Arab pupils in pre-university education is almost equal to their proportionate number in the Arab population (about 95 per cent are enrolled in schools) and does not differ, in this respect, from the situation in the Jewish sector. This remains true despite some early school-leaving by Arab girls, at the demand of their parents, and of boys, called upon to find jobs and assist their families financially. Such phenomena continue, to a certain extent, notwithstanding government efforts and a public campaign to limit school-leaving.[8] While Arab education in Israel is not without its shortcomings (to be discussed below), its quantitative achievement is generally impressive.[9]

Numerical increase is no less obvious among the Druzes. In the early days of the state, this community was, educationally, the least developed among Israel's minorities, probably owing to their low economic status and to the remoteness and isolation of their villages. In the 1948/9 school year, only 981 Druze pupils, 881 boys and 100 girls, were attending school. In 1986/7, 12,626 boys (53 per cent) and 10,979 girls (47 per cent) were at school—a notable increase, particularly for the girls, 97 per cent of whom were at school that year.[10] The above refers to primary schools; in secondary ones, however, there were cases of school-leaving, due to parents' opposition to their daughters continuing to attend school.

---

[8] See figures and their analysis by Suhayl Qabalān, 'Tasāquṭ al-ṭullāb wa-'l-qaḍāyā al-ijtimāʿiyya', al-Ittiḥād, 16 June 1989.

[9] Data, in addition to the Statistical Abstracts, in Sāmī Marʿī's 'al-Taʿlīm al-ʿArabī al-ibtidāʾī fī Isrāʾīl', al-Mawākib, 2/11–12 (Nov.–Dec. 1985), 16–39.

[10] Salmān Fallāḥ, 'Beʿayōt yěsōd ba-ḥinnūkh ha-Děrūzī bě-Israʾel', ha-Mizrah he-Hadash, 32/125–8 (1989), 115–28; Ūrī Thōn, 'ha-Ḥinnūkh ba-ʿeda ha-Děrūzīt', ha-Aretz, 14 Aug. 1970, 17; S. Rimāl, 'La-Děrūzīm děrūshīm merkēzey ḥinnūkh tīkhōn', ibid. 4 Sept. 1970, 17. For Druze complaints concerning their education, Majdī Halabī, ''Usfiyya janna fī aʿālī al-Karmil', Kull al-ʿArab, 8 Mar. 1991, 6.

VALUES AND ISSUES

While it is possible to solve the technical and physical problems of education, albeit with considerable effort, contending with values and content is more difficult. In the first months of the state, its Jewish leadership, acting out of a liberal, pluralistic approach, determined to let the Arab minority have its own educational sub-system, with Arabic as language of instruction and Arab civiliza-tion at the centre of its core curriculum—the intention being to encourage the Arabs to preserve their own religious, historical, and literary tradition. This policy has remained the cornerstone of the socialization of Arab pupils, together with the modernization through which their society and education have passed, both at school and in their continuous contacts with Jewish society as a modernizing agent. Socialization and the impact of modernization can, indeed, be observed in the cultural conflict in Arab education, particularly in the clash of expectations fostered by Arab society on the one hand, and the Ministry of Education and Culture on the other.

The identity conflict (to be discussed below, in Chapter 9) has created special problems in Arab education, torn between the perceptions of teachers, parents, and students, who see themselves as belonging to the Arab people (even beyond Israel's frontiers), and as citizens of the State of Israel (at war with their own kind). The Druzes excepted, members of the minorities are exempted from military service, not only because of security considerations, but also to spare the Israeli Arabs the decision to fight their own people. This situation has not been lost on Arab teachers and pupils. The teacher, representing the State of Israel in class, is expected to deliver messages with which he is not always in accord, and to reply to pupils' questions when he or she does not always have satisfactorily clear-cut answers. As to the state's education system, which is obviously unable to solve the minority's identity problems, it is nevertheless expected to react to the situation by determining objectives, contents, and curricula.

OBJECTIVES AND CURRICULA

Because of the difficulty in determining educational goals in the Arab sector acceptable both to the recipients and to the state, official policy seems to have been to postpone making decisions.[11] Thus in 1953, when important education laws were passed in the Knesset, goals were set for the entire state, without distinguishing between Jews and Arabs. While such objectives as scientific knowledge and interiorizing respect for work, for the principles of a free society, for egalitarianism, and for tolerance were appropriate for both sectors, as were love of country and loyalty to the state, one may argue that loyalty to the Jewish people and its cultural values was mostly applicable to the Jewish sector. Following the end of the Military Administration late in 1966, and the renewed contacts with people in the Israeli-held territories in 1967, pressure increased among the Arabs in Israel for a re-examination of educational goals.[12] In February 1972 the Minister of Education and Culture approved a document entitled 'Basic Goals for Arab Education in Israel'. Its main points were as follows: (1) educating for values of peace; (2) educating for loyalty to the State of Israel, with an emphasis on the common interests of all its inhabitants and the special character of the Arabs in Israel; (3) starting a project for facilitating social and economic integration; (4) educating the girls for independence and improvement of their social standing. 'The Yadlin Document', so called after Education Minister Aharon Yadlin (who was responsible for its preparation), was a significant step forward, in that it devoted special attention to the needs and aspirations of Israel's Arab population.

Another document was drawn up in 1975 and published in the following year, in a book prepared by the Ministry of Education and Culture on plans for education in Israel in the 1980s. As far as the Arabs were concerned, the following is relevant:

The goal of state education within the Arab sector in Israel is to base education on the elements of Arab culture, the achievements of science, hope for peace between Israel and its neighbours, loving the country common to all its citizens, and loyalty to the State of Israel, emphasizing interests common to everybody, while fostering the special character of the Arabs in Israel, and an acquaintance with Jewish culture.[13]

[11] Another opinion, extremely critical, in Khalil Nakhleh, 'The Goals of Education for Arabs in Israel', *New Outlook*, 20/74 (Apr.–May 1977), 29–35.
[12] Saʿd Sarṣūr, 'Ḥinnūkh ʿAravī bi-mēdīna Yēhūdīt', in A. Hareven (ed.), *Eḥad mi-kōl shishsha Isrěʾēlīm* (1981), 114.
[13] *Hatsaʿat tsevet lě-tikhnūn ha-ḥinnūkh li-shěnōt ha-shěmōnīm* (1976), 421.

Here one finds a well-thought-out combination of the objectives outlined in 1953 and 1972, paying greater attention to the Arab sector. The issues particular to the Arabs are taken up again at another point in this ministerial publication:

We feel that we cannot overlook the identity of the Arabs in Israel in all matters relating to their culture, traditions, and language. It is impossible to continue to ignore in the schools the existence of the Jewish–Arab conflict. We ought to clarify our positions unambiguously—Arab cultural uniqueness, on the one hand, and on the other, loyalty to the State of Israel, whose majority is Jewish and whose character is Zionist.[14]

Here clear goals were defined regarding both Arab culture and loyalty to the state, a combination of which was considered essential. Judging from the difference between these goals and those outlined for Druze education, defined as defence of the state and relations with other Druzes outside Israel, one gets the impression that the authors of the 1975–6 plans were still somewhat uncertain of the Arabs in Israel, thus not mentioning the encouragement of *their* relations with kinsmen across Israel's borders.

In Arab schools, as everywhere, the curriculum is the instrument for putting educational goals into practice. In principle, it ought to be equal to—although not identical with—that in Jewish schools in such disciplines as biology, geography, mathematics, and so forth, with some differences in other disciplines dictated by the language and culture of the two sectors.[15] In practice, however, matters are not so simple. Indeed, the language of instruction is Arabic, parallel to the use of Hebrew in Jewish schools. But while in Jewish schools a minimum of Arab history and literature is studied, and only a limited amount of Arabic is compulsory, pupils in Arab schools learn Hebrew, certain chapters of Hebrew literature (including chapters from the Bible), and Jewish history (including the basics of Zionist history). The next chapter will discuss issues of language and culture in more detail. Here it is sufficient to point out this asymmetry by which the Arab minority is supposed to learn more Hebrew and Judaism than the Jewish majority Arabic and Arab culture.[16] This is understandable in view of enhancing the chances of Arabs finding jobs in a society whose majority uses Hebrew rather than other languages, and perhaps bolstering the minority's loyalty to the state (hence the curriculum avoids the history of Arab nationalism). However, this asymmetry irritates Arab teachers and pupils;[17] the latter find other ways of obtaining nationalistic information, without the guidance of professional personnel. It is quite likely, therefore, that the official approach may well achieve results opposite to those intended, and encourage politicization all the more.

It seems, however, that the lesson has been learned: during the 1980s the amount of material dealing with Jewish history and Hebrew literature has been reduced in Arab schools. In the latter discipline, the new curriculum has mainly focused on Israeli literature, rather than that of the Jewish diaspora, which lacks appeal for Arab pupils, who have difficulty in finding common ground with it. On the other hand, the curriculum in Arab history and literature has been enlarged (although still avoiding nationalist content). There seems to be a growing tendency in official circles to redress the existing asymmetry, while persevering in educating for co-existence and loyalty to the state,[18] without offending the feelings of the Arab population, both Muslim and Christian, which is naturally proud of its significant cultural heritage. As part of this trend, the Ministry of Education has, in recent years, changed the curriculum in Arabic literature. The intention is to permit a wider selection of materials and to include poetry and prose written by Palestinian authors during the twentieth century. Again, some Arab critics have maintained that the reform does not go far enough.[19]

A different curriculum, specially adapted to the Druzes, was required, since that designed for Arab schools does not refer to them at all. While the Druze religion may not be taught at school, owing to its secret character, some spokesmen of this community

---

[16] For Arab complaints in the matter, see e.g. *Newsweek*, 8 Feb. 1971, 22.

[17] Cf. Peled's book (n. 14 above), esp. 15. See also ʿUmar Maḥāmīd, in *al-Ittiḥād*, 19 June 1989.

[18] All the principals in Arab schools have attended courses organized by the Department for Democracy and Coexistence in the Ministry of Education and Culture.

[19] See Ḥabīb Būlus, 'al-Adab al-ʿArabī al-Filasṭīnī fī manāhij tadrīs al-lugha al-ʿArabiyya fī Isrāʾīl', *al-Ittiḥād*, 30 June 1991.

have argued that at least its history, views, and special customs ought to be studied. Hence the goals of Druze education were drawn up by the Ministry of Education and Culture in a manner parallel to those relating to Arab education, as follows:

The objective of state education in the Druze sector is to base it on Druze and Arabic cultural values, the achievements of science, hopes for peace between Israel and its neighbours, love of the country common to all its citizens, loyalty to the State of Israel, and commonality in the construction of Israel and its defence, emphasizing interests common to all, encouraging the special relationship between Jews and Druzes, and acquaintance with Jewish culture, fostering the Israeli-Druze entity, rooting Druze youth in their community's heritage and in the commonality of fate among Druzes everywhere.

Consequently, textbooks had to be written, a task completed only in the 1985/6 school year, covering all disciplines and grades. In several areas, particularly in the lower grades, materials had to be adapted to meet requests of the Druzes; while for the upper grades, special new textbooks were prepared, chiefly in history, Druze heritage, civics, social studies, geography, Arabic, and Hebrew. All these were written by Druze teachers and educators. Of particular interest is the subject defined as Druze heritage, which began to be taught in 1976, and on which eight textbooks, together with a teacher's guide, have been published. Although the demand for studying this subject originated in the Druze community, some members of it had reservations: first, spiritual leaders, who were afraid that the secrets of their religion might be unveiled; however, after having examined the new textbooks they supported the project; secondly, the Druze Initiative Committee and circles close to it, which perceived this move as political, planned to drive a wedge between them and their Arab neighbours; their own approach was to consider the Druze heritage as part of the wider Arab one. Further, history books allotted special chapters to Druze history, in addition to discussing world, Jewish, and Arab history. In civics, the Druzes study their own history in modern times, and in social studies, Druze society. In literature, they read Druze literary works in addition to Arab ones; and Hebrew works on the Druzes, in their study of the Hebrew language.[20]

---

[20] Salmān Fallāḥ, in his book *Tōlĕdōt ha-Dĕrŭzīm bĕ-Isra'el* (1974); id., 'Be'ayōt vĕsōd' (n. 10 above). 121 ff.

ADMINISTRATIVE AND OTHER COMPLAINTS

The Arabs in Israel have devoted a great deal of attention to their education in recent years, and have set up a special committee to follow up grievances and act towards redressing them.[21] The first chairman of this committee was Dr Majid al-Haj, of Haifa University. The complaints articulated by Arab educators refer to the paucity of vocational schools[22] and their inadequate equipment,[23] forcing pupils who are vocationally inclined to enrol in other schools to which they are not suited, thus sometimes lowering the general level of achievement there; the absence of advanced technological schooling;[24] a lack of classrooms, spacious modern schools, computers laboratories,[25] sports equipment (chiefly in the villages),[26] and additional services, such as psychological counselling.[27] Difficulties of a social nature confronting the committee include the want of parental encouragement and family assistance (mostly in the case of villagers who had not gone to Israeli schools and still consider modern education as a waste of time); and premature school-leaving by girls in mixed schools and other institutions (on reaching puberty or soon afterwards).

Even though the general situation has considerably improved in many areas,[28] not everything has been done to bring education in the Arab sector up to the level of the Jewish one in all respects. For instance, there are still several villages where pupils study

---

[21] Cf. e.g. the meeting which the committee organized, 'Khuṭṭat tashwīshāt wa-khuṭuwāt kifāḥiyya ibtidāʾan min al-usbūʿ al-qādim tashhaduhā al-madāris al-ʿArabiyya', *Kull al-ʿArab*, 24 Aug. 1990, 15.

[22] Yechiel Harari, *The Arabs in Israel 1975–1976* (1977), 53, 58.

[23] ʿAzīz Haydar, *ha-Ḥinnūkh ha-miqtsōʿī-tekhnōlōgī ba-migzar ha-ʿAravī bě-Israʾel* (1985).

[24] Y. Algazī, 'Ba-derekh lě-Tōrōntō', *ha-Aretz*, 5 July 1991, B4.

[25] The situation of technological education in the Arab sector brought about, in 1985, the establishment of a foundation for developing it, see Ibrāhīm ʿAwda, 'Taṭawwur al-taʿlīm al-tiknūlūjī', *al-Mawākib*, 2/9–10 (Sept.–Oct. 1985), 80–2. See also 'Dōah ha-qeren lě-fittūaḥ tekhnōlōgī ba-ḥinnūkh ha-ʿAravī', *ha-Aretz*, 1 Dec. 1986, 6.

[26] A complaint by ʿAzīz Haydar, in his article in *al-Qaḍāyā*, Feb. 1990, 26 (n. 5 above), that in 1989 the average of Arab pupils per class was 31, while the Jewish was 27, is correct, but not particularly worrisome.

[27] Cf. arguments in this and other matters, Mundhir Gharīb, 'al-Taʿlīm al-ʿArabī fī Isrāʾīl fī iṭār taqārīr al-lijān al-dirāsiyya al-mukhtalifa', *al-Jadīd*, 7 (July 1978), 19–28.

[28] As reflected in the school-leaving examinations, see N. Mendler, 'Talmīdīm ʿAraviyyīm mi-Noṣrat maṣlīḥīm mi-bagrūt yōter mi-talmīdeyha ha-Yěhūdiyyīm', *ha-Aretz*, 7 Feb. 1990, A5.

in inadequate rented schoolrooms, occasionally even in decrepit buildings. The Ministry of Education and Culture has acknowledged that, speedy construction notwithstanding, in 1989 (that is, even before the large wave of Russian-Jewish immigration) there was still a shortage of 700 classrooms in the Arab sector and as many in the Jewish one.[29] Of course, in proportion to the population figures, the deficiency in the Arab sector looms larger. Further, equipment is still inadequate in certain schools in this sector. True, some grievances refer to exceptional cases. However, the details count for less than a prevailing feeling, at least among some teachers and pupils, that the physical conditions of schools in the Arab sector are inferior to those in the Jewish. This feeling of discrimination found some confirmation in the fact that until recently a Jew was director of the Arab education department in the Ministry of Education and Culture; only in 1987 was an Arab educator, 'Alī Ḥaydar Zahāliqa, appointed to this position.[30]

The sorry situation of the scarcity of Arab teachers in the first years after the 1948 Arab-Israeli War compelled the hiring of teachers lacking academic and pedagogical qualifications. The problem has been dealt with, since 1959, by intensive training of school and kindergarten teachers (Muslim, Christian, and Druze) through the establishment of two teachers' colleges, with a two-year curriculum, as in the Jewish colleges. These teachers were employed in primary schools, while positions in the secondary schools were filled by university graduates who had also been trained in the universities' departments of education. Indeed, teaching has become, over the years, the main occupation of Arab university graduates (Arab students will be discussed separately later in this chapter). Financially, the situation of Arab teachers is no worse than in the Jewish sector—in other words, not brilliant. However, their main problem may well be in having to take sides and adopt attitudes in class, under difficult conditions.

The following may provide an example of the ambiguous situation. On 12 January 1980, about thirty representatives of Arab local authorities met in Nazareth to discuss education. At the end of

[29] An interview with I. Navōn, then Minister of Education and Culture, in *al-'Ajamī*, 25 Nov. 1989. Other data are brought by Yūsuf Faraj, 'Kayfa tastaqbil madārisunā al-sana al-dirāsiyya al-jadīda?', *al-Ittiḥād*, 30 Aug. 1991, Suppl., 1, 5.
[30] For his views, cf. 'Alī Ḥaydar Zahāliqa, 'Mashākil al-ta'līm al-'Arabī fī al-waqt al-ḥāḍir wa-'l-sanawāt al-2000', *Kull al-'Arab*, 7 Dec. 1990, 10.

their meeting, they issued a joint condemnation of the Ministry of the Interior, which they maintained had not forwarded funds needed for school buildings and equipment. They also decided to hold a general strike in all schools in the Arab sector for one day, 23 January 1980. The Ministry of Education and Culture, for its part, instructed all teachers to show up in their classrooms as usual.

Arab teachers thus found themselves in an impossible dilemma, which was actually only one facet of their being both civil servants and members of their own particular group. An Israeli-Arab scholar has written that for the parents, the teachers are, indeed, 'agents of the authorities'.[31] In addition to tensions with the parents,[32] some teachers have difficulties in discussing political issues brought up by their pupils.[33] While they support free debate, in principle, in certain cases teachers hesitate to express their own opinions freely in matters connected with Israeli and Middle Eastern politics.[34] In addition, teachers in the Arab sector (as elsewhere) sometimes experience didactic and pedagogical difficulties, as well as tensions with their director or inspector,[35] which obviously do not facilitate their relations with their pupils.

Some recognition of the difficult issues facing these teachers may be found in a circular issued by the Director-General of the Ministry of Education and Culture, dating from May 1983. Addressed to Arab teachers, it dwells at some length on the issue of double loyalty. A few selected passages follow.

With the following we bring to the attention of teachers and educators in the Arab schools—chiefly the post-primary ones—a number of guiding points relating to their activity in the realm of civic Arab education. Most Israeli Arabs—including the teachers—expect to live in Israel peacefully, as citizens equal in rights and duties, actively loyal to the state and its democratic values. However, they are also sons of the Arab nation, and this arouses in them sentiments of identification with their brethren in the

---

[31] Marʿi, *Arab Education*, 37–8.

[32] Sāmī Marʿī, 'al-Madrasa wa-'l-ijtimāʿ fī al-qarya al-ʿArabiyya fī Isrāʾīl', *Āfāq*, 1/1 (July 1980), 3–29. An exchange of views about 'Shuʾūn al-madāris wa-'l-taʿlīm fī al-wasaṭ al-ʿArabī', *al-Sināra*, 7 July 1989, 8–9.

[33] For instance, Usāma Ḥalabī, 'Ḥurriyat al-taʿbīr dākhil al-madrasa wa-khārijahā', *al-Jadīd*, 9 (Sept. 1983), 17–19, 45.

[34] An interesting suggestion was put forth, to include official lessons of political education, which would provide answers relating to Jewish–Arab coexistence in Israel. See Samʿān Samʿān, 'al-Tarbiya al-siyāsiyya fī al-madāris al-ʿArabiyya', *al-Mawākib*, 3/7–8 (July–Aug. 1986), 78–83.

[35] The most comprehensive study of this topic is by Bien (n. 3 above).

Arab world. As long as a political struggle and an armed conflict persist between the State of Israel and most of the Arab States, Israeli-Arab citizens are in a quandary . . . Many teachers and educators—all the year round and more particularly so during extraordinary events, when political instincts boil up—wonder what to tell their pupils; how to explain what is going on and the attitudes of participants in the events. When pupils do not obtain at school reliable information and guidance to understand what is going on, they will look elsewhere for answers to the questions which trouble them. Teachers feel frustrated and losing face when avoiding pupils' queries . . . The education system should educate both Jewish and Arab pupils to a life based on peace, understanding and mutual respect, loyalty and active citizenship. The goal of Arab civic education, in the Arab schools, is to educate Arab youngsters to be citizens of the State of Israel, who take on duties and active citizenship, insisting on their civic rights out of identification with the state. Yet they also have to be Arabs, proud of their cultural national heritage and identifying with the Arab cultural world . . . Educators ought to encourage discussion on issues that trouble youngsters, attempting to have all views equitably aired. Pupils should be given an opportunity to hear and grasp varying and contrasting points of view, without the teacher forcing his own opinions on them. Pupils ought to be encouraged to analyse rationally whatever they have heard or read, to distinguish between the essence and the empty slogans. An important objective is to uproot prejudices and stereotypes . . . One way to achieve this is to have them meet other youths, including Jewish ones, for well-defined common activities.

While this important document could not resolve all problems, it went a long way in pointing out educational principles for teachers and others.

NON-GOVERNMENTAL SCHOOLS

Private schools in the Arab sector have been and still are mostly Christian.[36] These, both primary and secondary, have a long history in the Middle East and have generally enjoyed a fairly large measure of autonomy. During Israel's first twenty years, about 10 per cent of Arab children studied in Christian establishments; some of these were Muslims (but very few were Druzes). With the growing confidence of Muslims in the state schools, fewer of their children were enrolled in Christian establishments, all the more so

---

[36] See Winter (n. 7 above), 174–6.

since many villagers were distressed that the Koran was not studied in these schools. The latter were also hurt financially by a decline in the allocation of funds by church organizations. Consequently, they agreed to accept funds from the Israeli government in return for accepting its educational supervision and the introduction of the official curriculum, with the addition, however, of religious studies and the preservation of a special atmosphere (better discipline, uniforms, and so forth).

Christian schools in Israel today form a sort of outer circle among those comprising the state education system. Not a few have attained high standards, such as a Haifa secondary school called the Arab Orthodox College (founded in 1952 and reaching a student body of more than 600).[37] Most of these establishments, however, are Catholic, with a Protestant or Greek Orthodox minority. Most are regular academic schools, but some are vocational, for both boys are girls; their service in the education of girls is particularly noteworthy.

Education in East Jerusalem has a special character. Since, following the 1967 annexation by Israel, most inhabitants maintained their Jordanian citizenship rather than take an Israeli one, the official Jordanian curriculum has been preserved. This enables secondary school pupils to sit for the Jordanian matriculation examinations, and the diploma allows them to continue higher education in Jordan or other Arab states. The main innovation is the addition of Hebrew to the curriculum and the selection of one school to teach the Israeli curriculum so that its graduates may have the option of studying in Israeli universities,[38] as do others, too, after having sat for qualifying examinations.

Few organizations are available to Arab youths outside their schools, except for sports groups and some others which will now be briefly noted. These unattached young people comprise school drop-outs who have interrupted their education to look for jobs, or even secondary school graduates who are as yet unemployed or only partly employed. Their overall number is large,[39] and their frustra-

---

[37] Nasīm Abū Khayṭ, 'al-Kulliyya al-Urthūdhuksiyya fī Ḥayfā', *al-Ittiḥād*, 1 Nov. 1987.
[38] Winter (n. 7 above), 175–6. Cf. Gideon Weigert, 'Arabische Jugend in Ost-Jerusalem', in C. C. Schweitzer and M. Nemitz (eds.), *Krisenherd Nah-Ost* (1973), 93–100.
[39] Sami Jeraisi, *Reflections on Problems of Arab Youth* (n.d.), 2 ff.

tion finds an outlet in increased interest in politics. Wishing to prevent an open conflict between Israelism and Arabism, the Israeli education authorities refrain from imparting political values in the schools. Civics is taught more as a body of useful information rather than as a set of values;[40] even education for democracy, despite public consensus about its importance, is somewhat neglected.[41] As a result, Arab school graduates and drop-outs are more exposed to political propaganda. Government agencies and Histadrut representatives show little interest in these young people;[42] associations such as the scouts absorb but few of them.

MAPAM (United Workers' Party), a left-of-centre grouping, has attempted to step into this void. Its activity in this context, although modest in figures, is significant in its novelty. Soon after the state's establishment, MAPAM's youth organization, Ha-Shōmer ha-Tsaʿīr, attempted to recruit young Arabs. In 1950 an Arab architect close to MAPAM's views, Rustum Bastūnī, proposed the setting up of an Arab youth movement, patterned on Ha-Shōmer ha-Tsaʿīr. This started with thirteen boys and two girls, half of them Muslims and the other half Christians. They were invited to spend some time on a kibbutz (co-operative settlement), to acquire professional skills and meet intensively with the local Jewish youth. Similar groups were formed later to stay at other MAPAM kibbutzim, apparently with no little success in making them acquainted with kibbutz life. Members of this Pioneer Arab Youth, as the groups were called, were quite impressed by this experiment in coexistence as well as by kibbutz life. At its peak, in 1959–60, the movement numbered about 1,300 Arab members, in kibbutzim and summer-camps, where they associated with Jewish young people. However, after 1962, the attempt gradually disintegrated, perhaps because it was not an authentic movement with its own grass roots.[43] In 1990 MAPAM revived it and hundreds attended seminars and lectures.[44]

---

[40] On this complicated subject, cf. H. Rappaport *et al.*, *Těnūʿat ha-nōʿar ha-ʿAravī bě-Israʾel: Yedaʿ, ʿarakhīm wě-hitnahagūyōt bě-nōseʾ ḥevra w-mědīna* (1978).

[41] Mājid al-Hāj, *ha-Ḥīnnūkh lě-děmōqratiyya bě-veyt ha-sefer ha-ʿAravī bě-Israʾel: beʿayōt w-mēsīmōt* (1989).

[42] Elī Elʿad, 'ha-ʿArabīstīm ʿayefīm: haznaḥa ba-tīppūl ba-rěḥōv ha-ʿAravī w-va-nōʿar', *ha-Aretz*, 30 Jan. 1970, 17.

[43] The most readable summing-up of this movement was written by Yěhōshafat Netser and Tamar Raz, *Těnūʿat ha-nōʿar ha-ʿAravī ha-halūtsī* (1976).

[44] See *New Outlook*, 34/314–15 (Apr.–May 1991), back cover.

Meetings of Arab and Jewish young people have continued, meanwhile, in more institutionalized structures, such as secondary schools, as well as gatherings initiated by various organizations such as the Institute for Arab Studies at the Givʿat Ḥavīva kibbutz (affiliated to MAPAM or Communist groups).[45] All these affect only a small part of Arab youth. Others idle away their time (if they are unemployed), or are exposed to nationalist propaganda (sometimes extreme),[46] or join fundamentalist Islamic groups (which have some success in taking care of them and recruiting them).[47]

THE STUDENTS

In many countries, students constitute an active element, effervescent with hope to change state and society. Those at Israeli universities, who perceive themselves as leaders of the intellectual élite,[48] are no different. Among them, Arab students are very articulate in their demands regarding both their own hopes and the future of Arab society in Israel. Indeed, they have high expectations from themselves and from state and society.[49] In many respects, Arab students feel frustrated, while their education has prepared them, possibly better than some of their Jewish peers, to express themselves forcefully.

Although both the number of Arab students and their ratio in the student body have grown,[50] this hardly reflects their group's proportion in the overall population. Thus, in 1988/9 (the last school year for which we have detailed figures), 3,828 Arab students were registered in all Israeli institutions of higher learning, constituting 5.9 per cent of all students (while Arabs form about 16 per cent of Israel's population).

[45] Report and analysis by Havīva Ber and Jābir ʿAsāqila, *Mifgěshey noʿar Yěhūdī-ʿAravī bě-Givʿat Havīva: Haʿarakhat ʿamadōt 'lifney' wě-aharey'* (1988).
[46] See e.g. Abū Maʿādh, 'Hunāk man yaḥtāj ilà tarbiya dīmuqrāṭiyya wa-tarbiya waṭaniyya', *al-Maydān*, 6 Apr. 1990, 3.
[47] Ūd Gūndar, 'Gan yěladīm ba-ḥatsar ha-misgad', *ha-Aretz*, 9 Jan. 1991, B2.
[48] Elie Rekhess, 'Israeli Arab Intelligentsia', *Jerusalem Quarterly*, 11 (Spring 1979), 51–69.
[49] Among the works on Arab students in Israel, see Marʿi, *Arab Education*, Ch. 6.
[50] For their small number in the 1950s, Anīs Rashīd Abū Ḥannā, 'al-Ṭālib al-ʿArabī fī al-jāmiʿāt al-ʿIbriyya', *al-Ṣināra*, 27 Jan. 1989, 13.

TABLE 5.2. Students in Israeli institutions of
higher education, 1980/1 to 1988/9

	1980/1	1984/5	1988/9
TOTAL	54,394	59,929	64,880
Jews (%)	95.3	93.3	94.1
Non-Jews (%)	4.7	6.7	5.9
Muslims	2.7	4.1	3.4
Christians	1.7	2.1	1.9
Druzes	0.3	0.5	0.6

Source: Central Bureau of Statistics, *Supplement to
Statistical Monthly of Israel*, 6 (1990), 168, table 1.

There seem to be several reasons for the relatively low number of
Arab students in institutions of higher education:

1. The difficulty of studying in Hebrew:[51] all Israeli universities
   and colleges teach in Hebrew, as a great majority of their
   students are Israeli Jews; in several of them, such as the Hebrew
   University of Jerusalem, special courses in Hebrew are available
   to Arab students and to students from other countries.
2. The lower rates of achievement in many Arab secondary
   schools, as compared to the Jewish.
3. The small number of Arab women students, probably due to
   conservatism in their homes and parental opposition to leaving
   them. However, at the University of Haifa, for the first time, in
   the 1990/1 school year women constituted 52 per cent of the
   Arab students.
4. Arab graduates' limited chances of obtaining suitable jobs in
   their area of expertise, a problem besetting Jewish graduates as
   well, but to a lesser degree (we shall revert to this issue below).
5. Difficulties in finding housing in town, which probably explains the flow of Arab students, especially women, to Haifa
   University, close to their towns and villages in Galilee.

Many students enrol in the faculties of law, the humanities, and
the social sciences. One reason may be that they have failed in the

[51] Doris Angst, 'Arabs in Israel: In Search of Identity', *Swiss Review of World
Affairs*, 33/1 (Apr. 1983), 14–19.

TABLE 5.3. Students in Israeli higher education, by institution, 1988/9

	All	Hebrew University	Technological Institute (Haifa)	Tel-Aviv University	Bar-Ilan University	Haifa University	Ben-Gurion University	Weizman Institute
TOTAL (nos.)	64,880	16,112	8,905	18,779	8,650	6,056	5,748	630
Jews (%)	94.1	91.7	92.9	98.6	98.8	80.0	95.2	99.3
Non-Jews (%)	5.9	8.3	7.1	1.4	1.2	20.0	4.8	0.7
Muslims (%)	3.4	5.5	3.0	0.9	0.9	9.9	3.7	0.5
Christians (%)	1.9	2.4	3.0	0.4	0.1	7.3	0.8	—
Druzes (%)	0.6	0.4	1.1	0.1	0.2	2.8	0.3	—

Source: Central Bureau of Statistics, *Supplement to Statistical Monthly of Israel*, 6 (1990), 178, table 8.

TABLE 5.4. Students in Israeli higher education, by area of study, 1988/9

	All	Humanities	Social Sciences	Law	Medicine of Related Areas	Mathematics and Science	Agriculture	Engineering and Architecture
TOTAL (nos.)	64,880	15,574	18,784	2,247	4,849	10,269	1,136	9,626
Jews (%)	94.1	92.3	95.7	94.8	91.9	93.4	95.9	95.8
Non-Jews (%)	5.9	7.7	4.3	5.2	8.1	6.6	4.1	4.2
Muslims (%)	3.4	4.8	2.4	2.0	4.2	4.2	3.3	1.8
Christians (%)	1.9	2.2	1.5	2.7	3.1	1.8	0.6	1.7
Druzes (%)	0.6	0.7	0.4	0.5	0.8	0.6	0.2	0.7

Source: Central Bureau of Statistics, *Supplement to Statistical Monthly of Israel*, 6 (1990), 175, table 7.

competitive exams for entry to architecture and the sciences, or found these studies too difficult. Empirical research carried out in 1982 by Dr Nadim Rouhana and a number of assistants in Galilee and the Little Triangle showed that about a third of the students originally intended to study medicine and dentistry.[52] Those who entered these faculties did remarkably well; for instance, the first successful liver transplant in Israel was carried out in 1991 by an Arab surgeon. The difficulty in getting admitted into the science faculties was probably due to the low standards of science teaching in Arab secondary schools. However, in this matter, too, a turn for the better has occurred. According to a report issued by ʿAlī Ḥaydar Zaḥāliqa, Director of Arab Education in the Ministry of Education and Culture, in 1988/9, about 60 per cent of all Arab secondary school pupils studied science, which he believed would increase their chances of going on to mathematics, physics, and computer science at the university level.[53] It is characteristic for the Christians that their ratio is higher than that of the Muslims (considering their overall population figures), in all faculties, agriculture excepted.

Consequently, some Arab students are frustrated in their university studies, which are not always their first choice. They have naturally tended to be active not only in their own interests, but also in those of their society, most particularly in the struggle for complete equality and, increasingly, for the nationalist cause. Not a few, indeed, perceive such activities as a mission, due to their constituting an educated élite. Insofar as their opinions have been made known in their manifestos, newspapers, speeches, and demonstrations, Arab students have expressed various views bearing first on a continuous struggle for their standing as students; secondly on full equality of the Arabs in Israel (mostly voiced up to 1967); and thirdly, since 1967, along with students in the Israeli-held territories, on their national aspirations, in a trend towards Palestinization. The more politically aware among them, indeed, wrap all three approaches together in one package.

If one goes into more detail, certain topics are most frequently discussed by Arab students in their declarations and publications:

[52] Nadīm Rouhanā, 'Baʿd al-mumayyizāt li-ʾl-ṭullāb al-khirrījīn al-Jāmiʿiyyīn al-Filasṭīniyyīn min Isrāʾīl', *al-Jadīd*, 5 (May 1984), esp. 26–7.
[53] ʿAṭallāh Manṣūr, '60% me-ha-sṭūdenṭīm ha-ʿAraviyyīm ba-Aretz lamēdū ha-shana miqtsōʿōt reyʾaliyyīm', *ha-Aretz*, 22 Sept. 1989, A6.

(1) their particular relation to the land and its symbolic significance for all Arabs in Israel; (2) their refusal to carry out the guard duties in student dormitories, which their Jewish colleagues perform (university administrators have maintained that equality should be expressed in duties not merely in rights; Arab students argued in response that they could not possibly fulfil a task by virtue of which they would be perceiving their fellow Arabs as potential enemies); (3) their feeling of isolation at the university, due to the lack of friendly relations with Jewish students.[54] While it is quite possible that living together in the university dormitories creates some tensions,[55] these are evident (although perhaps less so) between the Jews themselves as well (say, between the orthodox and the secular).

A research project carried out in this context by Majid al-Haj has led to interesting conclusions. Nine hundred Arab and Jewish students at Haifa University replied to questionnaires containing 400 queries regarding their views and attitudes.[56] The study showed an almost total absence of hostility between the two groups, but also a complete absence of co-operation—despite their declared willingness to come together. Indeed, alienation from the state and harsh criticism were voiced in a one-time Arab students' newspaper at Haifa University, *Ṣawt al-Karmil* (Voice of the Carmel), published in May 1988. Similar issues have been argued by Druze students, although perhaps more moderately. Their grievances concerning their own economic problems and their debates about identifying with the political demands of Arab students reflect, in the university microcosm, the issues troubling the Druze community in general.[57]

Student politicization has found a powerful advocate in the Arab Students' Committees. These were set up first in Jerusalem in 1958/9, then in each of the other universities; afterwards a country-

[54] e.g. editorial of *Awḍāʾ Jadīda* (Arabic Suppl. to the Hebrew *Dorban*, organ of Tel-Aviv University's students), 20 Apr. 1967, 1. Cf. *Bat-Qōl* (organ of Bar-Īlan University's students), 11 Nov. 1970, 4–5.

[55] Sīgal Bar-Qōvets, 'Ḥayyey shittūf', *Pī ha-Atōn* (organ of the students at the Hebrew University of Jerusalem), Apr. 1991, 20–1.

[56] Rōn Shaḥar, 'Dū-Qiyyūm ba-avīrat haqtsana', *ha-Aretz*, 3 Jan. 1991, B4.

[57] Kamāl Fawwāz, 'Dĕrūzīm wa-ʿAravīm ba-qampūs', *Pī ha-Atōn*, 10 Feb. 1970; Yōkhī Qeydar and Yōsef Qīsṭer, 'Ma kōʾev la-sṭūdenṭīm ha-Dĕrūzīm mi-Daliyat al-Karmil', *Marʾōt* (organ of the student members of the Histadrut), 20 Apr. 1971, 3.

wide committee was elected. All these present themselves as the representatives of the Arab students. The committees began their activities by offering guidance to new students in the labyrinth of university bureaucracy, as well as other assistance, for example over examinations,[58] then moved towards raising the intellectual level of secondary school pupils and the Arab sector generally.[59] They organized political protests in favour of this sector,[60] and became increasingly radicalized in their political attitudes throughout the 1970s and 1980s.[61] In those years, the committees became politically increasingly identified not only with their sector within Israel, but also with the Arabs in the Israeli-held territories. Their extremism was particularly articulated at times of war—in 1973, 1982, and 1990-1.

As early as 1978, the Arab Students' Committee at the Hebrew University of Jerusalem published a thirty-page booklet, entitled al-Tahaddī (The Challenge). This was a collection of articles sharply attacking the State of Israel and the moderates willing to accommodate to its political dominance. Not surprisingly, politically aware and organizationally experienced students were usually the most prominent in the committees, attempting to influence and lead the others. Over several years members of the Israeli Communist Party (then of ḤADASH) preponderated in the committees, the Sons of the Village, an extreme group which will be discussed below (in Chapter 7), later overtaking them. The Progressive List for Peace, yet another nationalist grouping (to be discussed in Chapter 7) has also tried for representation in these committees.

An idea of the activities of the Arab Students' Committee at the Hebrew University of Jerusalem can be gathered from a detailed twelve-page report which it issued relating to its doings in the 1988/9 school year.[62] This report discusses three levels of activity— political, cultural, and academic. The political section is not merely the first, but the longest, filling up most of the report; moreover,

---

[58] Cf. al-Ittiḥād, 16 Mar. 1965; Pī ha-Atōn, 4 May 1971, 5 (a letter of the Committee to the editor).

[59] al-Ittiḥād, 4 Jan. 1966.

[60] Ibid. 6 July 1965; ibid. 19 Aug. 1966. On its activities in those years, see also Jacob M. Landau, The Arabs in Israel: A Political Study (1969), 54–7, 225.

[61] For an extreme example, see E. El'ad, 'Stūdentīm 'Aravīm Isrē'elīm mĕsayy'īm li-fĕ'ūlōt Fatḥ ba-qampūsīm bĕ-Artsōt ha-Bĕrīt', ha-Aretz, 10 Apr. 1970.

[62] Taqrīr 'an a'māl al-lajna li-dawrat 1988–1989 [1989].

it refers both to student and general politics. It mentions the
following political activities of the committee: (1) identifying with
Palestinian students in the Israeli-held territories; (2) demonstrat-
ing in favour of this identification and organizing a visit to Bir-Zeyt
University in the West Bank; (3) convoking a conference on the
role of Palestinian women in the *intifāda*; (4) protesting against the
curfew imposed in the Israeli-held territories; (5) collecting funds
to buy food for the village ʿĪsawiyya (near Jerusalem), on which a
curfew had been imposed; (6) visiting and offering flowers to those
wounded in the *intifāda*; (7) participating in political demonstrations and strikes, in a show of solidarity; (8) organizing meetings to
protest over Israel's continuing rule in the territories; (9) inviting
Fayṣal al-Ḥusaynī, the Palestinian nationalist leader, to speak at the
university campus; (10) organizing meetings in support for the
struggle to establish a Palestinian state.

On the cultural level, book exhibitions were organized, as well as
an evening on Palestinian costume, a debate on Land Day, sports
events, and a mass gathering against compelling Arab students
to guard their dormitories. On the academic level, advice was
offered to first-year students, visits were organized to secondary
schools and their pupils invited to tour the university campus, and
delegates were sent to a conference on Arab education. In all these
manifestations, a clear-cut political objective is evident, usually
expressed in criticism of the State of Israel and its policies in
the universities and Arab schools on the one hand, and in a growing identification with the nationalist struggle in the Israeli-held
territories on the other. Various rightist Jewish circles, both
student and otherwise, have repeatedly declared that the activities
of the Arab Students' Committees are an open incitement against
the State of Israel and even comprise a demand for its annihilation
by including it within a future Palestinian state, as had at times
been advocated by the Palestine Liberation Organization (further:
PLO).

An often-repeated demand by the Arab Students' Committees
and other groups is the establishment of an Arab university within
the State of Israel—Arab in language, teaching, course content,
professors, and students.[63] Up to the moment of writing, the Israeli
government has been reluctant to do this, for three reasons: first,

[63] However, spokesmen of the Arabs in Israel cannot fully agree in the matter.
See *Bat-Qōl*, 11 Dec. 1970, 4.

the shortage of funds for higher education which, indeed, in recent years has forced a reduction in the government allocations to the already extant universities; secondly, the non-availability of scholars and research fellows of recognized international standards such as are employed in Israeli universities; thirdly, the apprehension that an Arab university might turn into a hotbed of anti-Israeli political agitation, as in the case of universities in the Israeli-held territories. However, of late there have been certain developments in establishing institutions of higher education to serve the Arabs in Israel. In 1983, a Centre for the Revival of the Arab Heritage was set up in Ṭaiyyba, in the Little Triangle; its head, Ṣāliḥ Barānsī, considers it a first step towards establishing an Arab university. Upon completion, the Centre is intended to comprise a department of research, a centre for folklore, a public library, and a programming unit.[64] Meanwhile, several books on the Palestinian heritage have been published and a Palestinian museum is planned beside the already established library.

Further, the state reacted to the prevailing situation in which many Muslim officials had to complete their studies in Nablus, Hebron, or Gaza, in the Israeli-held territories, where they absorbed a large dose of anti-Israelism as well. Consequently, colleges for preparing religious officials were set up in Israel proper, at Ṭaiyyba, Bāqa al-Gharbiyya, and Umm al-Faḥm—three centres in the all-Muslim Little Triangle—possibly in the hope of reducing the politicization of future Muslim officials.[65] Other recent innovations were the establishment in November 1990 of an Arab college in Ṭīra, also in the Little Triangle, within the framework of the Open University, and another in Nazareth, in September 1991.[66] Yet another is planned, in February 1992, for the large Bedouin concentration in Rahaṭ, in the Negev. All this has had little effect on the continuing demands by various Arab circles for an Arab university in Israel, equal in status to the existing ones—as voiced, for instance, in an article by Shākir Farīd Ḥasan, of the village of Muṣmuṣ, in the Arabic weekly *Kull al-ʿArab* (All the Arabs),[67]

[64] 'New Centre in Triangle', *Middle East*, 109 (Nov. 1983), 12.
[65] ʿAṭallāh Manṣūr, 'Mikhlalōt lĕ-hakhsharat anshey dat Mūslĕmiyyīm yippatĕḥū bĕ-Bāqa al-Gharbīyya w-vĕ-Umm al-Faḥm', *ha-Aretz*, 10 Oct. 1989, 3.
[66] Cf. *Arabs in Israel* (Tel-Aviv monthly), 1/3 (25 Nov. 1990), 4; ibid. 1/22 (10 Nov. 1991), 2.
[67] Dated 5 Oct. 1990.

and more recently, in December 1991, in the Knesset, by an Arab MK, ʿAbd al-Wahhāb Darāwshe.

However, it should be noted that only a part of the points raised by Arab students and their friends originate from extreme political involvement. Many of their arguments express keen anxiety about their personal careers, conditioned by the slight chance of finding employment appropriate to their aspirations upon graduation.[68] Higher education in Israel lends its Arab graduates prestige, but also occupational frustration, as when they must, willy-nilly, work as teachers (about 50 per cent of university graduates) or in other occupations which would not be their first choice. In brief, it is not easy for them to pursue their preferred careers in Israel.[69] Hence, some renounce higher education, which does not seem to produce an adequate return for their efforts.[70] In general, there is no differential salary policy,[71] but they suffer from the disadvantages of most minorities in the labour market, while in their special case an additional difficulty prevails as regards junior and senior positions in the civil service, particularly if these have security associations,[72] at least as long as Israel remains at war with its neighbours. Together with the continued growth in the number of Arab university graduates in Israel (12,000 in 1989, with some 1,200 added annually[73]) and the increase of unemployment among them (as well as generally among the population),[74] one may expect that disappointment and frustration will feed radicalism in their views and deeds.

All this notwithstanding, not a few Arab university students have

---

[68] Avraham Binyamīn and Rachel Peleg, *Sheʾīfōt le-ʿatīd shel talmīdey shĕmīniyyōt ʿAraviyyīm w-mashmaʿūtan ha-hevratīt* (1976).

[69] ʿAzīz Haydar, *ha-Hīnnūkh ha-miqtsōʿī-tekhnōlōgī*, 57 ff.; Elie Rekhess, *A Survey of Israel Arab Graduates from Institutions of Higher Learning in Israel (1961–1971)* (1974).

[70] ʿAmōs Gilbōʿa, 'Taʿasūqa la-ʿAravīm', *Maʿarīv*, 1 June 1990, E4.

[71] Ruth Klinov, 'Yĕhūdīm va-ʿAravīm' (Ch. 2 n. 2 above).

[72] Diyāb Mahmūd Mūsā, 'Shĕʿat heshbōn ha-nefesh lĕ-ʿArviyyey Israʾel', *ha-Aretz*, 27 Oct. 1990, 9; Z. Schiff, 'Pĕʿilūt ha-Shīn Beyt ba-Ūnīversīṭaʾōt', ibid. 22 Jan. 1971, 9.

[73] Mājid al-Hāj, 'Aqademaʾīm bĕ-tsawārōn kahōl', *Pōlīṭīqa*, 29 (Nov. 1989), 24–7.

[74] Id., 'al-Aqādīmiyyūn al-ʿArab fī Isrāʾīl: mumayyizāt raʾīsiyya wa-dāʾiqat al-ʿamal', *al-Aswār*, 2 (Summer 1988), 41–58. Cf. the interview with al-Hāj in *Kull al-ʿArab*, 31 Aug. 1990, 13; also Yosef Goell, 'True Unions', *Jerusalem Post*, 6 Feb. 1987, 10.

striven to maintain good relations with their Jewish colleagues and with the Jewish Establishment. This is more marked as regards Druze students, of whom one, Mas'ad Qaddūr, was elected, as mentioned, president of the Tel-Aviv University Students' Association in 1991—the first time a non-Jew was elected to such a position at any Israeli university. This is merely one instance of the integration of Druze students in Israeli universities, where only a small minority is directly involved in the politics of the various Arab Students' Committees. The rise in their overall number is impressive. During the years of British rule in Palestine, only one Druze student completed his university studies. In the 1987/8 school year, by contrast, 530 Druze students were studying in Israeli universities and another 50 at universities abroad. Among these, the number of women students is still very small, probably because of family opposition as well as early marriage. In order to encourage Druze secondary school graduates to pursue their studies, the Ministry of Education and Culture has since 1986/7 been granting them financial incentives, in addition to already existing scholarships. These chiefly apply to free study in the preparatory classes specially available for them at Haifa University and elsewhere. And indeed, in the first year that these incentives were offered, about 200 Druze students took advantage of them at Haifa University alone (compared to only fifteen previously).[75]

[75] Salmān Fallāḥ, 'Be'ayōt yĕsod' (n. 10 above), 117–18.

6

Language and Culture

INTRODUCTORY

Educated Arabs in Israel are interested both in the Palestinian heritage and in the current cultural status of their own minority—in language, literature, the press, and the arts. In a lecture given in 1983, Emile Ḥabībī, writer, journalist, and former Communist leader, maintained that Arab culture in the State of Israel would largely determine the outcome of the Palestinian national struggle.[1] Other Arab intellectuals in Israel, too, have referred to the need for developing their culture as a primary objective.[2] Not a few are trying to do research into Arab culture in Palestine in previous centuries, and assess its significance.[3] A more radical group among them has lately been demanding cultural autonomy—in education, language, university teaching, radio and television programmes, and so on—in response to a large minority's aspiration to express its national character in complete equality with the majority.[4]

LANGUAGE ISSUES

Every social group has a special relationship to its own language. The Arabs, however, throughout their history, have shown a particularly high regard for it, considering it an important value in itself, an epitome of perfection. That the Koran was revealed in Arabic naturally enhanced the significance of the language for all Muslims. For the Arabs in Palestine and then in Israel, as for

[1] The lecture was later printed as 'Istimrār al-thaqāfa al-ʿArabiyya al-Filasṭīniyya fī Isrāʾīl', al-Jadīd, 3 (Mar. 1984), 13–18.

[2] e.g. Sharīf Muḥammad Sharīf, 'Nidāʾ al-judhūr—waqfa maʿa al-turāth al-Filasṭīnī fī al-dākhil', al-Aswār, 3 (Spring 1989), 76–82. The author, born in Nazareth, was then a student at the Hebrew University of Jerusalem.

[3] e.g. Munʿim Ḥaddād, 'al-Liqāʾ bayn al-thaqāfa al-Filasṭīniyya al-taqlīdiyya wa-bayn al-thaqāfa al-gharbiyya fī Isrāʾīl', ibid. 9 (Spring 1991), 119–31.

[4] Cf. Varda Yĕrūshalmī, 'Beyn ōṭōnōmiyya lĕ-neʾemanūt', ha-Aretz, 13 Dec. 1990, B4.

the Jews there, language has served not merely as a means of communication, but also as a symbol of ethnic and cultural identity and a vehicle for expressing nationalist aspirations—an instrument that ought to be fostered as an integral part of those aspirations. It is no accident that a well-known Israeli-Arab writer like Ḥannā Abū Ḥannā has defined land and language as 'the two essential bases for the preservation of our existence'.[5] Further, many Arabs feel that, although the majority language in the State of Israel is Hebrew, in the region of the Middle East and North Africa it is Arabic.

By law,[6] both Hebrew and Arabic are official languages in the State of Israel: both are employed in the Knesset, the lawcourts, and government offices; on identity cards, stamps, coins, paper money, and many public signs; on radio and television. It has already been said (above, Chapter 5) that Arabic is the medium of instruction for all Arab children, as Hebrew is for Jewish ones. A substantive difference, in the legal domain, is that Hebrew (rather than Arabic) is granted precedence over English in interpreting the law in cases when different interpretations are possible.

In practice, Hebrew is favoured over Arabic in several aspects of daily life, dictated by the economic and political weight naturally attached to the majority in any society. According to the 1983 population census, 30 per cent of all Arabs in Israel speak Hebrew as a second language, while only 11.5 per cent of the Jews speak Arabic as a second language, many of them emigrants from Middle Eastern countries, where they studied Arabic. This situation derives from the asymmetry in education, by which all Arab children study Hebrew at school for a substantial number of hours over several years, while Jewish pupils learn Arabic, generally as an elective study, for fewer years. Hence it is not surprising that government offices prefer Hebrew, in practice. This is the case, for instance, with road signs in a number of mixed towns and elsewhere.[7] Only recently, in January 1989, the Central Committee of the Histadrut held a special debate on this issue and decided to use its influence

---

[5] Ḥannā Abū Ḥannā, 'al-Arḍ wa-'l-lugha', *al-Ṣināra*, 29 Mar. 1990.
[6] A part of the following is based on Jacob M. Landau's 'Hebrew and Arabic in the State of Israel: Political Aspects of the Language Issue', *International Journal of the Sociology of Language*, 67 (1987), 117–33.
[7] Yaʿacov Friedler, 'Israeli Arabs are strongly committed to Democracy', *Jerusalem Post*, 1 June 1986, 4.

to have all public signs written in both Hebrew and Arabic.[8]
It should also be noted that *Divrey ha-Knesset*, the stenographic
reports of parliamentary debates, are published solely in Hebrew;
laws are published in both languages, but the Arabic version generally appears in print later than the Hebrew.

Since most economic life, banking, politics, and military matters,
as well as the whole of higher education, are in Hebrew, the Arabs
in Israel find themselves in a dilemma. On the one hand, some of
their spokesmen argue that they have to devote too much time at
school to learning Hebrew as a foreign language, perhaps at the
expense of Arabic; on the other hand, others maintain that too little
Hebrew is studied, hence the school graduates are not well enough
equipped, linguistically, to compete in the free labour market and
in higher education. Considering all the above, bilingualism has a
special character in the State of Israel: Arabic is equal to Hebrew,
but in some aspects is somewhat less than equal. Nevertheless,
language has not become a focal area of controversy, perhaps
because the above aspects are not central and also because the
Jewish majority has usually demonstrated a liberal, pluralistic
approach to the Arab minority on issues of language and culture.
Indeed, Arabs are free to publish literary works and newspapers
in their own language, which they do. Symptomatically, when
1989/90 was officially proclaimed 'the year of Hebrew', some
Arabs,[9] but also some Jews,[10] immediately demanded that it be 'the
year of Hebrew and Arabic'.

POLITICAL LITERATURE

Arabic literature in Israel, at least in the state's early years, was a
continuation of literary expression in the years of British rule in
Palestine.[11] As then, it continued to develop separately, without

---

[8] 'Kol shiltey ha-histadrūt bĕ-yishshūvīm ʿAraviyyīm w-vĕ-yishshūvīm
mĕʿōravīm, yihyū bi-shĕtey ha-safōt', *ha-Aretz*, 30 Jan. 1989, 3.

[9] e.g., ʿAbd al-Rahmān al-Shaykh Yūsuf, "ʿĀm al-lugha al-ʿArabiyya', *al-Ittihād*,
13 June 1990; Muhammad Habīb Allāh, 'La-narudd al-iʿtibār li-lughatinā al-
ʿArabiyya', *al-Ghad*, 2 (Apr. 1990), 18–19.

[10] Nīr Shōhat, 'ha-Hagīga ha-mĕshūttefet li-khvōd shĕnat ha-lashōn ha-ʿIvrīt
wĕ-ha-lashōn ha-ʿAravīt', *Mifgash*, 13–14 (Summer–Autumn 1990), 108–21.

[11] For which see e.g. Kāmil al-Sawāfīrī, 'al-Adab fī Filastīn fī zill al-intidāb',
al-Ufq al-Jadīd, 4/1 (Jan. 1965), 23–4.

any regular contacts between Arab and Jewish intellectuals. Each of the two sectors had its own writers' association,[12] derived inspiration from different civilizations, and addressed itself to different readers. Meetings between the two have indeed been attempted,[13] but these were merely occasional and uninstitutionalized encounters between the two camps. In each of the two sectors stereotypes have been formed about the other,[14] often bearing no relation to reality. Although the debate continues on whether Arabic literature in Palestine, in Israel, and in the Israeli-held territories is an organic part of wider Arabic culture or, rather, a local literature with its own specifics,[15] it can still be maintained that it has evolved its own characteristics in the last forty years. This is, indeed, a rich and varied literature. It can boast of prose and poetry focusing on topics central to world literatures. However, it comprises a prominent component of political writing, addressed to a readership which has passed from a majority into a minority and is struggling to maintain its particular character.[16] This phenomenon is referred to by Professor George Qanāziʿ, of Haifa University, as 'ideological elements in Arabic literature in Israel'.[17] Such characteristics,

[12] After several attempts, an association of Arab writers was set up in Nazareth, on 30 Sept.–1 Oct. 1987. See al-Mawākib, 4/11–12 (Nov.–Dec. 1987), 69–89. For the association's rules and regulations, cf. Ittiḥād al-Kuttāb al-ʿArab (Autumn 1988), 167–9; also al-Ṣināra, 6 July 1990, 18, 30.

[13] Mōshe Dōr, 'ha-Sifrūt ha-ʿAravīt ha-tsōmaḥat ba-aretz', Maʿarīv, 18 Feb. 1972, 34. Cf. Amos Kenan, 'Communication between Jewish and Arab Citizens', New Outlook, 14/120 (Jan.–Feb. 1971), 19–21.

[14] Fauzi El-Asmar, 'The Portrayal of Arabs in Hebrew Children's Literature', Journal of Palestine Studies, 16/1 (Autumn 1986), 81–94.

[15] R. Snīr, 'Petsaʿ eḥad mi-pětsaʿav—ha-sifrūt ha-ʿAravīt ha-Palesṭīnīt bě-Isra'el', Alpayim, 2 (1990), esp. 244–6.

[16] I shall focus on the political dimensions of Arab literature in Israel, which has been discussed in several works. See e.g., in addition to Snīr's study, mentioned in n. 15, the following: Ghassān Kanafānī, Adab al-muqāwama fī Filasṭīn al-muḥtalla; Luṭfiyya al-Shihābī, 'Dīwān al-waṭan al-muhtall', al-Adīb, June 1969, 39–40; Maḥmūd al-Samra, 'Dawāwīn shiʿr min al-arḍ al-muḥtalla', ibid. Nov. 1969, 12–14; Riyāḍ Sharāra, 'Adab al-muqāwama fī Filasṭīn al-muḥtalla', al-Hawādith, 10/507 (29 July 1966), 24; Anṭūn Shammās, ha-Sifrūt ha-ʿAravīt bě-Isra'el aḥarey 1967 (1976); S. Moreh, 'ha-Sifrūt ba-safa ha-ʿAravīt bi-Mědīnat Isra'el', ha-Mizraḥ he-Hadash, 9/33–4 (1958), 26–38; Avraham Yinōn, 'Kamma nōs'ey mōqed ba-sifrūt shel ʿArviyyey Isra'el', ibid. 15/57–8 (1965), 57–84; Salmān Maṣālḥa, 'Anashīm bě-tōkh millīm', Pōlīṭiqa, 21 (June 1988), 44–50; Natan Zakh, 'ʿAl reqaʿ tsaʾaqat ha-yamīm ha-ṭěrūfīm', ibid. 51–6; Shmuel Moreh, 'Arabic Literature in Israel', Middle Eastern Studies, 3/3 (April 1967), 283–94; Stefan Wild, Ghassan Kanafani: The Life of A Palestinian (1975).

[17] George Qanāziʿ, 'Yěsōdōt idey'ōlōgiyyīm ba-sifrūt ha-ʿAravīt bě-Isra'el', ha-Mizraḥ he-Hadash, 32/125–8 (1989), 129–38.

naturally enough, appear in the writings of ethnic and religious minorities in other places as well.

Owing to the high cost of publishing books in Israel, many Arab writers and poets have preferred to print their work in newspapers and periodicals (to be discussed below in this chapter), or to seek subsidies from institutions. This situation has largely conditioned Arab political writing, with the dividing line being either support for the state and its Establishment or, conversely, criticism of it. Supporters wrote in pro-government organs or enjoyed grants and awards from the authorities, the Histadrut, and other bodies. The critics, on the other hand (for example Emile Ḥabībī[18]), published their writings in the Communist press, which over the years has been no less nationalist than Marxist, or, later, in nationalist organs in Israel, in the Israeli-held territories, or abroad.[19] In so far as such writing was published in the State of Israel, its authors had to take into account the existence of censorship, necessitated by the war between Israel and the Arab states. True, censorship was usually applied to security matters alone; however, there have been isolated cases when it intervened in others as well. An exceptional example is the case of Shafīq Ḥabīb, charged with writing a politically inciting poem and given a suspended sentence by the courts in April 1992.[20] Seen from this perspective, Arabic literature in the State of Israel reflects the general situation as well as the ideological attitudes of the minority: the critics, spokesmen of oppositionist circles, have been increasingly radical in their political expression,[21] while supporters, identifying with the State of Israel, have been silenced, to a growing extent, in their writing. The works of both sides have dealt, of course, with subjects of concern to many Arabs in Israel: relations between Jews and Arabs, in general, and Palestinians, in particular; the struggle for full equality; and various events within Israel or the Middle East which affect the Arab minority.

The 1967 War did away with the cultural blockade on Arabic literature in Israel, by renewing contacts with the Israeli-held

[18] For his literary work, see S. Balas, 'Mal'akh ba-geyhinnōm', *ha-Aretz*, 5 June 1970, 22.

[19] Details in Landau, *The Arabs in Israel* (1969), 57–68.

[20] Shafīq Ḥabīb, 'al-Riqāba ḥarrafat tarjamat qaṣā'idī', *al-Ṣināra*, 22 June 1990, 3.

[21] See various examples in the stories transl. by S. Balas into Hebrew, entitled *Sippūrīm Palesṭīna'iyyīm* (1970).

territories and through them with Jordan and other Arab states.[22] Since then, Israel has ruled over a large additional number of Arabs, all of whom had been nurtured on a strongly anti-Israeli (sometimes anti-Jewish) literature and press. This influence was a starting-point in shaping post-1967 Arabic writing in Israel.[23] The renewed encounter with Palestinians in the Israeli-held territories as well as with the literature of the Arab states has had a visible impact on the Arabs in Israel. The Communist Druze poet, Samīḥ al-Qāsim,[24] writing in Arabic, characterized the 1967 encounter as 'being born anew'. Indeed, in addition to the 1967 War, which ended the cultural and linguistic isolation of the Arab minority in Israel, the Military Administration, abolished half a year earlier, also disappeared. Consequently, more openness became possible, almost imperative. Moreover, soon after this war, an era of economic growth and prosperity began—factors facilitating the printing and publication of books and periodicals. Symptomatic of this change is the fact that several writers, formerly supporters of the Establishment, showed signs of moving to the camp of its critics. Such are Michel Ḥaddād and some others.[25] Several joined the extremist stand of those Arab writers in Israel who not only call for equality, but openly take sides with a radical nationalist struggle within the state. This is not merely a more acute form of alienation among Arab writers in Israel.[26] Rather, to use their own simile, it is a literary eruption like that of a volcano whose lava consists of nationalist sentiments suppressed during the first twenty years of Israel's existence.[27]

Increasingly, works of a clear-cut political nature are being published. An example is a book in Arabic by ʿUmar G͟hazzāwī, entitled *Zionism and the Arab Minority in Israel*,[28] in which the

[22] Shammās, *ha-Sifrūt ha-ʿAravīt bĕ-Isra'el* (n. 16 above), 1 ff.
[23] Emile Habībī, 'Ta'thīr ḥarb 1967 ʿalà al-adab al-Filasṭīnī fī Isrā'īl', *al-Jadīd*, 1–2 (Jan.–Feb. 1976), 51–65; Maḥmud G͟hanāyim, 'Namādhij min qaṣaṣinā al-maḥallī fī al-sabʿīnāt wa-'l-thamānīnāt', *al-Ittiḥād*, 6 July 1990.
[24] Cf. Sarah Graham-Brown, 'The Poetry of Survival', *Middle East*, 122 (Dec. 1984), 43–4.
[25] See about him Muhammad Hamza G͟hanāyim, 'Riwāya ʿArabiyya Filasṭīniyya bi-ḥurūf ʿIbriyya', *al-Jadīd*, 35/6 (June 1986), 57–9.
[26] George Qanāziʿ, 'Beʿayat ha-zehūt ba-sifrūt shel ʿArviyyey Isra'el', in A. Hareven (ed.), *Eḥad mi-kol shishsha* (1981), 149–69.
[27] Snīr (n. 15 above), 255.
[28] ʿUmar G͟hazzāwī, *al-Ṣahyūniyya wa-'l-aqalliyya al-qawmiyya al-ʿArabiyya fī Isrā'īl*.

author perceives Israeli rule as a state of Nazi-type apartheid,[29] oblivious to all evidence contradicting his thesis. Similarly, the nationalist poetry of a permanent oppositionist such as Maḥmud Darwīsh (who has left Israel) grew more bitter over the years in its radical contents and style. In the writings of Darwīsh and others like him, the 'private ego' and the 'national ego' are as one, while the dominant political tone gives the latter the upper hand. A certain sense of satisfaction and security is derived by these writers from their assumption that theirs is a majority literature (considering Middle Eastern conditions), not a minority one; the writing is directed outwards no less than inwards. Hence it increasingly resembles, in motifs and emphases, literature in the Israeli-held territories. No less than their peers in the territories, Arab authors in Israel seem to feel that they must write politically, even radically, according to their perceptions of the situation in the State of Israel. An example is the above Samīḥ al-Qāsim.[30] Aware of this, Itzhak Navon, while Minister of Education and Culture, in 1988 appointed a committee headed by an Arab, Muwaffaq Khūrī, deputy head of the Iʿblīn local council, to award annual prizes to authors of Arabic *belles-lettres*, both prose and poetry,[31] probably in order to encourage writing not centrally bearing on politics.

The professional associations of Arab writers well reflect the polarization and fragmentation within Arab society in Israel. In 1990, at least three competing associations were in existence: (1) the General Union of Palestinian Arab Writers in Israel (al-Ittiḥād al-ʿāmm li-ʾl-kuttāb al-ʿArab al-Filasṭiniyyīn fī Isrāʾīl), in Nazareth, headed by Jamāl Qaʿwār, a writer who has moved, politically, from the Progressive List for Peace to the Democratic Arab Party; (2) the League of the Palestinian Men of Letters within [Israel] (Rābiṭat al-udabāʾ al-Filasṭiniyyīn fī-ʾl-dākhil), also in Nazareth, headed by Aḥmad Darwīsh, an adherent of the Progressive List for Peace and with the active participation of the above George Qanāziʿ, who teaches Arabic literature at Haifa University, and the writer Ḥannā Abū Ḥannā; (3) the Union of Arab Writers in Israel (Ittiḥād al-Kuttāb al-ʿArab fī Isrāʾīl), headed by Samīḥ al-Qāsim, active in Communist politics, the

---

[29] Ibid. 40–52.

[30] 'Nadwat al-Quds ḥawl al-adab al-Filasṭīnī fī Isrāʾīl', *al-Jadīd*, 11–12 (Nov.– Dec. 1983), 6–11, esp. 9–10.

[31] Muwaffaq Khūrī, in *al-Ṣināra*, 24 May 1991.

Druze Salmān Nāṭūr and the writer Fārūq Muwāsī, a Ph.D. graduate in Arabic literature from Bar-Ilan University.[32]

THE THEATRE

Besides narrative prose, poetry, and political works, Arab authors in Israel have written plays. The theatre, a well-tried vehicle for expressing and shaping public opinion, has served the Arab minority in this role.[33] Arab theatrical activity under the British Mandate in Palestine had no immediate continuation in Israel. When theatrical troupes sprang up in centres of Arab population, such as Nazareth and Haifa, their first steps were hesitant, artistically and as regards content, and were characterized by feeling their way. After Arab actors had studied, together with their Jewish peers, at the Ben-Zvi drama school in Ramat-Gan, or elsewhere (even abroad), and after the revival of Arabic literature since 1967 and the potential rise in the number of spectators, speedy development took place in the Arab theatre. Although several troupes presented the best of the world repertoire, others selected Arabic plays written in Israel. Among these, the number of political plays grew steadily, particularly those dealing, explicitly or implicitly, with issues concerning the Arabs in Israel and their coexistence with the Jews. An example is *Coexistence*, performed in Haifa, in 1970. It was written by Muḥammad Watad, a Muslim Arab active in MAPAM and later elected to the Knesset on its slate (more recently he has moved to the Israeli Communist Party).[34] The play presents a collection of stories about the daily life of both simple people and well-educated ones—a gallery of types representing split personalities which meditate on Jewish–Arab coexistence in Israel. The play was

[32] Details in *Arabs in Israel*, 1/7 (15 Mar. 1991), 7.
[33] For the Arab theatre in Israel, see *inter alia*: Yūsuf Haydar, 'al-Haraka al-masrahiyya fī al-bilād', in Khālid Khalīfa (ed.), *Filasṭīniyyūn 1948–1988* (1988), esp. 248 ff.; Riyāḍ ʿIṣmat, 'Ta'ṣīl al-masraḥ al-ʿArabī', *al-Shaʿb*, 15 Nov. 1978; Naḥman Ben-ʿAmmī, 'Sīaḥ ʿal ʿAravīm', *Maʿarīv*, 15 July 1970, 19; D. Rubinstein, 'ha-Ballōnīm matsīgīm et ha-hōweh he-hashūkh', *Davar*, 30 Nov. 1972, 7, 11. Shōsh Maymōn, 'Nim'as lī lēmasher et ha-kěʿev shellī', *Yědīʿōt Aharōnōt*, 28 Oct. 1988, Suppl., 12–13; Mendel Kohansky, 'An Israeli-Arab's Coexistence', *Jerusalem Post Magazine*, 17 July 1970, 16.
[34] Muhammad Watad, 'Co-Existence', *New Outlook*, 13/117 (Sept.–Oct. 1970), 68–73.

performed in both Arabic and Hebrew, and offered a moderate political message—the search for solutions for coexistence. Another play, performed in East Jerusalem two years later, by the Balloons' Troupe, was rather different in content and intent. Entitled *Darkness*, it attacked the ills of contemporary Arabic society, forcefully pleading for doing away with darkness—meaning both feudal Arab society and Israeli rule. An East Jerusalem troupe, al-Ḥakawātī, has in subsequent years performed political plays with even more trenchant messages, chiefly applying to the Israeli-held territories.[35]

THE PRESS

In Israel numerous newspapers and periodicals are published in various languages—Hebrew, Arabic, and the languages of the different diasporas from which Jews have migrated. During the new state's first ten years, three main categories were evident in the Arabic press: first, that supported by the state or the Histadrut; secondly, that financed by political parties and critical or rival groupings; thirdly, publications edited and distributed by Christian denominations.[36]

Following the 1967 War, the first category disappeared. Prominent among these older publications were the weekly *Ḥaqīqat al-Amr* (The Truth of the Matter), appearing since 1937; the daily *al-Anbā'* (News), followed by the daily *al-Yawm* (The Day),[37] or the literary periodical *Liqā'* (Meeting). The main reason for their closing down (although *Liqā'* was later revived) seems to have been Arab reluctance to read them, due to successful competition from other newspapers and periodicals, published in Jerusalem and

---

[35] The cinema, too, strove to promote Palestinian views among the Arabs in Israel and others. See Ḥusayn al-ʿAwdāt, *al-Sīnimā wa-'l-qaḍiyya al-Filasṭīniyya²* (1989).

[36] For the Arab press in Palestine under Ottoman and British rule, the most exhaustive treatment is in three volumes by J. Yěhōshūaʿ, entitled, respectively, *Taʾrīkh al-ṣiḥāfa al-ʿArabiyya fī Filasṭīn fī al-ʿahd al-ʿUthmānī (1908–1918)* (1978); *Taʾrīkh al-ṣiḥāfa al-ʿArabiyya al-Filasṭīniyya 1919–1929* (1981); *Taʾrīkh al-ṣiḥāfa al-ʿArabiyya al-Filasṭīniyya fī nihāyat ʿahd al-intidāb al-Brīṭānī ʿalā Filasṭīn, 1930–1948* (1983). See also ʿAbd al-Bāqī Shannān, 'Bidāyat al-ṣiḥāfa al-Filasṭīniyya', *al-Mawākib*, 4/7–8 (July–Aug. 1987), 42–6.

[37] Ellen Geffner, 'An Israeli Arab View of Israel', *Jewish Social Studies*, 36/2 (Apr. 1974), 134–41.

in the Israeli-held territories. The Histadrut, however, continued to issue, for its more or less steady readership, Arab periodicals of a vocational, educational, or cultural character, as well as a periodical for women, entitled *al-Mar'a* (The Woman).

The second category was led by Communist publications, such as the daily *al-Ittiḥād* (The Union, or Unity), which continue to appear and to criticize the Establishment aggressively. Their contents sometimes border on incitement, and the authorities took a very unusual step and closed down *al-Ittiḥād* for a week in March 1988.[38] Another example is a non-Communist political newspaper, *al-'Arabī* (The Arab), published irregularly, without any mention of place, publisher, or responsible editor, every issue being labelled as 'a one-off newspaper' (which means that, legally, it does not need a publication permit).[39] The tactic, probably learned from al-Arḍ, a group active thirty years previously (to be discussed below, in Chapter 7), implies introducing a slight change in the newspaper's title, in every issue, such as 'The Voice of the Arab', 'The Opinion of the Arab', 'The Appeal of the Arab', and so forth.

The third category, the press of the Christian denominations, continued publication, with various modifications, but generally maintaining political attitudes critical of the State of Israel and of its agencies in the Arab sector.

The main innovation, in the 1980s, was in the publication of several local Arab newspapers, which fill the void left by the demise of the pro-Establishment press. Some are regular, while others appear at irregular intervals. They are mostly published in relatively large centres like Nazareth and Acre (for Galilee), Umm al-Faḥm (for the Little Triangle), Jaffa, and other places. Thanks to their focusing on local affairs, including some gossip, and printing political articles as well, they penetrate wider circles. Thus, they exploit both the remarkable increase in the number of literate Arabs in Israel and the rise in their interest in politics; indeed, they have probably contributed their own share to politicization.[40] One instance is the popular weekly *al-Ṣināra* (The Hook), published in Nazareth, which combines anti-Establishment propaganda

---

[38] Cf. *ha-Aretz*, 25–30 Mar. 1988; *Jerusalem Post*, 5 Apr. 1988.
[39] We have the issues from 10 Nov. 1989 to 12 Jan. 1990, but it is possible that subsequent ones were published.
[40] Khālid Khalīfa, 'al-Majāl al-ṣuhufī—al-ṣiḥāfa al-Filasṭīniyya ilà ayna?', in Khālid Khalīfa (ed.), '*Filasṭīniyyūn 1948–1988* (1988), 317–20.

TABLE 6.1. Main Arabic newspapers and periodicals

Name	Frequency	Place of Publication	Publisher	Editor	Political Affiliation
al-Ittiḥād	Daily	Haifa	Tawfīq Ṭūbī	Sālim Jubrān	Communist
al-Ṣināra	Weekly	Nazareth	Widāʿ Mashʿūr	Luṭfī Mashʿūr	Independent
Kull al-ʿArab	Weekly	Tel-Aviv	Laylā Ḥaṣdāya	Muḥammad Watad	Independent
al-ʿArabī	Weekly	Acre	George Abū Raḥmūn	George Abū Raḥmūn	Independent
al-Ṣirāṭ	Weekly	Umm al-Faḥm	Sulaymān Aghbāriyya	Sulaymān Aghbāriyya	Islamic Movement*
Nidāʾ al-Aswār	Weekly	Acre	Hanān Ḥijāzī	Dīb ʿAkkāwī	Independent
al-Maydān	Weekly	Nazareth	Maḥmūd Abū Rajab	ʿAwaḍ ʿAbd al-Fattāḥ	Village Sons
Panorama	Weekly	Ṭaiyyba	ʿĀʾida Jābir	Bassām Jābir	Independent
al-Nadwa	Weekly	Jerusalem	Maḥmūd Zahāliqa	Maḥmūd Zahāliqa	Independent
Ṣawt al-Ḥaqq wa-ʾl-Ḥurriya	Weekly	Umm al-Faḥm	Khālid Muhannà	Khālid Muhannà	Islamic Movement†

al-Diyār	Weekly	Nazareth	ʿAbd al-Wahhāb Darāwshe	ʿAbd al-Wahhāb Darāwshe	Democratic Arab Party[‡]
al-Waṭan	Weekly	Nazareth	None specified	None specified	Progressive List for Peace[§]
al-Qindīl	Weekly	Bāqa al-Gharbiyya	Jamāl Majdala	Muḥammad Ghanāʾim	Independent
al-Rāšid	Weekly	Nazareth	Ḥabīb Musallam	Ḥabīb Musallam	Independent
al-Fawwāl	Monthly	Ṭira	Manṣūr Manṣūr	Jamāl ʿAbd al-Raḥīm	Independent
al-Fuṣūr	Monthly	Ṭaiyyba	Muntaṣar Ḥājj Yaḥyà	Muntaṣar Ḥājj Yaḥyà	Independent
al-Siyāsa	Monthly	Haifa	Khālid Khalifa	Khālid Khalifa	Independent
Ṣawt al-Qurà	Monthly	Haifa	Maḥmūd Abū al-Hayia	Khālid Khalifa	40 villages
al-Wurūd	Monthly	Lydda	Angel Munayyir	Edmond Munayyir	Independent
al-Jadīd	Monthly	Haifa	Ibrāhīm Mālik	Ibrāhīm Mālik	Communist
al-Quds	Daily	E. Jerusalem	Maḥmūd Abū Zuluf	Maḥmūd Abū Zuluf	PLO

TABLE 6.1. (*continued*)

Name	Frequency	Place of Publication	Publisher	Editor	Political Affiliation
al-Nahār	Daily	E. Jerusalem	ʿUthmān al-Halaq	ʿIṣām al-ʿInānī	Kingdom of Jordan
al-Fajr	Daily	E. Jerusalem	Ḥilmī Ḥanūn	Ḥannā Sinyōra	FATAH
al-Shaʿb	Daily	E. Jerusalem	Maḥmūd Yaʿish	ʿAli Yaʿish	PLO
al-Bayādir al-Siyāsī	Weekly	E. Jerusalem	Jacques Ḥazmō	Jacques Ḥazmō	PLO and Kingdom of Jordan
al Usbūʿ al-Jadīd	Weekly	E. Jerusalem	Ḥannā Sinyōra	Ḥannā Sinyōra	PLO
al-Manār	Weekly	E. Jerusalem	Ismāʿīl ʿAjwā	Ismāʿīl ʿAjwā	PLO
al-Mawqif[¶]	Monthly	E. Jerusalem	Zuhayr al-Raʾīs	Isḥāq al-Budayrī	Pan-Arabism
Qaḍāyā	Every two months	E. Jerusalem	Maḥmūd Muḥārib	Maḥmūd Muḥārib	Independent?[‖]

* Started to appear in July 1990, one week after *Ṣawt al-Ḥaqq wa-ʾl-Ḥurriyya* was closed down by an order of the authorities.
† Probably connected to the Muslim Brethren.
‡ Its publication was renewed in 1991.
§ *al-Waṭan* did not mention the names of the publisher and the responsible editor, probably owing to conflicts within the PLP. In order not to break the law, which lays down that every newspaper and periodical has to apply for a publication permit and submit the names of the above functionaries, *al-Waṭan* constantly represents itself as a 'Bulletin for the Voter' (*nashra li-ʾl-nākhib*).
¶ Started publication in Jan. 1991.
‖ Started publication in Nov. 1989.

with spicy reports of local scandals. The weekly hosts various radical newspapermen, including several who have left the Israeli Communist Party, such as Ṣalībā K͟hamīs. About half of each issue is reserved for politics,[41] thus contributing to the radicalization of its readers. The paper competes not only with the Communist press, but also with the nationalist, like the Nazareth weekly of the Progressive List for Peace, *al-Waṭan* (The Fatherland) which is also published without name of publisher and responsible editor. Yet another is *al-Rāya* (The Banner), succeeded by *al-Maydān* (The Combat Area), both issued by the Sons of the Village, an extreme group (to be discussed below, in Chapter 8). To these, several dailies and periodicals can be added, published in East Jerusalem and addressing themselves to the Arabs in the Israeli-held territories; both contents and style are aggressive. For instance, during the Gulf War, early in 1991, these newspapers enthusiastically supported Ṣaddām Ḥusayn, getting approving feedback from readers in Isreal and the territories.[42]

If one omits various Arab newspapers issued sporadically and for short periods, as well as those that have closed down, the list in Table 6.1 reflects the Arab press as of the end of the year 1990.[43]

---

[41] D. Rubinstein, "Ittōn Isrĕ'elī mĕ'ōd', *ha-Aretz*, 4 Jan. 1991, 13–14.

[42] Yizhar Be'er, 'Empty Shoes in the Sand: Israel's Arabs Take Stock', *New Outlook*, 34/314–15 (Apr.–May 1991), 31–3.

[43] Based on *The Arabs in Israel*, 1/3 (25 Nov. 1990), 8, and other sources.

7

Political Organization
and Leadership

INTRODUCTORY

During the first decade of Israel as a state, the Arabs did not
achieve any significant degree of political organization, a fact con-
spicuous against the background of speedily increasing politicization in the Jewish sector. There were various reasons for this: (1)
the shock of turning from a majority into a minority, dispersed in
several separate regions; (2) the absence of an experienced political
leadership (which found itself outside the frontiers of the new
state); (3) unfamiliarity with Hebrew as well as with the new rules
of the political game on a country-wide scale; (4) The Military
Administration; (5) that most Jewish parties and organizations
(with a few exceptions to be mentioned below) have not encouraged
Arabs to join their ranks.[1]

Consequently, although no legal ban existed on the formation of
Arab parties and political groupings, it took a while until a second
generation of Israeli citizens became aware of the significance of
political organization and activity. This occurred chiefly under the
impact of demographic growth, learning Hebrew, and acquiring a
broader education, and the abolition of the Military Administration
in 1966. Earlier, in so far as the Arabs in Israel demonstrated an
interest in politics at all, this occurred mostly on the local level,
a process continuing until today, although now it goes together
with participation in country-wide politics. The latter dimension
has developed concurrently with the growth of a wider political
awareness within the Arab sector, and the rise of a new leadership,
which tried to shape organizational instruments for expressing
this awareness. This leadership comprised both intellectuals and
practical politicians who, having given due consideration to developments within Jewish society, reached the conclusion that solely
by broad political organization (not merely by individual or small

[1] See also S. Shamir, *ha-Perspeqṭīva ha-hīsṭōrīt—divrey mavō'* (1976), 1–10.

group activity, as formerly), could the interests of the Arab sector be promoted. Since 1967, moreover, speedy politicization has penetrated and affected a large part of the Arabs in Israel, so that numerous topics, essentially non-political, are increasingly coloured by politics.[2]

FROM MODERATE ORGANIZATION TO EXTREMISM

Barring the al-Arḍ affair (to which we shall revert below), the characteristic lack of political organization was more a sign of inexperience and perplexity in Arab society after 1948 than the result of any explicit government policy (most Jewish leaders in Israel were uncertain what character such a policy should adopt). Considering this situation, when conditions changed with the abolition of the Military Administration and with the renewal of contacts with people in the Israeli-held territories half a year later, extremists in both the Jewish and the Arab sectors increasingly prescribed the essence and style of politics. This resulted in the practical radicalization of the entire system, and the Arabs within it, so that moderate groups continued to exist, but to some degree were paralysed.[3]

Local organizations, sometimes politically influenced, continued their activities throughout, whether these were initiated by heads of *hamula*s, or by political parties (such as the Communists), or later by groups of young people, generally from among the better-educated. Local politics will be discussed in detail below (in Chapter 8). Here political organizations of a national, country-wide significance will be considered.

NON-PARTY POLITICAL ORGANIZATIONS

The first political organization which exceeded the limits of local issues was the al-Arḍ group.[4] In 1959, a number of nationalist

---

[2] One instance is a convention relating to health matters of the Arab sector, which met in April 1986 and immediately turned to heated political arguments concerning the economic conditions of the Arabs in Israel. See *al-Rābiṭa*, 40 (Sept. 1960), 34–40.

[3] Maḥmūd ʿAbbāsī, 'Hilkhey rūaḥ ḥadashīm bĕ-qerev ʿArviyyey Isra'el', *Migwan*, 53 (Nov. 1980), 41–4.

[4] Fuller details in Landau, *The Arabs in Israel* (1969), 92–107.

young Arabs broke away from the Popular Front, a Communist Front organization established a year earlier.[5] These young men set up a new political group, symbolically named al-Arḍ (the Earth), claiming to represent the Arabs in Israel and their nationalist aspirations. The group was small, consisting of about twenty members, but it was very active. It published a weekly over thirteen weeks, without applying for the required permit; it registered itself legally as an association, thus acquiring legitimacy; it distributed holding shares; and it sent letters to the United Nations, to foreign embassies, and to newspapers abroad. It even attempted to set up a recognized political party, but failed, despite its appeal to the Supreme Court in 1964. When it became evident that the group had established connections with Israel's enemies across the borders, its activity was banned. The last move of al-Arḍ was to attempt to run for the Knesset in the 1965 elections, but it was frustrated in this by a decision of the Supreme Court which ruled that even in its new guise (as the Socialist Arab List) it was a subversive organization. Indeed, an entire paragraph in al-Arḍ's programme defined its objectives as fighting for Arab Palestinian nationalism—completely disregarding the political aspirations of the Jewish majority and of the State of Israel as such. This tendency was obvious also in the group's weekly and in the proclamations of its leaders.

Several events occurred in the decade following the ban on al-Arḍ, encouraging the Arabs in Israel, in one way or another, to look again for ways and means towards country-wide political organization: (1) the establishment in 1965, outside Israel's borders, of the Palestine Liberation Organization (PLO) whose slogans and, later, activities, could not but inflame the imagination of some Arabs in Israel; (2) the renewal of association with friends and relatives in the Israeli-held territories after 1967, where the existence of active political organization could be observed; (3) decline in the prestige of Israel in the 1973 War and subsequently in the international arena; (4) the intensified activity of practically all the Israeli political parties within the Arab sector in the parliamentary electoral campaigns of 1965, 1969, and 1973, when their court-

---

[5] On the Front and its history, see Asʿad Ghānim, 'al-Jabha al-ʿArabiyya al-shaʿbiyya wa-al-ṣirāʿ ḍidd muṣādarat al-arāḍī 1958–1961', *Qaḍāyā*, 3 (May 1990), 50–8.

ing of Arab votes gave the Arabs in Israel a feeling of power and importance, combined with an increasing awareness of the advantages of political organization. Thus, mainly following the 1973 War, various independent political structures sprang up, largely based on geographical commonality. Such were associations of young people or of the better-educated, for example a country-wide committee of secondary school pupils (in 1974), or a general union of Arab Students' Committees at the universities (in 1975), besides associations of university graduates or intellectuals in many large localities. Further, a country-wide organization of elected members of local authority councils was set up in 1974 as 'the National Committee of Heads of Arab Local Councils in Israel', and another, in 1975, to deal with matters relating to Arab Lands, entitled 'the National Committee for the Defence of Lands'.[6] During those years and subsequently, other associations were formed, several of which are still in existence. The main ones will be discussed below, disregarding those which had a short life-span and no real impact on the Arab sector.[7] The organizations will be treated under three headings: political committees, radical groups, and political parties.

POLITICAL COMMITTEES

Arab Students' Committees have been mentioned above (Chapter 5).

The National Committee of Heads of Arab Local Councils

This committee was set up in 1974 by the Arabs themselves, but without the participation of the Druzes, who later set up their own parallel committee.[8] This occurred largely as a result of a report which showed that a substantial gap existed between state

---

[6] Elie Rekhess, ʿArviyyey Israʾel lĕ-aḥar 1967: haḥrafata shel bĕʿayat ha-ōriyentatsiyya (1976), esp. 30.

[7] For details, ʿAṭallāh Manṣūr, 'Histaggĕrūtam shel ʿArviyyey Israʾel', ha-Aretz, 18 Oct. 1982, 7–8.

[8] Avīva Shābī, 'Memshala ba-derekh', Yĕdīʿōt Aḥarōnōt, 25 Dec. 1987, Suppl., 6, 28; 'Lajnat al-ruʾasāʾ wa-mabdaʾ al-taṭawwur wa-ʾl-ḍarūra', Kull al-ʿArab, 24 May 1991; Majid al-Haj and Henry Rosenfeld, 'The Emergence of an Indigenous Political Framework in Israel: The National Committee of Chairmen of Arab Local Authorities', Asian and African Studies, 23/2–3 (Nov. 1989), 205–44.

allocations to Jewish and Arab local authorities respectively. The committee's first objective was, indeed, to eliminate this gap. Its first head was Ḥannā Muways, a Communist MK; after his death the role was assumed (since 9 June 1981) by Ibrāhīm Nimr Ḥusayn, mayor of Shafā ʿAmr. The committee became, in time, the main supra-party body representing Arabs in Israel. At all events, it was rapidly swept into political activity which had little to do with local government. The events of Land Day in 1976, in which it was involved, turned it into a representative body (at least, this was its self-perception), not merely in municipal issues, but also in national ones. The committee's membership has generally been almost equally divided between the extremists (such as the Communists) and the moderates. Since it has often acted as a vehicle for protests and demands, the committee has been considered by many Arabs in Israel as a miniature government— although it has never been recognized as an official body by the state authorities, which perceive it merely as a grouping of democratically elected heads of local authorities. In other words, while in the first two years of its existence this committee busied itself chiefly with issues affecting local matters, housing, roads, electricity, water, drainage, and cultural activity, it moved on to demand recognition of the Arabs in Israel as a national minority and, after 1983 (when the power of the Communist members grew), to deal with such country-wide issues as land expropriation, financial allocations, and employment; it also took steps to strengthen relations with Arabs in the Israeli-held territories, by identifying with their nationalist struggle and supporting it, while denouncing what it termed 'the crimes of the State of Israel against them'. For instance, at a meeting in February 1984 the committee decided that 'the Arab population in Israel is an inseparable part of the Palestinian Arab people, striving speedily to attain its legal, recognized national rights.' None the less, the power struggle between moderates and extremists in the committee has continued, with the latter frequently winning the day. A significant first step in this direction occurred in 1976, when the committee met with Itzhak Rabin, then Prime Minister, and asked him to grant the Arabs in Israel the status of a national (and not merely a religious and cultural) minority—a request which Rabin turned down. However, over the years the committee increasingly perceived itself as an advocate both of Arab aspirations for complete equality and of their nationalist ambitions, in the double context of the Arabs in Israel and in the Israeli-held territories. An example of its influence was the generally successful strike in 1987, in the name of Equality Day,[9] which the committee initiated and led, and another general strike in December 1989. Another manifestation occurred in May 1991, when the state authorities accepted the committee's demands and undertook to equate the allocations for Arab local authorities with the Druze (which had been arranged several days previously). When the promised funds arrived only in dribbles, some heads of Arab local councils struck time and again, until, on 26 August 1991, an official government decision was taken to equate the Arab local councils fully with the Jewish ones and to transfer all the promised funds.[10] Only then did the strikes end (as of writing). These events encouraged many Arabs to perceive this body as representing them.

The National Committee for the Defence of Lands

This was set up in 1975 to protest against what its members believed to be government moves for the expropriation of Arab lands. It was first headed by a priest, Shaḥāda Shaḥāda, of Shafā ʿAmr, and among its founders was Ṣalībā Khamīs, then one of the leaders of the Israeli Communist Party; indeed, the committee was Communist-dominated for years.[11] It has served both moderates and extremists as a framework for protests against the expropriation of Arab lands; it was largely instrumental in organizing the first Land Day in 1976, and also subsequent ones, as well as demonstrations, strikes, and meetings.[12]

The Arab Co-ordination Committee

This was set up on 21 February 1981, with the declared aim of serving as an umbrella organization for several militant groups, such as the Nationalist Progressive Movement, the Sons of the

[9] Joel Beinin, 'From Land Day to Equality Day', *Middle East Report*, Jan.–Feb. 1988, 24–7.
[10] Full text of the government decision, in Arabic, in *al-Ittiḥād*, 1 Sep. 1991.
[11] ʿAṭallāh Manṣūr, 'Zēqenīm baʿaley hashpaʿa', *ha-Aretz*, 21 Apr. 1987, 13.
[12] Details in Naẓīr Majallī's 'Yawm al-arḍ 1990', *al-Ittiḥād*, 23 Mar. 1990, 6–7 (interviews with Shaḥāda Shaḥāda and others). Cf. 'Nadwat yawm al-arḍ', *Nidāʾ al-Aswār*, 30 Mar. 1990, 4–5.

Village, and others (to be discussed below). Among the active participants were ex-members of al-Ard; one of its avowed objectives was to prepare the cadres for a revolution, together with anti-Zionist Jewish circles. The committee was officially banned in 1982.

The Follow-up Committee for Arab Citizens

This was established on 30 October 1982, on the initiative of Ibrāhīm Nimr Ḥusayn, chairman of the National Committee of Heads of Arab Local Councils, with the aim of acting as an even more representative organization.[13] He himself has been serving as chairman of both bodies. This committee comprised, at its outset, eleven heads of Arab local authorities, and all the Arab MKs. Arab members of the Central Committee of the Histadrut, representatives of the Sons of the Village, Islamic groups, university students, and the Union of Arab Secondary School Pupils, were co-opted later. In December 1990 Arab residents of the mixed towns began demanding due representation on this body. The committee works through five commissions, which report both to it and to the National Committee of Heads of Arab Local Councils on education, health, sports, social services, and agriculture. Though the Follow-up Committee for Arab Citizens has no official recognition, it organizes protest meetings and strikes,[14] to bolster its position as a self-alleged 'miniature parliament' of the Arabs in Israel. Several other institutions branch out from this committee, such as the Follow-up Committee for Arab Education. The following is an illustration of the political activities of the Follow-up Committee.

Consequent to several years of argument by certain Jewish circles that the Arabs (excluding the Druzes and several small groups) should not be equal citizens, because they do not serve in the Defence Forces, the Minister responsible for the affairs of the Arabs, David Magen, came up, in 1991, with an interesting suggestion. He proposed that Arab youths be recruited for national, instead of military, service, to be carried out in the Arab localities. The Follow-up Committee for Arab Citizens convened to reject the

---

[13] ʿAṭallāh Manṣūr, 'Mī měnahel et Vaʿadat ha-Maʿaqav ha-ʿElyōna', *ha-Aretz*, 20 Mar. 1988, 11.
[14] See e.g. *al-Ittiḥād*, 23 May 1989.

proposal unreservedly. Among its arguments were the following: the proposal was intended to mobilize Arabs for service work in order to free Jewish soldiers to deal with the *intifāḍa*; and it had the character of forced labour. Several members of the committee argued for civil disobedience, if national service should be enforced.[15] The entire matter has been dropped meanwhile and is now being considered as a voluntary option only.

Even though all the above committees have no legal standing whatsoever, they contain ingredients of institutions building towards 'a state in the making', which resemble, to a large degree (and not coincidentally), the process adopted by the Jewish community in British-ruled Palestine. As defined by Ibrāhīm Nimr Ḥusayn himself, in 1989,[16] the National Committee of the Heads of Arab Local Councils is something of a government, while the Follow-up Committee for Arab Citizens is somewhat of a parliament, for the Arabs in Israel. In fact, the debates in those two committees and the decisions passed by them and by subsidiary bodies reflect the struggle between the trends supporting Arab integration within the state and those opposing its very existence and striving for the realization of a separate entity.

The Druzes do not participate in these committees, having in 1982 set up a Follow-up Committee of their own, made up of seven public personalities (not including the community's spiritual leader). This Follow-up Committee set as its first objective to watch over events in the Lebanon War and the immediate fate of their co-religionists; afterwards, it focused on other matters related to the Druzes in Israel.[17]

RADICAL GROUPS

The Sons of the Village (Abnā' al-Balad)

This militant grouping was set up in 1973, approximately, and is the most radical organization among secular Arab circles in Israel. Heir to al-Arḍ, in many respects, it is still rather small but none

[15] e.g. *ha-Aretz*, 7 Jan. 1991, A3 ('Aṭallāh Manṣūr's report). Cf. D. Rubinstein, 'Lō' lĕ-sherūt lĕ'ūmī', ibid. 10 Jan. 1991, B1.
[16] In an interview to the Jaffa newspaper *al-'Ajamī*, 20 May 1989.
[17] Shakīb Ṣāliḥ, *Tōlĕdōt ha-Dĕrūzīm* (1989), 255.

the less vociferous. It preaches the message of the Zionist state's delegitimization, while adopting the PLO position that 'a secular state should be established for both peoples', in which Jews would no longer be a majority. As the Sons of the Village and similarly minded groups perceive the situation, an Arab majority would be attained by a merger of the Arabs in Israel and in the territories, or, as they phrase it, 'Hebron is like Galilee.' These groups were encouraged by what they interpreted as Israel's defeat in the 1973 War. As part of their struggle for the state's delegitimization, they insisted on non-participation in Knesset elections at the end of that year, and subsequently.

Among Arab political groups, the Sons were probably the most extreme and certainly the most articulate.[18] The organization was set up in Umm al-Faḥm, in opposition to the Communists, whom they considered too moderate in their nationalism and too prone to grant legitimacy to the Israeli Establishment by playing according to its rules of the game and refusing to reject UN declaration no. 242 (which admits the possibility of two states). The Sons were willing, however, to participate in local elections, starting with Umm al-Faḥm in 1973, and attacking both the *ḥamula* heads and the Communists. Their leader, a lawyer named Muḥammad Tawfīq al-Kayawān, gained a seat on the local council, a success that had an impact on nearby Arab villages, and even on more remote ones. Al-Kayawān, a lawyer from Umm al-Faḥm, was reported to have declared, 'I have only a single identity—that of a Palestinian, even if I carry an Israeli identity card.'[19] Similar groups have emerged, connected to the Sons in one way or another. Such are al-Nahḍa (the Revival, or Awakening) in Ṭaiyyba; al-Fajr (the Dawn) in ʿAra and ʿArʿara; and others elsewhere. These were tiny, but vocal, groups. For instance, ʿAbd al-ʿAzīz Abū Iṣbaʿ, secretary of al-Nahḍa in Ṭaiyyba, recently maintained in a newspaper interview that his group was a continuation of al-Arḍ, adding that the attitude of his own towards other groups was shaped by the positions assumed by those others to the Palestinian

---

[18] For them, see Rafīq Ḥalabī, 'Anaḥnū ha-yĕlīdīm', *Kōteret Raʾshīt*, 3 (15 Dec. 1982), 22–3; ʿAṭallāh Manṣūr, 'Radīqalīzatsiyya ba-rĕḥōv ha-ʿAravī', *ha-Aretz*, 9 Mar. 1978.

[19] David Lennon, 'Israel's Unwilling Arabs', *Middle East International*, 120 (14 Mar. 1980), 7.

question and its sole legitimate representative (that is, the PLO).[20] In the 1978 local authority elections, the Sons of the Village improved their vote in various places, attaining about 4,000 votes,[21] proportionately increasing their representation in Umm al-Faḥm from one to two, and gaining one councillor each in Ṭaiyyba, Kābūl, Maʿīliya, and Bāqa al-Gharbiyya, respectively. In 1983, their overall representation reached nine, on various local councils. In 1989, they ran in thirteen places, gaining a councillor in each of the following villages: Jat, Kafr Kannā, Ṣakhneyn, Majd al-Kurūm, Maʿīliya, and Jish. According to their own claims, they had opened twenty branches in Arab villages and were counting on support in others.[22] Organizational ties between the groups in various villages were sporadic, but essential ideological agreement maintained the connection. However, since there was no full ideological identification between all members and supporters, the Sons refrained from setting up a movement with a rigid constitution, which would only have led to rifts. They preferred (following the example of al-Arḍ) to set up various associations—for issuing certain publications, including a weekly; for protecting political prisoners; for women; and for youth.

The Sons of the Village have attempted to work in terms of both main aspirations of the Arab sector in Israel—demanding the end of all discrimination and the obtaining of full equality; and voicing insistent nationalist demands for a Palestinian state, as envisaged by the PLO. Despite this duality, or perhaps because of it, the Sons have enjoyed little support among Israel's Arab minority, obtaining some popularity only among university students. The Arab students, as we have said, set up an Arab Students' Committee in each university, not officially recognized but serving, among other things, as an indicator of their political mood. Over the years, these committees have been a battleground between Communists and nationalists, with the former frequently gaining the upper hand; more recently, however, the latter have become stronger.[23] The

[20] Shawqiyya ʿUrūq Manṣūr, 'Liqāʾ maʿa ʿAbd al-ʿAzīz Abū Iṣbaʿ sekreter ḥarakat al-nahḍa', *al-Ṣināra*, 26 Jan. 1990.

[21] Yael Yishai, 'Challenge Groups in Israeli Politics', *Middle East Journal*, 35/4 (Autumn 1981), 544–56.

[22] Yaʾīr Nĕhōraʾī, 'Eretz Israʾel ha-shĕlema, tsad beyt', *Yĕrūshalayim*, 19 Jan. 1990, 8–10.

[23] Erik Bender, "Arviyyey artsĕkha wĕ-ʿArviyyey eretz aḥeret', *Pī ha-Atōn*, 28 Dec. 1977, 2.

decline of the Israel Communist Party among the Arabs in Israel, on the one hand, and the increasing solidarity with the *intifāda*, on the other, were probably the reasons why, in the November 1988 Arab Students' Committee elections at the Hebrew University of Jerusalem, the Sons obtained eight representatives (versus nine for the Communists), based on 800 participating votes,[24] while in the December 1989 elections they, together with some allies, won a majority of nine seats (versus eight for the Communists and their allies), based on 844 (out of 1,200) Arab students' votes.[25] Several weeks later, the Sons got a majority in the Arab Students' Committee at Ben-Gurion University in the Negev: together with the Progressive List for Peace, they obtained five seats (versus four for the Communists). Further, they received a significant representation in the Arab Students' Committee at Tel-Aviv University; their strength grew at Haifa University and the Technion as well.

The Sons' university activities are not directed only towards their fellow students (for example by advising them) but also—possibly, mostly—towards Arab nationalist issues. Their avowed intention is to move from local issues to country-wide ones. For instance, they collected signatures against the immigration of Soviet Jews for a petition which they meant to send to the UN Secretary-General.[26] An article in their weekly, *al-Maydān*, had the characteristic title 'Our Legal Right to Oppose [Jewish] Immigration at the Expense of our Daily Bread and the Expropriation of Our Land'.[27] In this context, the Sons proved to be more aggressively involved than other Arabs in Israel, who were also worried about Jewish immigration from the Soviet Union.[28] Equally, in January 1991, they tried to organize demonstrations in favour of Ṣaddām Ḥusayn, arguing that Iraq would solve the problems of the Palestinians.[29] Their intentions and aspirations are revealed by their manifestos and pamphlets, bearing such typical titles as 'Let the Day of the Prisoner be a Day for Strengthening Our Fighters in Gaol and those among the Masses of the *Intifāda*' (distributed in April

[24] *Kol ha-ʿĪr*, 30 Dec. 1988, 17; *Pī ha-Atōn*, Jan. 1989, 4.

[25] *Pī ha-Atōn*, 3 (Jan. 1990), 7.

[26] *al-Maydān*, 9 Mar. 1990; *Pī ha-Atōn*, Apr. 1990, 7.

[27] An article, so entitled, was published in *al-Maydān*, 9 Mar. 1990.

[28] A. Dayyan, "ʿŌlīm ʿaleyhem", *Kol ha-ʿĪr*, 9 Mar. 1990, 41–4.

[29] ʿAṭallāh Manṣūr, 'Běney ha-kěfar měʾargěnīm hafganat těmīkha běʿemdat ʿIrāq', *ha-Aretz*, 11 Jan. 1991, A3.

1989);[30] 'Yes to Attaining the Independence of the Palestinian State' (dated 12 November 1989);[31] or 'The Immigration of Soviet Jews Threatens Our Existence in Our Motherland' (dated 9 February 1990).[32] The issues are defined even more sharply in the student Sons' 1988/9 electoral platform,[33] which is apparently intended for all the universities. There are two clear camps—friends and enemies. The former are the Socialist states, liberation movements, and the progressive Jewish forces which are opposed to Zionism; the latter are imperialism, Zionism, and the local Arab reactionary forces (Zionism bears most of the brunt).

A perusal of the Sons' first weekly, *al-Rāya*, of which 82 issues were published during 1987/8, until it was closed down (for being financed by the subversive Popular Front for the Liberation of Palestine); and of their second weekly, *al-Maydān*, published in Nazareth since 24 November 1989, provides a full survey of their politics. For instance, *al-Maydān*'s first editorial calls on 'all patriotic forces to write in the weekly'.[34]

No less revealing is a 150-page book, recently compiled and published by the Sons of the Village about their organization, entitled *The Sons of the Village Movement: Positions and Premisses*.[35] This starts with an appeal to 'the Palestinian masses of our people', so that from the very first it is emphasized that the Sons consider themselves as Palestinians, not Israelis. This motif is repeated time and again. In a flowery literary style, the authors address their cadres and members, urging them to struggle for national liberation within an organized and centralized framework. Their political programme—written in February 1988 and approved by a convention in Nazareth held in July of the same year—is one of the more interesting documents in the book.[36] According to this manifesto,

---

[30] *Li-yakun yawm al-sajīn yawman li-daʿm munādilīnā fī al-sujūn wa-jamāhīr al-intifāda.*

[31] *Naʿam li-injāz istiqlāl al-dawla al-Filasṭīniyya.*

[32] *Hijrat al-Yahūd al-Sōfyet tuhaddid baqāʾanā fī waṭaninā.* Several of the arguments of the Sons of the Village are also known from the counter-arguments of their opponents, such as RAQAH: see e.g. ʿal-Murāhana al-khāsira li-ḥarakat Abnāʾ al-balad', *al-Ittiḥād*, 3 Apr. 1990.

[33] *al-Barnāmaj al-siyāsī li-ʾl-ḥaraka al-waṭaniyya al-taqaddumiyya—Abnāʾ al-balad fī al-jāmiʿāt* [1988–9].

[34] ʿAwaḍ ʿAbd al-Fattāḥ, 'Li-naʿmal ʿalā khalq ṣiḥāfa mawḍūʿiyya wa-multazima', *al-Maydān*, 1/1 (24 Nov. 1989), 3.

[35] *Harakat Abnāʾ al-balad mawāqif wa-munṭalaqāt* (1989).

[36] Ibid. 10–14.

which does not once mention the State of Israel, the Arab states form an integral part of the developing countries exploited by imperialism, both economically and militarily. Zionism is labelled an instrument of imperialism and defined as a reactionary colonialist movement representing the interests of the Jewish bourgeoisie (such slogans are frequently used by anti-Semitic Marxist circles). The Arab minority in the Jewish state serves it as a cheap labour force. Zionism and Arab reactionarism prevent the establishment of a united Arab state based on a socialist society. Consequently, that part of the Palestinian Arab people which remained in its motherland after 1948 ought to lead the struggle for liberation and progress in the area. Since the 1960s the PLO heads this struggle, both politically and militarily. The Arab masses in the Jewish state profess their Palestinian identity and strive for a national awakening, while integrating with the Arab masses in the socialist camp and working against capitalism.

The programme defined the aims of the Sons as follows: (1) to represent the interests of the oppressed masses, both Arab and Jewish, for coexistence in a framework free from discrimination; (2) to obtain the right of deciding their fate within an independent Palestinian state; (3) to ensure the right of Palestinian refugees to return to their motherland; (4) to achieve all democratic freedoms for the masses; (5) to strive for equality in nationhood, religion, sex, and colour; (6) to stop the destruction of houses and expropriation of lands and return those expropriated to their owners; (7) to establish a democratic society; (8) to set up a large mass organization to fight imperialism and Zionism; (9) to ensure for the masses livelihood, cultural services, health, housing, employment, and everything necessary for self-rule. The *modus operandi* of the Sons was then set out as follows:

1. Everyone who accepted these objectives and ways of struggle could become a member of the movement.
2. The movement would employ legal means.
3. The struggle would be carried out via various representative bodies, such as the National Committee for the Defence of Lands, the National Committee of Heads of Arab Local Councils, unions of Arab students, and secondary school pupils, trade unions, women's associations, and the like.
4. Democratic and liberal Jews would be co-opted to the struggle.

5. Parliamentary efforts were useless, in the light of experience.
6. Local elections, on the other hand, were essential in strengthening the relationship between local authorities and the Arab masses, in order to improve their situation.
7. Relations between the movement and any party, organization, or group would be determined by one criterion—safeguarding the interests of the Arab masses.

Other documents in the same volume consist of extreme pronouncements and articles. Several attack the radical Islamic groups (which, according to the writers, oppose nationalist activity), while others phrase their arguments in a Marxist style (with its characteristic jargon). Here one notes a paradox. Considering their bitter opposition to the Israeli Communist Party and its legitimization of the State of Israel, it is odd that the Sons of the Village employ Marxist slogans which since the late 1980s have been disappearing all over the world. Perhaps they intend to fight the Communists with their own weapons, competing with them for the support of the better-educated Arabs in Israel. However, their tendency to employ an arrogant style and harsh language have probably contributed to their overall number remaining low. The Sons of the Village claim to have twenty branches in various Arab localities, but they do not reveal membership figures. They maintain that 80 per cent of their membership are Muslims and 20 per cent Christians, with only a few Druzes. None the less, one gets the impression that almost all the members are Muslims, as are practically all their active supporters.

The Nationalist Progressive Movement

The Sons of the Village have found allies, albeit few in number, among a group calling itself the Nationalist Progressive Movement. This was established in 1978 by university students in Jerusalem, Haifa, Tel-Aviv, and Be'er Sheba. While its guiding principles resemble those of the Sons, one may consider this an organization paralleling the latter, rather than rivalling it. Anyway, co-operation between the two is customary.[37]

In brief, the significance of the Sons of the Village and the

---

[37] Tim Coone, 'Strangers in the State', *Middle East*, 67 (May 1980), 36–8.

Nationalist Progressive Movement is not in numbers (lately even reduced, due to a rift), but rather in their very existence and availability to act as a hard core for a wider movement, nationalist rather than Marxist, if it were to be established.

The Nationalist Socialist Front

Other radical groups have recently joined the political scene, such as the Nationalist Socialist Front (al-Jabha al-Qawmiyya al-Ishtirākiyya), set up in Nazareth on 28 September 1990. The thirteen founders included Ṣāliḥ Barānsī and Manṣūr Qardōsh, both once leading members of al-Arḍ. The group's ideological guidelines differ but little from those of the Sons of the Village, namely the resolution of the Palestine question and co-operation with non-Zionist Jewish circles; however, this group has expressed stronger reservations regarding religious trends in politics, which it labels reactionary.[38] The Nationalist Socialist Front, while accusing the Sons of the Village of being Marxist, maintains that it itself is not.

POLITICAL PARTIES

A different pattern of organization may be observed within the political parties, at first Jewish–Arab, then exclusively Arab. In the first years of the State of Israel, Arabs were registered as full members solely in the Communist Party (which was already admitting both Jews and Arabs during the British Mandate). Since 1954, MAPAM has followed suit. These two were the only political parties to speak for a binational society and state. Both have consistently sent both Jews and Arabs to the Knesset, the Israel Communist Party since 1949 and MAPAM since 1951.[39] Both strove to mobilize Arab youth; MAPAM even set up a Pioneer Arab Youth movement (discussed above, Chapter 5). The Zionist platforms of other Jewish parties were not sufficiantly attractive to

[38] A summary of their programme was published in *al-Sināra*, 11 Nov. 1991, 18. Cf. ʿAṭallāh Manṣūr, ʿVatīqey al-Arḍ heqīmū gūf ḥadash ʿim ʿeqrōnōt zehīm', *ha-Aretz*, 10 Jan. 1991, A5.

[39] The MAPAM Arab MK in the Knesset elected in 1988 is Ḥusayn Fāris, for whose views see his article, entitled 'Lā narā amalan kabīran fī al-ḥall al-silmī ṭālamā baqiya al-Likkūd fī al-ḥukm', *al-Usbūʿ al-Jadīd*, 1 Mar. 1990, 20–1.

the Arabs. MAPAI (the Workers' Party of Israel) consequently set up slates of Arab candidates, allied with it, to run for the Knesset elections; but it is difficult to see these as political parties. Later, Arabs joined MAPAI itself, subsequently called Ha-ʿAvōda, or Israel Labour Party (henceforth: ILP), and other parties, but in modest numbers. Even though they reached 10 per cent, or 15,000, of the ILP membership in 1991,[40] their influence seems limited. This applies also to Arab MKs. Indeed, MAPAI/ILP's relations with the Arabs in Israel were stronger while it was forming and heading Coalition Cabinets, but grew weaker afterwards.[41] Mass voting by the Arabs in Knesset elections, however, compelled various other Jewish parties, too, to rethink their relations with the minorities, and devote more attention to promoting their interests, to their own political benefit.

Here we limit our discussion to three non-Jewish parties in which Arab membership and interests predominate—the Israeli Communist Party, the Progressive List for Peace, and the Democratic Arab Party.

The Israeli Communist Party

The ICP has been of mixed Jewish–Arab membership throughout, but has none the less succeeded in creating for itself the image of a nationalist Arab party—at least among Israel's minorities, and recruiting their electoral support to a great extent.[42] This was particularly true after August 1965, when the Communists split into two, chiefly owing to the reluctance of Arabs and Jews to continue together in the same party: the smaller ICP remained mostly Jewish, while RAQAH (the New Communist List) was mainly Arab.[43] Before the 1977 elections RAQAH established a

---

[40] Yōram Katz, '10% min aʿḍā' ḥizb al-ʿAmal ʿArab', *Kull al-ʿArab*, 5 July 1991.

[41] Some opinions in the matter in Sālim Jubrān's 'al-Dawr al-siyāsī li-'l-jamāhīr al-ʿArabiyya—baʿīdan ʿan al-adḥnāb wa-'l-muzāyada!', *al-Ittiḥād*, 31 May 1991, 6. A more extreme view, without any documented basis, is the accusation levelled at the Alignment of anti-Arab policies, see T. A. Karasova, *Blok Maarakh v partiyno-politichyeskiy sistyeme Izrailya* (1983).

[42] Nissīm Mishʿal, 'RAQAH hitslīḥa līstōr le-ʿatsma tadmīt shel miflaga ʿAravīt,' *ha-Tsōfeh*, 23 June 1972, Suppl., 2; Saleh Baransi, 'All This Time We were Alone,' *Merip Reports*, 96 (May 1981), 16–23.

[43] For this party, cf. M. M. Czudnowski and J. M. Landau, *The Israeli Communist Party and the Elections for the Fifth Knesset, 1961* (1965). Many subsequent works relied on this work and even copied entire pages from it. See also

wider front, together with certain educated Arabs and some other small groups. Entitled HADASH, this front jealously maintained the guidelines of RAQAH's ideology. As a consequence of this move, RAQAH/HADASH obtained its greatest electoral success, over 50 per cent of the Arab vote. As a rule, in all the elections to the Knesset, RAQAH obtained more votes from the Arabs than from the Jews, even though the former are only a minority of the population (this will be discussed in more detail below, Chapter 8). The main reason was the increasing distancing of the Arabs from Jewish parties and their gradual acceptance of RAQAH's image as promoter of the civil rights of the Arabs in Israel, their demands for full equality, and their nationalist aspirations. Similarly, RAQAH identified itself with nationalist Arab movements outside Israel.[44] In short, from 1965 RAQAH succeeded in assuming the red mantle of Arab nationalism.[45] It invested much effort in publishing books and newspapers, and in organizational activities among Arab youths. Most of its functionaries, also, consist of Arabs, who are salaried (while Jewish parties expect volunteer work from many of their members and supporters). *Prima facie*, the unswerving adherence of a Marxist party to nationalism, even chauvinism, may seem strange; however, Middle Eastern Communists have often identified with minority groups and their nationalist aspirations, thereby obtaining their grateful loyalty and co-operation.

At first, much of RAQAH's success was obtained among the Christians, and some of its leading Arab members were Christians, such as Tawfīq Ṭūbī, Emile Ḥabībī, Emile Tōmā, and others. However, since 1967 the party has focused more on the Muslims, promoting them to leading positions, as in the case of Tawfīq

Muḥmūd Muḥārib, *al-Ḥizb al-shuyūʿī al-Isrāʾīlī wa-ʾl-qadiyya al-Filasṭīniyya 1948–1981: dirāsa naqdiyya* (1989), esp. 191–206. Cf. Alain Greilshammer, *Les Communistes israéliens* (1978); Ori Stendel, 'The Rise of New Political Currents in the Arab Sector in Israel, 1948–1974', in Moshe Maʿoz (ed.), *Palestinian Arab Politics* (1975), esp. 109–30; L. A. Barkovskiy, *Arabskoye nasyelyeniye Izrailya* (1986), esp. 86–122.

[44] Clinton Bailey, 'The Communist Party and the Communists in Israel', *Midstream*, May 1970, 49 ff.

[45] Havīv Knaʿan, 'ha-Adderet ha-adūmma shel ha-lěʾūmanūt ha-ʿAravīt', *ha-Aretz*, 26 Oct. 1969, 11. Cf. Q. Měnaḥem (=Měnaḥem Qapelyūq), 'Hefqerūt "demōqrāṭīt"', *Davar*, 26 Oct. 1969.

Ziyād,[46] Mayor of Nazareth and MK, or Hāshim Maḥāmīd,[47] Mayor of Umm al-Faḥm, and Muḥammad Naffāʿ, both of them now MKs. Concurrently, the Communists have increased their activity among the Druzes as well. Throughout, they have been most careful not to attack religion; on the contrary, they have fostered a self-image of protectors of the institutions of all religions (chiefly Islam's). Indefatigably, they have addressed their propaganda to all groups and classes, but more emphatically to workers (particularly those employed outside their villages), intellectuals, and youths. This explains, in some measure, the composition of their membership. According to RAQAḤ's own figures in 1969 (no other data were released later) this consisted of: 57 per cent workers, 20 per cent officials, 8 per cent from the liberal professions, 8 per cent artisans, and 5 per cent housewives.[48] RAQAḤ members have also attempted to assist Arabs in their personal affairs,[49] employing every opportunity to improve the party's image.

The party has focused its attention, also, on cultural and literary matters, for which many Arabs feel much sympathy. In addition to books and pamphlets, RAQAḤ publishes various newspapers, including the daily *al-Ittiḥād*, the Arabic daily with the longest existence in Israel and at times the only one available. Both *al-Ittiḥād* and several periodicals—notably the monthly *al-Jadīd* (The New)—as well as the speeches of the party's MKs and its other leaders and their writings, political meetings, and literary debates—have consistently followed the ideological and propaganda guidelines of the Soviet Union. Like the Soviet Union, RAQAḤ enthusiastically supported Arab nationalism and even more Palestinian, through its propaganda, while harshly condemning official Israeli policies in almost all matters. However, for all practical purposes, the party has admitted Israel's existence and has followed the state's rules of the game in its politics. The party

---

[46] Joyce Anne, 'Interview With Tawfiq Zayyad', *American Arab Affairs*, 25 (Summer 1988), 48–54.

[47] Cf. the interview of Maḥāmīd in *al-Usbūʿ al-ʿArabī*, 15 Feb. 1990, 13–15; and of Naffāʿ in *al-Sināra*, 20 Sept. 1991, 10–11.

[48] Havīv Knaʿan, '57% me-ḥavrey RAQAḤ hem pōʿalīm', *ha-Aretz*, 21 Feb. 1969, 16.

[49] Examples in Rafī Benqler's 'ha-Dīlemma shel Nōṣrat', *ʿAl ha-Mishmar*, 17 Oct. 1969, 5, 8.

propaganda has consistently advocated, for many years, both full
equality for the Arabs in Israel and establishment of a Palestinian
state, side by side with Israel.[50] As RAQAH sees it, the best way
for the Arabs to attain both goals is via co-operation with the
Jewish sector in Israel.[51] In addition to an ongoing debate with
Israeli policies, both internally and externally, RAQAH finds itself
in sharp confrontation with the Islamic circles that are increasingly
becoming involved in the politics of the Arab minority, with the
party blaming fundamentalist Muslims for disrupting what it
perceives as the unity of the Arab front in Israel.[52]

RAQAH's contribution to the radicalization of a part of the
Arab sector has been twofold. Firstly, its nationalist propaganda
has stirred aspirations and expectations and garnered more Arab
votes than any other political party. Secondly, its organizing of
various political structures, like the Popular Front in 1958, later
HADASH, as well as associations of women, youth, and so forth,
has pointed the way to political organization later adopted by other
groups as well. Still, RAQAH/HADASH has accepted the political
rules of the game in Israel, even supporting the establishment of a
Palestinian state side by side with Israel.

The Progressive List for Peace

The PLP is a quasi-party organization, also headed by nationalist
politicians and inspired by their guidelines.[53] Its beginnings were in
a group entitled the Nationalist Faction which split away from
RAQAH in Nazareth on 27 November 1981, in a bid to become the
main power in the local municipal council, emphasizing its own
nationalist ideology and accusing RAQAH of various sins of
omission. So as not to antagonize the state authorities and the
Jewish sector unduly, the group's name was changed, in January
1982, to the Arab Progressive Movement in Israel and, on 24
April of that year, again, to the Progressive List for Peace—to

---

[50] As expressed by Tawfīq Tūbī, in his farewell speech from the Knesset, in July
1990. Cf. *al-Ittiḥād*, 5 July 1990, 3.

[51] As phrased by one of RAQAH's prominent Arab members, Sālim Jubrān,
'Qaḍiyyatunā al-ʿādila, kayfa naksib al-raʾy al-ʿāmm taʾyīdan lahā?', ibid. 31 Mar.
1989.

[52] e.g., Shākir Farīd Ḥasan, 'Naqd dhātī li-masīrat ḥizbinā al-shuyūʿī', ibid. 27
Feb. 1990.

[53] Avner Regev, *ʿArviyyey Israʾel: Sūgiyyōt pōlīṭiyyōt* (1989), 18–24.

demonstrate its intention to co-operate with sympathetic Jewish elements. The eighty founders then elected an executive council and launched their political activity, at first locally, in Nazareth, and later on a country-wide basis. At that time, its leading figure and chief ideologue was one of the erstwhile founders of ḤADASH and a past Associate-Mayor of Nazareth, Kāmil al-Ẓāhir (born in 1942). The new grouping appealed for municipal reform, supported the struggle for full Arab equality in Israel, and the establishment of a Palestinian state in the Israeli-held territories. Competing with RAQAḤ/ḤADASH and other groups in the 1983 local elections in Nazareth (see below, Chapter 8), it obtained four seats on the municipal council, out of a total of seventeen. While it failed to dislodge RAQAH/ḤADASH from this council, the results were far from negligible, and the group felt encouraged to turn to national, rather than local, politics.

Enlarging its scope by uniting in 1984 with several other groups, the Nazareth nucleus set up the PLP, as it is still known. Among the constituent elements were the al-Anṣār group, made up of Arab intellectuals in Umm al-Faḥm (who had split off from the Sons of the Village when these refused to run for the Knesset) and Alternative, a Jewish leftist group favouring recognition of the PLO and establishment of a Palestinian Arab State in exchange for peace with Israel. Immediately after the foundation of the PLP in its new structure, it elected a twenty-one member Central Committee and a seven-member presidium. In its founding proclamation, dated 30 May 1984, the PLP announced its intention to run for the Knesset. It also detailed its main goals, as follows: (1) obtaining complete equality between Arabs and Jews, by an unceasing fight against discrimination; (2) mutual recognition by the Israeli-Jewish and Palestinian-Arab peoples of the right of self-determination, accompanied by an Israeli retreat from all occupied territories and East Jerusalem, where the Palestinian-Arab people would establish its own independent state; (3) mutual recognition by the State of Israel and the Palestinian State, following negotiations in which the PLO would be the only legitimate representative of the Palestinian people (the PLP never concealed its relations with the PLO); (4) an immediate and unconditional retreat of the Israeli Defence Forces from Lebanon.[54]

[54] ha-Rĕshīma ha-Mitqaddemet lĕ-Shalōm, *Hōdaʿat ha-yissūd* (1984).

The head of the reconstituted PLP was Muḥammad Mīʿārī (born in 1939), a lawyer who sees himself as a spokesman for educated Arabs.[55] He was once a member of al-Arḍ, and, after it had been banned, in 1965 joined the list of candidates headed by al-Arḍ members which was legally prohibited from running for the Knesset. Before joining the PLP and becoming its chairman, Mīʿārī had tried to establish relations with several other groups, such as RAQAḤ and MAPAM, but he never joined them. He strove consistently to act within the framework of law—but, within these constraints, he never hesitated to proclaim his strongly radical views.

Organizationally, the PLP was not a fully constituted party in its first years. Rather, it was a movement with five branches: in the Negev; the Little Triangle; Nazareth; Upper Galilee and Acre; Lower Galilee and Haifa. It was led by a seven-member presidium, which met whenever necessary. Its most visible expression was a list of 120, actually a slate of candidates for the 1984, then for the 1988, Knesset elections. This list was made up of Arab and Jewish candidates, listed alternately (probably as an insurance against eventual accusations of Arab subversiveness). The first was Mīʿārī himself; the second Matityahū Peled (born in 1923), a retired major-general and senior lecturer in Arabic literature at Tel-Aviv University; the third and fourth, two Arabs, Riyāḥ Abu al-ʿAsal, ex-HADASH member, Anglican priest and the PLP's secretary-general between 1985 and 1990, and Walīd Ṣādiq, erstwhile MK; then a Jew, an Arab, and so on. If one may rely on this slate as an indicator of the PLP's composition, it comprised, in 1984, 32 per cent Muslims, 10 per cent Christians, 6 per cent Bedouin, 3 per cent Druze, and 49 per cent Jews. Women (seven in all) represented 12 per cent, a sign of the PLP's socially progressive character. Attempts by various political parties to have the PLP disqualified from the electoral contest fell through, since the courts ruled that its activities were within the law. The party won two Knesset seats in 1984 but only one in 1988, probably due to lack of sufficient co-operation between its Arab and Jewish components (as will be explained below, in Chapter 8). Political radicalization, expressed in the Arab sector in 1984 by the election of Muḥammad Mīʿārī to the Knesset, was similarly noticeable, in an even more

[55] Cf. Maḥmūd Mīʿārī, 'Beʿayat ha-zehūt beyn ha-maskīlīm ha-ʿAravīm bĕ-Israʾel', in A. Hareven (ed.), *Eḥad mi-kol shishsha* (1981), 170–4.

extreme form, in the Jewish sector in the election of Meʾīr Kahanā.[56] The PLP offered its supporters a double message. In its official platform, it stressed its desire for Arab–Jewish and Palestinian–Israeli peace, a democratic constitution, separation between religion and state, national and civil equality for the Arabs in education, economic standing and housing (in 1988, support for the *intifāḍa*, too, was expressed). However, the party seems to have maintained another, more radical platform, proclaimed by Riyāḥ Abū al-ʿAsal at an electoral rally in Ṭaiyyba, in 1984. According to this, the PLP was dedicated to the Arab refugees' right of return to Jaffa, Haifa, Acre, Ramleh, and other places; and to negotiations with the PLO concerning Israel's pre-1967 frontiers, which the PLP did not consider as finite.[57] The extremism in the party's positions is attributable not only to its leaders' views, but also to its tactical need to compete with RAQAH/ḤADASH, its main rival in the Arab sector. It is no mere accident that the PLP elected an Arab to head it, while RAQAH's long-time leader was a Jew, Meʾīr Wīlner, its secretary-general. None the less, several of the PLP's prominent leaders were dissatisfied with the weight given to its Jewish members, feeling that this arrangement contradicted their own nationalist aspirations. Consequently, they attempted, by word and deed, to limit the scope of Jewish influence within the party.[58]

In a way, this is compatible with Mīʿārī's view that three main trends have been competing with one another in Israel's Arab sector—the nationalist, the Marxist, and the religious.[59] It seems obvious that he wishes to imply that the PLP is the only true representative of the nationalist trend, which has been gaining over the others. This, of course, leaves some of Mīʿārī's difficulties unresolved, particularly as his leadership has been challenged,[60]

[56] E. A. Nakhleh, 'Post-Israeli Election Polarizations and Changes', *Middle East Insight*, 3/6 (1984), 18–25.

[57] Acc. to the evidence of Tsvī Alpeleg, in an interview given to Amnōn Dōtan, 'Leʾan mitqaddemet ha-Rēshīma ha-Mitqaddemet', *ʿAl ha-Mishmar*, 21 Sept. 1984, 11.

[58] See e.g. the short story published by ʿAlī al-Hindāwī, a member of the PLP in Shafā ʿAmr, entitled 'Khudh al-ḥikma min afwāh . . . al-ḥaṭṭābīn', *al-Ṣīnāra*, 1 Dec. 1989, 7—whose moral is that Arabs lose in their partnership with Jews.

[59] 'al-Nāʾib Muḥammad Mīʿārī fī ḥadīth maʿa al-Usbūʿ al-Jadīd,' *al-Usbūʿ al-Jadīd*, 15 Apr. 1989, 16–18.

[60] Rashīd Salīm, 'al-Haraka al-taqaddumiyya bi-ḥāja ilà intifāḍa li-isqāṭ al-qiyāda wa-mumārasatihā', *al-Ṣīnāra*, 9 Feb. 1990, 4.

and all the more so since he rushed, in speech and writing, to take the part of Ṣaddām Ḥusayn when the latter invaded Kuwait in August 1990.

The Democratic Arab Party

The DAP was established in July 1988, with a view to participating in the Knesset elections that same year. This is the first political party in Israel to be made up solely of Arabs (mostly Muslims) and appealing to them alone, without expecting any Jewish electoral support. In this it evidently differs from both RAQAḤ/ḤADASH and the PLP. Its founder and leader is ʿAbd al-Raḥmān Darāwshe (born in 1943), a Muslim from the village of Iksāl, near Nazareth, with a BA degree in history and education, formerly a teacher and inspector of schools. In 1984, the ILP decided that, instead of having a nominating committee appoint its Arab candidates for the Knesset, the Arabs themselves, members of the party's central bodies, would select them. Thus Darāwshe, a party member since 1965, was nominated and in due course became an MK. Later, in October 1986, he was appointed a Deputy Minister, as a gesture by the ILP towards those Arabs who have justifiedly maintained that they are under-represented in senior administrative and elective positions. Darāwshe seems to have been apprehensive that this very appointment would identify him totally with Israel's Jewish Establishment. Moreover, his own political views and activities were not necessarily compatible with those of the ILP, most particularly in his favouring a Palestinian state patterned on the PLO initiative. Therefore, in the spring of 1988 Darāwshe left the party, setting up a one-man faction in the Knesset.[61] He then wrote, in Hebrew, a long article on the electoral potential of the Arabs in Israel,[62] and subsequently started to try to exploit this potential by founding the DAP.

About 600 people, including sixteen heads of Arab local authorities, twenty deputy heads, 120 members of local councils, religious functionaries (both Muslim and Christian), two Druzes, and several Arab businessmen participated in the inauguration

---

[61] Dan Margalīt, 'ha-Shūttaf mistalleq me-ha-ʿisqa', *ha-Aretz*, 9 Feb. 1988, 13.
[62] ʿAbd al-Wahhāb Darāwshe, 'Mishqal ḥasar taqdīm', *Pōlīṭīqa*, 21 (June 1988), 22–3.

ceremony. Darāws̲h̲e declared that Arabs had previously elected Jews to the Knesset, but the time had come for Arabs to vote for their own. Despite the proclaimed ethnic basis of his party, which could have promoted extremism, Darāws̲h̲e has insistently striven not to break away completely from the Israeli consensus—a move in the direction of moderation. None the less, Darāws̲h̲e felt that, tactically, he ought to block accusations by his rivals that he himself might be 'an agent of the ILP'. In consequence, the DAP presented itself in the image of an independent Arab party, of a nationalist character, which would focus on the affairs of the Arabs in Israel and those in the Israeli-held territories, and their rights. However, the impression spread that Darāws̲h̲e and his party would give priority to the struggle for equal rights of the Arabs in Israel over that for their nationalist aspirations (even if not totally neglecting them), and would strive to achieve at least a part of Arab economic demands by joining a Coalition Cabinet.[63] Darāws̲h̲e was naturally aware of this mood; hence the line he adopted before the 1988 Knesset elections and after them[64] was to argue that the Arabs in Israel have been loyal to the state and its laws and their wish is merely to support the establishment of a Palestinian state side by side with Israel.

Darāws̲h̲e was elected to the Knesset in 1988 with enough votes for a seat and a half. At all events, the fact that the new Coalition Cabinet was formed without the DAP, and that Darāws̲h̲e has maintained a lone seat in the Opposition ranks, seems to hurt the party, which did not do as well as it had expected in the 1989 local elections. Still, Darāws̲h̲e himself appears to have maintained his popularity in the meetings convened by his party,[65] striving to keep it together by his public support for Iraq's invasion of Kuwait—a gesture which caused Rā'id Manṣūr, general secretary of the party's younger groups,[66] to resign in protest.

The absence of pre-election agreements among RAQAḤ/ ḤADAS̲H̲, the PLP and the DAP—because of ideological dif-

[63] Ṭaha As̲h̲qar, 'Mustaqbal al-tanẓīm al-siyāsī 'ind al-'Arab fī Isrā'īl', *al-Ṣināra*, 1 Dec. 1989, 7.
[64] Abdel Wahab Darawshe, 'The Intifada and Israeli Arabs', *New Outlook*, 32/ 297–8 (Nov.–Dec. 1989), 30–1.
[65] 'Aṭallāh Manṣūr, 'Livnōt et ha-bayit teḥilla', *ha-Aretz*, 1 Aug. 1990, 22.
[66] N. Kahanā, 'Hitpaṭṭer mazkal ha-dōr ha-tsaʿīr ba-Miflaga he-Demōqraṭīt ha-'Aravīt biglal tĕmīk̲h̲ata bĕ-Ṣaddām', ibid. 24 Aug. 1990, A3.

ferences and personal rivalry—adversely affected the total count for all three in 1988 (as will be explained below, in Chapter 8). None the less, the sum total of their electoral support in that year, approaching 59 per cent of all valid Arab votes, does suggest a radicalization in Arab support for the more extreme political parties.

ISLAMIC ORGANIZATIONS

As already said, these organizations frequently contain a clear-cut political element, owing to the basically political character of Islam. Until the time of writing (1991), however, this has not yet been expressed in a country-wide organization, for example towards the 1992 Knesset elections—although this is not excluded. The spiritual leader of the Muslim fundamentalists in Israel, ʿAbdallāh Nimr Darwīsh, who is based in Kafr Qāsim, in the Little Triangle, has already hinted at his intention to form an Islamic slate of candidates for those elections.[67] In contrast, other prominent persons in these circles, such as Rāʾid Ṣalāḥ Mahājna (born in 1958), Mayor of Umm al-Faḥm, are taking an opposite stand,[68] probably in order not to take part in Israel's rules of the game and thereby legitimize it. After all, Islam's political ideology grants legitimization solely to the Islamic state.

Many spokesmen of the fundamentalists content themselves at present with their attainments in the February–March 1989 local elections (for which see below, Chapter 8) and with the consequent rise in their power.[69] True, they refrained from running in the Knesset elections of 1988 or the Histadrut ones of 1989. Their members comprise not a few who are shy of openly adopting extreme positions that might embroil them with the Israeli authorities who, after all, subsidize the local authorities.[70] The political direction of the Islamic fundamentalists in Israel is partly

[67] 'Hal tahūd al-haraka al-Islāmiyya intikhābāt al-Knesset?', *al-Nadwa*, 3 (16 Mar. 1990).
[68] Ibid. See also ʿal-Shaykh Rāʾid Sālāh raʾīs baladiyyat Umm al-Faḥm yarudd ʿalà al-hajma al-iʿlāmiyya al-mukaththafa', *Ṣawt al-Ḥaqq wa-ʾl-Ḥurriyya*, 9 Mar. 1990, 7.
[69] A. Bar-Yōsef, 'Kafr Qāsim: ha-kětōvet ʿal ha-qīr', *Maʿarīv*, 10 Mar. 1989, 4.
[70] Oz Frankel, 'Living with Fundamentalism', *Jerusalem Post*, 10 Mar. 1989, 9.

affected by *de facto* relations with the authorities and partly by the impact exercised on them by Muslim circles in the West Bank and the Gaza Strip.[71] This seems particularly applicable to the Little Triangle, tangential to the West Bank and entirely inhabited by Muslims, thus creating a Muslim zone on both sides of the Green Line.

Since Islamic organization in Israel tends to be cautious in its political behaviour, it focuses meanwhile on numerous community services, both variegated and effective. This trend is not determined merely by the seeking of popularity, although this, too, is naturally taken into account. It seems, indeed, that the fundamentalists are shaping institutional structures—educational, cultural, social, and economic—parallel to those of the State of Israel and its agencies. If so, they are fostering, and experimenting with, such structures in order that they may serve as an alternative framework for a future Islamic state, or, at least, for a state-within-a-state. Although the Islamic movement keeps a low profile on the political level (to prevent official intervention), there can be no doubt that its aim is to become the leading political force in the Arab sector. Indeed, its slogan 'Islam is the Solution' is well understood as referring not merely to the religious and spiritual or social and educational domain. Since 1990, leaders of the Islamic groups in Israel have been participating in various moves intended to create a comprehensive political alliance for electoral reasons. With this purpose in mind they have contacted the PLP, the DAP, and RAQAH/HADASH.[72] Of course, doubts remain as to the substance of such negotiations: for instance, Muḥammad Mī'ārī has expressed reservations; moreover, one may wonder about the practicability of an electoral alliance between the fundamentalists and the atheist RAQAH/HADASH. However, in Israeli-Arab politics, electoral co-operation between at least some of these elements is not impossible, in the near or distant future.[73]

[71] Ghada Talhami, 'Islamic Fundamentalism and the Palestinians', *Muslim World*, 78/3–4 (July–Oct. 1988), 173–88.

[72] 'Hal al-ḥadīth ḥawl tashkīl ḥizb 'Arabī muwaḥḥad huwa mujarrad kalām?', *al-Nadwa*, 23 Mar. 1990.

[73] See also Ibrāhīm Mālik, 'ha-Tĕnū'a ha-Islāmīt bĕ-Isra'el—beyn ha-dĕveqūt ba-mĕqōrōt lĕ-maḥaseh ha-pragmaṭīzm', *Sĕqīrōt 'al 'Arviyyey Isra'el*, 4 (Aug. 1990), 1–14.

DRUZE ORGANIZATION IN ISRAEL

This, too, reflects the political rifts characteristically fragmenting Israeli society, both Jewish and Arab. Two examples, briefly alluded to earlier, should suffice.

1. The Druze Initiative Committee was set up in 1972 with three main objectives: first, to oppose what they regarded as the intention of the authorities to cause a split between Druzes and Arabs; secondly, to abolish the compulsory service of Druze men in the Israeli Defence Forces; thirdly, to prevent expropriation of Druze lands. The first leader of this group was Sheikh Farhūd Qāsim, followed by Jamāl Muʿaddī, both vociferous opponents of Druze military service. RAQAH was involved in establishing the Druze Initiative Committee; when it set up ḤADASH, in 1977, it co-opted this group to its new front. The committee maintains that Druzes are both Arabs and Muslims, and that they perceive themselves as Palestinian Arabs professing a somewhat different religion. Most of its activities have centred on encouraging Druzes to refuse service in Israel's Defence Forces—and assisting those few who have resisted conscription. They had some limited success in 1982, when Israel's Defence Forces clashed with the Druzes in Lebanon.

2. The Zionist Druze Circle was established in 1974, perhaps in response to the Druze Initiative Committee. Its founders were young Druzes from Dāliyat al-Karmil, led by Yūsuf Naṣr al-Dīn, from the same village. Its objective is support for the State of Israel and integration into it, without any reservations whatsoever, emphasizing that Druzes are neither Muslims nor Arabs. Despite its somewhat contradictory name, the circle encompasses about 4,000 members, according to Yūsuf Naṣr al-Dīn's claim (at the end of 1991), branching into various villages. Significantly, it was joined by heads of local authorities, *qadi*s, sheikhs, students, and others. The circle has remained small, but it is the first of its kind in Israel. It does not claim to constitute a political party and, in so far as ascertainable, has no exclusive ties with any party in Israel.

POLITICAL LEADERSHIP

Traditional-Religious and Local Leadership

The crisis of the political leadership of the Arabs in Israel, which is as old as the state itself, has not yet been resolved. Most of the former political leaders left or fled the region in 1948, while others remained in the West Bank or the Gaza Strip.[74] The gradually emerging alternative leadership at first lacked impressive political stature. In fact, as in other developing countries, this was chiefly a religious or local leadership (rural or tribal). Only after long years did a more meaningful political leadership arise, party-related or otherwise. The process was delayed by the fact that both the state authorities and the political parties were accustomed, in the Arab sector, as well as in the Jewish one, to co-opt people to an already existing leadership. This applied, for instance, to Arab MKs, few of whom were made of the stuff of country-wide political leadership. All these factors retarded the formation of a grass-roots leadership among the Arabs in Israel.

During the first twenty years of the state, no Muslim leaders were generally accepted, perhaps because most Muslim officials were appointed by the Israeli authorities. Only after the 1967 War, following the meeting of the Arabs in Israel with their co-religionists in the Israeli-held territories, and, later, with the growth of Islamic fundamentalism, did the situation change. As explained above, a new, politically-minded Islamic leadership has developed, in which personalities like ʿAbdallāh Nimr Darwīsh, Rāʾid Salāḥ Mahājna, and Ibrāhīm Ṣarṣūr present themselves as potential political leaders,[75] imbued with aspirations beyond local affairs and reaching out to country-wide politics.

The Druze Elders, who function as priests of the community, have ruled—and still do—this denomination, thanks to their traditional prestige and religious position. However, not a few young Druzes who have served in the Defence Forces, as well as a small urban group of intellectuals, have been looking around for an alternative leadership, better experienced in Israeli politics and

---

[74] The most recent study of the pre-1948 Arab leadership is ʿAbd al-Sattār Qāsim's 'al-Qiyāda al-Filasṭīniyya qabl ʿām 1948 wa-atharuhā fī al-nakba', *al-Mawākib*, 4/11–12 (Nov.–Dec. 1987), 4–25; 5/1–2 (Jan.–Feb. 1988), 14–28; 5/5–6 (May–June 1988), 57–68.

[75] Shawqiyya ʿUrūq Mansūr, 'al-Shaykh Ibrāhīm Ṣarṣūr', *al-Ṣināra*, 2 Feb. 1990.

socio-economic conditions, and more compatible with these young men's ideas. The outcome of the contest between the two camps has yet to be determined. The three main Druze *hamulas*—those of Ṭarīf, Khneyfes, and Muʿaddī—are represented in the religious courts of appeal of the denomination. The old Sheikh Amīn Ṭarīf is still the spiritual leader of all Druzes in Israel, while Ṣāliḥ Khneyfes and Jabr Muʿaddī have served as MKs with the support of MAPAI/ILP. These *hamulas* and those allied with them take the most significant decisions in the denomination and generally determine the results of local elections in Druze localities. Several Druzes have reached important positions in the civil service and elsewhere, with national connotations: Rafīq Ḥalabī in television reporting and editing, Salmān Fallāḥ in the Ministry of Education and Culture, Shākib Ṣāliḥ as a lecturer in history at Bar-Ilan University, Zaydān ʿAṭshe as Israeli consul abroad and as MK, and others. As yet, these are not state-wide figures, but some of them may assume the mantle of Druze leadership, if the traditional power of the Elders decreases. True enough, the number of young Druzes has been growing, in both absolute and relative figures; however, the traditional leadership is well aware of this and strives to prepare appropriate followers from among the youths.

Leadership patterns differ somewhat among the Christian denominations in Israel, some of whom have a political tradition, connected to their own institutions abroad. Particularly among the Greek Catholics and the Greek Orthodox, religious leadership has had a political role as well, with considerable involvement. This was especially true, as mentioned above, of Archbishop George al-Ḥakīm, head of the Greek Catholic denomination from 1949 to 1967, who even attempted to pose as leader of all Arabs in Israel. Following al-Ḥakīm's departure for Damascus, and the 1967 War, the relative significance of the Christians declined somewhat, owing to the proportionate diminution of their share in the minority population (many more Muslims were added in East Jerusalem, where besides, they had a large hinterland in the Israeli-held territories). Equally, after an entire generation of Arabs and Jews had benefited from free compulsory education, the relative position of well-educated Christians has been reduced somewhat, in particular since many Muslims and not a few Druzes have graduated from the universities. All this has had an impact on the quality and effectiveness of Christian leadership.

Local and National Leadership

While the status of the religious leadership has been eroded to a considerable degree among the minorities in Israel, at least in the political domain, this has not been the case with local leadership. True, there, too, the influence of the religious leadership has been somewhat reduced, but it has preserved a not inconsiderable share of its traditional power in local politics as well as in the Knesset elections, when village or *hamula* heads, tribal chieftains, and sometimes even prominent urban personalities seek to recruit support for one slate of candidates or another. As already indicated above, the economic power of the *hamula* heads has declined over the years, but not necessarily their political influence. Despite the rivalry in the earlier years of the state between the Haifa and Tel-Aviv branches of MAPAI (in whose hands, as the most powerful party in Coalition Cabinets, decision-making regarding the Arabs remained),[76] they were at one in striving to influence the Arabs in their favour. *Hamula* leaders, then and later, have exploited these facts in their power struggles. Other political parties competed with MAPAI since the 1960s, then with the ILO, in courting the *hamula* heads,[77] especially close to election dates. Nevertheless, for many years, most rivalries were focused among the *hamula*s themselves, rather than between the parties. Thus, for some time, Israeli-Arab politics continued to centre on local rather than national matters,[78] as the Arabs had much more experience with the former.

The Communists were among the first who tried their hand in both local and country-wide politics. However, their overall achievements were at first modest mainly owing to their clashing, locally, with *hamula* heads and other traditional forces, and, nationally, remaining outside the political consensus. Indeed, local politics, in which tradition still had a significant role, continued to be central for the Arabs.[79] Even after 1967, when Arab political activity expanded on a country-wide scale, would-be national

---

[76] 'Aṭallāh Manṣūr, 'ha-Aḥūza ha-'Aravīt niṣhmeṭet mi-ydey Abbā Ḥūṣhī', *ha-Aretz*, 1 Oct. 1968, 3.

[77] Měnaḥem Rahaṭ, 'Pěqīdey ha-memshala w-fě'īley ha-miflagōt ma'adīfīm et ziqney ha-kěfar ha-'Aravī', *Ma'arīv*, 1 Feb. 1971, 13.

[78] J. M. Landau, 'A Note on the Leadership of the Israeli Arabs', *Il Politico*, 27/3 (1962), 625–35.

[79] Mājid al-Ḥāj, 'al-Hamūla al-'Arabiyya fī Isrā'īl', *Āfāq*, 1/2 (Apr. 1981), 17–28; id., 'al-Ḥamūla al-'Arabiyya bayn al-tafakkuk wa-'l-tarābuṭ', *al-Mawākib*, 2/7–8 (July–Aug. 1985), 60–8.

leaders started in local politics and continued to perceive these as their power bases. It is no accident that the first body claiming to be representative of all the Arabs in Israel, the National Committee of Heads of Arab Local Councils, is a framework clearly deriving its force from the leaders of Arab villages and towns. Even a political organization like the Sons of the Village, although claiming to focus on country-wide politics, is still tied to the village not only in its name, but also in much of its activity and propaganda. All this is true as well of extreme Islamic circles, which employ—in their villages—an increasingly political style.

Further, a large part of the contest for Arab political leadership has moved, in recent years, to the area of the generation gap, particularly in matters regarding modern structures. In the traditional frameworks, both of religious denominations and of *hamulas*, the older men have continued to dictate norms and make decisions. However, a growing number of younger people, mostly well-educated and proficient in the ways of Israeli society and the political regime, have been aspiring to positions of local and national leadership.

In recent years, notables of religious denominations and of rural *hamulas*, serving as MKs, encouraged and assisted by MAPAI/ ILO, have vacated their seats in favour of those in the middle age groups. Even the parliamentary representation of RAQAH/ HADASH has changed, with older persons like Emile Ḥabībī and Tawfīq Ṭūbī retiring from the Knesset, and younger men, such as Muḥammad Naffāʿ[80] and Hāshim Maḥāmīd,[81] taking their place. Nowadays, the Arabs are represented in the Knesset by half a dozen MKs whose average age is in the forties. This applies not only to the Communists, or independents like Mīʿārī and Darāwshe, but also to those elected on the ticket of Zionist Jewish lists, such as Nawāf Maṣālḥa of the ILO or Ḥusayn Fāris of MAPAM. These express themselves in the Knesset and elsewhere in a style differing from that of their predecessors—not obsequiously, but demandingly, as is appropriate to citizens proud of their heritage and seeking full equality in civic rights and/or fulfilment of their nationalist aspirations.

---

[80] Secretary of the Young Communist League. See about him *al-Ittiḥād*, 23 Feb. 1990, 6.

[81] Dan Petreanu, 'Pragmatic Fighter for Arab Rights', *Jerusalem Post*, 20 May 1988, 6.

Several of the younger people mentioned above and their peers in the same age groups have been trying to achieve local political leadership, which in time may perhaps become country-wide. Again, this local leadership is of various kinds, its single common factor being that it differs from earlier patterns. Moreover, many of those elected as mayors or heads of local councils in 1989 are not only younger, but perceive themselves as being motivated ideologically rather than as representatives of *hamula*s or of Jewish parties (they consider the latter to be moved by self-interest alone in approaching the Arab population). It is natural, perhaps, that these younger Arabs, most of whom had been cold-shouldered by the Israeli Establishment, (which usually allied itself with heads of *hamula*s),[82] would tend to have reservations about the state and its Jewish majority.

Summing up the characteristics of Arab political leadership in the 1980s and early 1990s, one notes that, in the local authorities, in the Knesset, and elsewhere, there is no lack of aspirants. Many are middle-aged or younger, chiefly well-educated men, each of whom has been fostering his own political estate, vying with others and attempting to outdo them, with few serious attempts at political alliances.[83] This situation in nationalist, Communist, and Islamic circles, involved in politics and increasingly experienced, parallels conditions in Israel's Jewish sector. Thanks to a long history of political rifts and rivalries, no charismatic personality has yet appeared to lead the Arabs in Israel, not even a majority of them. Leading figures and their supporters have been striving to take over political organizations (such as the various committees mentioned above)[84] or institutions (like local authorities, parties, and Knesset representation). Owing to rivalry and competition, they have succeeded at best in neutralizing one another.

Some potential leaders are connected, along with their adherents, to factors beyond Israel's borders—the Vatican, international

---

[82] Hillel Danzig, 'Dĕrūsha gīsha ḥadasha el ha-miʿūṭ ha-ʿAravī', *Davar*, 9 Feb. 1971, 7, 10.

[83] Yizhar Bĕ'er, 'Mashber ḥarīf bĕ-hanhagat ʿArviyyey Israʾel', *ha-Aretz*, 20 Dec. 1990, A4; Aḥmad Saʿd, 'Hal tūjad azmat qiyāda ladà al-jamāhīr al-ʿArabiyya fī Israʾīl?', *al-Ittiḥād*, 4 Feb. 1990.

[84] For his views and aspirations, see Ibrāhīm Nimr Ḥusayn, 'Lam nafqud quwwat ʾthīrinā wa-lākin yajib an nughayyir al-taktīk', *al-Ṣināra*, 20 June 1989, 7, 10.

Islam,[85] the Soviet Union (or its heirs), the PLO, and others. Hence, their political advancement in Israel depends not only on securing the support of local Arabs, but also on continuing relations with external factors and the proportionate power of the latter. Still, the sum total of Arab personalities in Israel most probably comprises a serious potential for national political leadership. As of now, the various public committees discussed above, and other bodies, make up rather effective political forces. Their successful efforts, in recent years, to impose restraint and non-violence on the Land Day demonstrations indicates their strong internal position. Nevertheless, the variety and number of political opinions and aspirations among the Arabs in Israel make it difficult for them to agree on one, generally accepted, political leadership.[86]

---

[85] J. M. Landau, *The Politics of Pan-Islam* (1990).
[86] Sammy Smooha, *Arabs and Jews in Israel*, vol. i (1989), 113–15. I have been unable to consult the second volume, if it has been published meanwhile.

8

Elections: Parliamentary, Local, Trade-Unionist

INTRODUCTORY

In democratic regimes participation in elections and voting results are a good reflection of the political, economic, and social attitudes of various groups of people. Electoral analysis allows partial conclusions only, owing to the personal secrecy of the ballot; nevertheless, processes and trends can be discerned, although any attempt to interpret election outcomes should be approached with considerable caution. Arab voting behaviour in Israel will be discussed on three levels: the Knesset, local authorities, and the Histadrut.

KNESSET ELECTIONS

The main concern here is with parliamentary voting in the Arab sector since 1967, that is, in the six electoral contests in the years 1969–88, but reference will occasionally be made to previous years as well, for comparison.[1] In this context, it should be remembered that the inhabitants of the Israeli-held territories do not participate on any level of elections, since they are not Israeli citizens; in East Jerusalem and the Golan Heights, very few Arabs or Druzes vote, for the same reason (most refuse to accept Israeli citizenship). Arab voters in Israel have been influenced, to a large extent, by the outcome of the 1967 War, as one more component of processes already discussed above.

I shall attempt to note various trends in Arab parliamentary voting, based on Table 8.1, and then make some observations on the main characteristics of each separate electoral contest.

[1] For the Arabs and the Knesset elections, see Avraham Diskin, *Běhīrōt w-vōharīm bě-Isra'el*, ch. 4. For the elections between 1949 and 1965, Cf. Landau, *The Arabs in Israel* (1969), 108–55.

1. The available data refer chiefly to voting in exclusively Arab localities—towns, villages, and Bedouin encampments—as it is very difficult to isolate Arab votes in mixed towns with any certitude. This should hardly affect the conclusions, however, since the Arabs in mixed towns comprise not much more than 1 per cent of all Arabs having the franchise.

2. The rate of Arab participation in voting, which had ranged between 85.5 per cent and 92.1 per cent during the 1950s, declined in the two following decades to between 69.7 per cent and 80.3 per cent, approaching the rate of Jewish participation, even though not identical with it. The changes very probably reflected growing modernization, resulting in the *hamula* heads not sweeping their relatives off to the voting booths, nor husbands their wives. Moreover, it was partly an expression of disappointment, possibly alienation, from many parties and slates, as well as partly a response to calls for delegitimization of the State of Israel (by not turning up at the polls). Appeals to the Arabs in Israel to absent themselves from voting for the Knesset were indeed voiced, time and again, by the PLO, the Sons of the Village, and extreme Islamic politicians. Even a veteran Communist like Ṣalība Khamīs wrote a lengthly article on the matter, entitling it 'Is the Knesset a parliament for Jews and Arabs alike?' (His conclusion was negative, and he appealed for a separate parliament for the Arabs in Israel.)

3. The allied Arab lists consisted of slates of candidates affiliated to MAPAI/ILO, or more rarely to other Jewish parties. These were headed by local notables, recruited by Jewish political parties on family, religious, or regional grounds. These lists declined steadily in their electoral achievements from one campaign to the next, until in 1981 none of them crossed the minimal barrier of 1 per cent of the total votes cast, and they entirely disappeared from the campaigns of 1984 and 1988. This was in no small measure due to the reluctance of an increasing number of Arabs to vote for lists of Arab notables, generally formed on the basis of denominational and regional considerations, and sponsored by Jewish parties. Moreover, such *ad hoc* slates showed little activity except on election-eve, so that votes floated, out of pragmatic considerations, to parties or groups more prone to assist their supporters at all times; for the young educated voters, this move away from the allied Arab lists also suited their modernizing tendencies.

4. The groups which I have labelled 'national' have enjoyed

TABLE 8.1. Distribution of Arab votes in Israel, for Twelve Knessets (%)

The Slate	1 1949	2 1951	3 1955	4 1959	5 1961	6 1965	7 1969	8 1973	9 1977	10 1981	11 1984	12 1988
Arab Allied lists	53	55	57	58	46	42	40	36	21	13	—	—
National lists:												
ICP	22	16	16	12	23	1	1	—	—	—	—	—
RAQAH/HADASH	—	—	—	—	—	23	29	37	51	38	33	34
PLP	—	—	—	—	—	—	—	—	—	—	18	14
DAP	—	—	—	—	—	—	—	—	—	—	—	11
TOTAL, National lists	22	16	16	12	23	24	30	37	51	38	51	59
Jewish parties:												
MAPAI/Alignment*	10	17	22	20	24	24	16	12	10	26	23	17
Herūt/Likkūd†	4	10	2	4	3	2	1	3	3	8	5	6
National Religious Party (NRP)	11	1	3	4	4	6	9	9	5	4	4	3
Others	—	1	—	2	—	2	4	3	10	11	17	15
TOTAL, Jewish Parties	25	29	27	30	31	34	30	27	28	49	49	41
Participation in the Arab sector	79.3	85.5	92.1	88.9	85.6	87.8	85.8	79.7	76.3	69.7	75.1	72.9
Participation in the Jewish sector	86.9	75.1	82.8	81.6	81.6	83.0	81.7	78.6	79.2	78.5	78.8	80.3

* The Alignment (Ma'arakh) is made up of MAPAI, MAPAM, and a party called Aḥdūt ha-'Avōda.
† The Likkūd is made up of Herūt, the Liberals, La-'Am, and the Free Centre.
Sources: Publications of the Central Bureau of Statistics; A. Diskin, *Běḥirōt u-vōḥarim bě-Israel* (1988).

electoral support at least in part ideologically moved or serving as a protest vote. In the 1960s, they obtained 23 to 30 per cent of the Arab vote, rising in the 1970s to between a third and a half, approximately; in the 1988 Knesset elections they reached 59 per cent. Until the 1981 elections, it was RAQAH/HADASH alone that got these votes, after having broken with the ICP and become a mostly Arab party, with a nationalist image. Its record poll was in the 1977 elections, when it obtained more than half of all Arab votes (51 per cent). Its decline to about a third since the 1981 elections was very probably brought about by the rise of rival political forces in the Arab sector, whose nationalist image may well have been more persuasive, for instance, thanks to their relations with the PLO. It is possible, also, that RAQAH/HADASH may have suffered from its legitimization of the State of Israel as well as from the rapprochement of the Soviet Union to Israel from the mid-1980s.[2] The PLP appears to have taken votes away from RAQAH/HADASH: In 1984, the vote for the two of them together equalled 51 per cent, precisely the ratio obtained by the latter seven years previously, at the height of its electoral success. The combined Arab vote in 1988 was not very different, but on that occasion an exclusively Arab party entered the contest; this was the DAP (which, however, did not hurry to break away from the Israeli political consensus).[3] The three together obtained impressive results. It seems that the rise in nationalist considerations in voting indicates politicization in the Arab sector, at the expense of electoral support for the traditional allied Arab lists and the Jewish parties. Statistical analysis demonstrates that most of the voting support for the national Arab parties, both in figures and in percentages, came from Muslims (particularly since the decline and subsequent disappearance of the allied Arab lists).

5. The electoral results of the Jewish parties in the Arab sector have been fairly stable, if their *combined* vote is considered. However, if we add to them the votes obtained by the allied Arab lists, initiated and promoted by Jewish parties (chiefly MAPAI/ILP), the decline in Arab support is striking. This is particularly applicable

[2] I. Greilshammer, 'RAQAH wĕ-ha-bĕḥīrōt la-Knesset ha-12', in J. M. Landau (ed.), *ha-Migzar ha-ʿAravī bĕ-Iśraʾel wĕ-ha-bĕḥīrōt la-Knesset, 1988* (1989), 50–62.
[3] Yitzhak Reiter, 'ha-Miflaga ha-Demōqraṭīt ha-ʿAravīt w-mĕqōma ba-ōryenṭatsiyya shel ʿArviyyey Iśraʾel', ibid. 63–84.

to the Alignment headed by the ILP, and mostly so since 1977, fitting into its general electoral decline that year, when it was defeated by the Likkūd, which then set up its first Coalition Cabinet. This decline was even more relevant to the Alignment and other Jewish slates in the 1984 and 1988 Knesset elections, when the allied Arab lists disappeared completely, leaving all the Jewish slates combined with less than 50 per cent of the Arab vote. These phenomena may be attributed to a protest vote against the Israeli Establishment's lack of interest in the specific problems of the Arab population of the state and to a growing trend to support national Arab parties, that is, to prefer the ideological vote to the pragmatic one.

6. As a general rule, the Knesset vote in the smaller Arab villages has tended to be more conservative and moderate, while that in the larger ones and even more so in the towns has favoured the national parties. This provides yet another manifestation of the impact of modernization in larger localities, where educated young people tend to radicalization. The Bedouin vote, on the other hand, favours the Israeli Establishment and Jewish parties. An exception occurred in 1988, when many gave their support to the DAP—but it seems likely that quite a few of the Bedouin believed Darāwshe, the DAP's founder and leader, to have remained in the ILP (that is, that he was heading an allied Arab list; this, however, was not the case). Further, there are signs that Bedouin electoral behaviour increasingly resembles that of other Arabs in Israel in the distri-bution of their vote.[4] A majority of the Druzes have continued to support Jewish parties. In the early years of the state, they voted for MAPAI/ILO, and later for the Likkūd, especially since 1977, when the latter started to form Coalition Cabinets and included amongst its MKs a Druze, Amāl Naṣr al-Dīn. However, some Druzes vote for RAQAH/ḤADASH, as a sign of the disappoint-ment felt by some of their youths with the insufficient interest displayed by the Establishment in their concerns.

7. The above has been discussed mainly with reference to percentages. In absolute numbers, the electoral power of the Arab sector increases, of course, from one campaign to the next. The importance of this factor is evident in a multi-party system

---

[4] Joseph Ben-David, 'Dĕfūsey hatsbaʿa mishtannīm bĕ-qerev Bedwiyyey ha-Negev', ibid. 85–114.

endowed with proportional representation which determines the make-up of each Coalition Cabinet. The potential of the Arab vote is not yet fully reflected in the number of seats it obtains in each Knesset—usually between five and eight. The reasons are to be sought in relatively low voter participation over the last twenty years, and in the splitting of the vote, which causes a part of it to be wasted in the final count, particularly since the competing Arab parties shy away from pre-electoral agreements which would obviate some of this wastage. Thus the potential of the Arab vote, which could easily lead to a dozen seats in the Knesset, is flawed. While it is impossible to predict (in 1991) the course of the Knesset elections in 1992, it is likely that on that occasion, or on a subsequent one, the Arab sector, which adds some 35,000 to 40,000 qualified voters to the arena in each election, could conceivably get more seats through the vote of the numerous youngsters who will have reached voting age. This depends, of course, on the ability of Arab parties to set up joint slates of candidates who would be able to inspire confidence,[5] raising both ideological and pragmatic expectations—and persuading the voters that they mean what they say.

8. During the campaign for the seventh Knesset, in 1969, various topics were discussed in electoral propaganda in the Arab sector, at least by several of the competing parties and groups.[6] Among them were Jewish–Arab relations in Israel, full equality for the Arabs, village development, satisfactory employment, and the resolution of the conflict between Israel and the Arab states. The voting results indicate a decline of the ILP-headed Alignment (even though MAPAM had joined it, placing on its slate of candidates an Arab, ʿAbd al-ʿAzīz al-Zuʿbī).[7] RAQAḤ seems to have gained most from the Alignment's decline among Arabs, after having accused MAPAM of 'joining the Zionist Establishment'. Indeed,

---

[5] Cf. the questionnaire results in 'Fī istiṭlāʿ taḥlīl li-ʾl-raʾy al-ʿāmm al-ʿArabī al-Filasṭīnī dākhil al-khaṭṭ al-akhḍar tawaqquʿāt al-raʾy fī intikhābāt al-Knesset al-muqbila', *al-Usbūʿ al-Jadīd*, 1 July 1990, 33–9.

[6] On these elections and the Arab vote, see Emanuel Gutmann, 'ha-Bĕḥīrōt la-Knesset ha-shĕvīʿīt', *Gesher*, 15/61 (Dec. 1969), 15–21; Subhi Abu-Gosh, 'The Election Campaign in the Arab Sector', in Alan Arian (ed.), *The Elections in Israel—1969* (1972), 239–52; J. M. Landau, 'The Arab Vote', ibid. 253–63.

[7] But see E. Elʿad, 'ha-Aḥūza ha-ʿAravīt ʿavra lĕ-Allōn: hadīfat RAQAḤ ba-bĕḥīrōt neheshevet kĕ-hatslaḥatō', *ha-Aretz*, 7 Nov. 1969, 10.

RAQAH increased its Arab vote by 25 per cent, compared to 1965. Most of the electoral contest in the Arab sector took place between RAQAH and the Allied Arab lists, with the former getting its main support in towns and larger villages and the latter mostly in the smaller localities. In many places, a see-saw between these two competitors was apparent: When RAQAH's vote increased, that of the allied Arab lists declined, and vice versa. To sum up, RAQAH advanced in the Arab sector in comparison with 1965,[8] while the allied Arab lists and the Jewish parties—the NRP excepted[9]—retreated. The entire electoral campaign was livelier, following the abolition of Military Administration, and the nationalist impact of the inhabitants of the Israeli-held territories. These may well have affected the increased voting support for RAQAH, at the expense of the allied Arab lists and the Jewish parties, since Arabs, and even a few Druzes,[10] seemed to consider their support of RAQAH as a protest vote, at least, and a vote for Arab nationalism, at most.

9. The parliamentary elections for the eighth Knesset, in 1973, were postponed and held only after the end of the 1973 War, and were undoubtedly influenced by its course and results.[11] Some local Arabs seem to have felt a decline in their Israelism along with a rise in their Arabism. Not a few voters—both Jews and Arabs—blamed the Alignment-led Coalition Cabinet for serious errors of judgement on the eve of the war, the final outcome notwithstanding. Thus its prestige as a dominant party declined. This factor was understandably highlighted in the electoral campaign by the Alignment's rivals. Indeed, the matter was pounced upon not only by the Likkūd, but also by RAQAH, whose electoral propaganda among the Arabs emphasized the party's criticism of the Alignment-led Cabinet as well as the party's own support of Arab nationalism in

---

[8] Dōrōn Rōsenblūm, 'Ma beyn RAQAH lĕ-MAQĪ', *Davar*, 2 Oct. 1969; Havīv Kna'an, 'ha-Adderet ha-adūmma' (Ch. 7 n. 45 above); Hezī Karmel, 'ha-Qōl ha-'Aravī ba-bĕḥīrōt: kōḥa shel RAQAH gadel mĕ'aṭ', *Ma'arīv*, 30 Oct. 1969, 11.

[9] This was probably due to the religious assistance offered by the NRP to the minorities, via the Ministries of the Interior, Welfare, and Religious Affairs.

[10] E. El'ad, 'RAQAH nivlĕma ba-rĕhōv ha-'Aravī', *ha-Aretz*, 31 Oct. 1969, 17; Zaydān Abū 'Aṭsheh, 'Meha'a neged ha-'Avōda: Sṭūdenṭ Dĕrūzī masbīr et ha-hatsba'a lĕ-RAQAH', *Pī ha-Atōn*, 3 Mar. 1970, 2.

[11] Yechiel Harari, *ha-Bĕḥīrōt ba-migzar ha-'Aravī 1973* (1975), 29–49; Elī Eyal, 'Gam ha-Bedwīm ratsīm la-Knesset,' *Ma'arīv*, 17 Aug. 1973, 18; Moshe Shokeid, 'Strategy and Change in the Arab Vote: Observations in a Mixed City,' in Asher Arian (ed.), *The Elections in Israel—1973* (1975), 145–66.

Israel and in the Israeli-held territories. The Alignment's propaganda focused, for the first time, less on socio-economic affairs (like village development, education, and a rise in the standard of living) and more on political and ideological ones, highlighting the view that the Alignment alone was capable of achieving peace with Israel's neighbours. Although the Alignment officially invited Arabs to join it,[12] voting support for it and the allied Arab lists declined, while RAQAH increased its Arab vote by almost a third, compared to 1969, with its greatest success in all-Arab and mixed towns, as earlier, but also in localities in the Little Triangle, that is, among Muslims. As to the allied Arab lists, supported by the Alignment, one of them obtained two seats, for Sayf al-Dīn al-Zuʿbī, a Muslim, and Jabr Muʿaddī, a Druze, respectively. For the first time, a Bedouin slate ran as well. It obtained only about 3,800 votes in the large Bedouin encampments in the Negev, among 11,054 qualified voters (seemingly because of rivalries between tribal chiefs). However, this slate got 3,120 votes in the Little Triangle (that is, non-Bedouin) and some more elsewhere. The head of the slate, Ḥamad Abū Rabīʿa, won a seat in the Knesset.

10. The elections for the ninth Knesset, in 1977, reversed the ratio of political forces in Israel, as the Likkūd came to power after twenty-nine years of MAPAI/Alignment rule.[13] This change was brought about by various processes, chiefly in Jewish society, which was mainly responsible for the reversal; hence we shall not discuss it here. The Arabs in Israel were not directly responsible for this outcome, as they did not transfer their votes from Alignment to Likkūd (except for a small number). Indeed, for the first time, their proportionate rate of participation fell behind the Jewish and reached merely 76.3 per cent of qualified voters. However, the polarization in Arab electoral behaviour continued undiminished, especially between their support for the Alignment and the allied

---

[12] Naḥman Fabian, "Aravīm ka-ḥaverīm ba-ʿAvōda', *ha-Aretz*, 3 June 1973, 14.

[13] Gabriel Ben-Dor, 'Electoral Politics and Ethnic Polarization: Israeli Arabs in the 1977 Elections', in Asher Arian (ed.), *The Elections in Israel—1977* (1980), 171–85; Elyakim Rubinstein, 'The Lesser Parties', in Howard R. Penniman (ed.), *Israel at the Polls: The Knesset Elections of 1977* (1979), 193–5; J. M. Landau, 'Electoral Issues: Israel', in J. M. Landau, E. Özbudun, and F. Tachau (eds.), *Electoral Politics in the Middle East* (1980), 69–91; Asher Arian, 'Voting Behaviour: Israel', ibid. 173–84; Emanuel Gutmann, 'Parliamentary Elites: Israel', ibid. 273–97.

Arab lists on the one hand, and RAQAḤ/ḤADASH on the other. The latter was assisted by the Palestinization of a part of the Arab sector in Israel during the decade after the 1967 War and Israel's occupation of the territories. During that decade, a certain alienation from the State of Israel became manifest in the Arab sector, particularly among some of the younger people. This may have influenced a more nationalist, or at least a protest, vote. The Arab vote may have been affected, also, by the election being held not as usual in the autumn, but on 17 May, a mere six weeks after Land Day. Further, not long before election day, a report by Israel Koenig, representative of the Ministry of the Interior in Galilee, rejecting the possibility of Arab integration within the state as unreal, and using rather unpleasant language, was leaked to the press and caused much indignation amongst the Arab population. Because of all these factors, Arab support for the Jewish slates declined, affecting the Alignment as well as the allied Arab lists, of which only one ran in 1977, obtaining a Knesset seat for Sayf al-Dīn al-Zuʿbī. RAQAH/ḤADASH reached the peak of its power, about 51 per cent of all Arab votes: it increased its support not only in large places, as previously, but also in smaller localities, obtaining also about 12 per cent of Bedouin, and 29 per cent of Druze, votes. This is partly explicable by the electoral front it had set up, entitled ḤADASH (as mentioned above) which, without renouncing an iota of the party's ideological and strategic guidelines, presented itself as a tactical ally and patron of intellectual elements, young and energetic. All this reflected rather accurately the radical polarization in Israeli political society in 1977, with a relative majority of the Jews (over a third) giving its vote to the Likkūd and an absolute majority of the Arabs (over half) giving it to a party presenting a nationalist attitude largely contradicting that of the Likkūd.

11. Arab voting participation in the elections for the tenth Knesset, in 1981, was the lowest ever, only 69.7 per cent.[14] The fact

---

[14] Ōrī Sṭendel, 'Mĕgammōt ha-hatsbaʿa la-Knesset ha-ʿasīrīt bĕ-qerev ʿArviyyey Israʾel', *ha-Mizraḥ he-Ḥadash*, 30/117–20 (1981), 138–48; ʿAṭallāh Manṣūr, 'ha-Meyrūts aḥarey ha-qōl ha-ʿAravī', *ha-Aretz*, 2 June 1981, 12; Yōʾel Dar, 'Maʿarekhet ha-bĕḥīrōt ba-migzar ha-ʿAravī wĕ-ha-Dĕrūzī', *Davar*, 21 June 1981, 7; Tawfīq Khūrī, 'ha-Mahapakh ba-migzar ha-ʿAravī', *Migwan*, 62 (Aug. 1981), 40–2; Sh. Toledano, "Arviyyey Israʾel: haʿarakhōt shenitbaddū', *ha-Aretz*, 4 Sept. 1981, 14; id., 'Mashmaʿūt ha-hatsbaʿa ha-ʿAravīt', ibid. 7 Sept. 1981, 9; Don Peretz and

that elections were held in June, at the height of the farm labour season, is only a partial explanation. Perhaps the propaganda distributed by the Sons of the Village and kindred groups, based on the PLO's appeal to boycott the elections (thereby delegitimizing the state and its institutions), along with similar pronouncements by several extremist Muslim leaders, may have contributed, and perhaps also the indifference of those who suffered from their inability to determine the political process substantially. Among the Bedouin, for instance, participation declined by about 14 per cent, compared to 1977, perhaps because in 1981 no Bedouin slate was competing. Among the notable phenomena was the non-running of any Arab list allied to the Alignment; three Arab slates which ran independently got nowhere and their votes were lost. At least a part of the Arabs who used to vote for the lists allied to the Alignment gave the latter their votes directly—particularly as the Alignment set up branches in the larger villages before election day, and also included two Arab candidates on its own slate, both of whom got seats. They were Ḥamad Ḥalāʾila of the ILP and Muḥammad Watad of MAPAM. It is quite likely that some Arabs who were opposed to the Likkūd, and hoped to get rid of it, voted pragmatically for the Alignment, which in 1981 increased its strength in the Arab sector as well as in the Jewish one, compared to 1977. Among other Jewish parties, the Likkūd strengthened its Arab support, not necessarily in absolute figures (it obtained approximately 10,765 Arab votes), but rather proportionately (a rise of about 250 per cent, compared to 1977). This may be attributed to various causes: the Likkūd, leading the Coalition Cabinet since 1977, was able to disburse various benefits; its achievement of peace with Egypt was widely appreciated; lastly, it included on its slate a Druze candidate, Amāl Naṣr al-Dīn, who won a seat (about a third of the Likkūd's minority votes were Druzes). RAQAḤ/ HADASH's vote dropped from its 1977 record, the party losing about a quarter of its Arab electoral support. The decline may have been partly brought about by verbal attacks from the Sons of the Village and other nationalist circles, which took issue with RAQAḤ/ḤADASH's nationalist image and accused it (not sur-

Sammy Smooha, 'Israel's Tenth Knesset Elections—Ethnic Upsurgence and Decline of Ideology', *Middle East Journal*, 35/4 (Autumn 1981), 506–26; J. M. Landau, 'The Arab Vote', in D. Caspi, A. Diskin, and E. Gutmann (eds.), *The Roots of Begin's Success: The 1981 Israeli Elections* (1984), 169–89.

prisingly) of Communism. Yet others blamed Marxism and the Soviet Union, which had shortly before invaded Afghanistan, a Muslim state. Nevertheless, RAQAH/HADASH succeeded in preserving a good part of its positions, especially among Christian Arabs, being the only party to include them in top places in its electoral slate. Besides, 38 per cent of all Arab votes constituted a substantial achievement, the highest yet for the Communists (1977 excepted), better than that of any rival. If one considers the Arab vote for RAQAH/HADASH a nationalist one, it was roughly equal, proportionately, to the Jewish support for the Likkūd in 1981.

12. Arab participation in the elections for the eleventh Knesset, in 1984, rose, compared to 1981, and almost reverted, proportionately, to its level in 1977.[15] This was the first time that no Arab list made up of local notables, either allied to the Alignment or independent, ran for election, very probably thanks to the lesson of the 1981 Knesset elections, which demonstrated that under the new conditions, such candidates had little chance of success. However, this new development does not seem to have helped the Alignment which, indeed, placed two Arab candidates on its slate, ʿAbd al-Wahhāb Darāwshe for the ILO and Muhammad Watad for MAPAM. Both entered the Knesset but, since they are Muslims, this may have adversely affected Christian and Druze support. The Likkūd, too, declined in its Arab vote from about 8 per cent to about 5 per cent, possibly in criticism of its initiating and carrying out the 1982 War in the Lebanon and against the Palestinians there. However, among the Druzes the Likkūd obtained some support, thanks to its placing a Druze on its slate. All the other Jewish parties combined saw a slight increase in the Arab vote. This was particularly evident in the case of Shinnūy ('Change'), a middle-of-the-road liberal party, which placed a Druze, Zaydān ʿAtshe, in one of the top places on its slate. RAQAH/HADASH lost a few more votes, proportionately, obtaining a third of all the Arab votes, not at all a bad result, but less than the party expected.

---

[15] Husayn Mūsà, "Arab Isrāʾīl ilà ayna?', *al-Sināra*, 13 Apr. 1984; Nadim Rouhana, 'Collective Identity and Arab Voting Patterns', in A. Arian and M. Shamir (eds.), *Elections in Israel—1984* (1986), 121–49; Hillel Frisch, 'Between Instrumentalism and Separatism: The Arab Vote in the 1984 Knesset Elections', in D. J. Elazar and Shmuel Sandler (eds.), *Israel's Odd Couple: The 1984 Knesset Elections and the National Unity Government* (1990), 119–34.

The main reason was the establishment of a new grouping, the PLP, which attracted some RAQAH/HADASH supporters via a lively, often bitter, debate. As has been said, the PLP was a non-Marxist, nationalist grouping, competing with RAQAH/HADASH in the Arab sector, with noteworthy success for a first attempt at running.[16] Many of the 18 per cent of Arab votes that the PLP received must have come at the expense of RAQAH/HADASH from those who considered it a more authentic nationalist Arab party.[17] It apparently is no accident that, as already said, the 51 per cent of Arab votes obtained by RAQAH/HADASH in 1977, tally with the combined vote of RAQAH/HADASH and the PLP in 1984 (33 and 18 per cent, respectively). Anyway, these two combined obtained, in 1984, more than half of all Arab votes, while all Jewish parties combined got less than half (49 per cent). As to the denominational voting support for RAQAH/HADASH and the PLP, respectively, about 42 per cent of the Christians voted for the former and some 14 per cent for the latter; while among the Muslims (for example in the Little Triangle), almost a third voted for the former and about 20 per cent for the latter. In other words, while in the Little Triangle, which is all-Muslim, RAQAH/HADASH obtained approximately the same rate of Arab voting support as throughout the entire state, the PLP made a stronger show there than country-wide, perhaps owing to the recent Islamic revival which has been adopting a marked anti-Communist stance.

13. Arab voting participation in the twelfth Knesset elections, in 1988, declined again, despite intensive pre-election propaganda.[18] In view of the dramatic increase of 18 per cent in qualified Arab voters between 1984 and 1988, more Jewish parties intensified their campaign in the Arab sector. The results of these efforts were varied. The elections were held almost one year after the start

[16] Amnōn Dōtan, 'Lĕ'an mitqaddemet ha-rĕshīma ha-mitqaddemet' (Ch. 7 n. 57 above).
[17] ʿAṭallāh Manṣūr, 'Miflaga lĕ'ūmīt la-ʿAravīm', *ha-Aretz*, 30 July 1984, 9.
[18] *Israel Statistical Bulletin*, 12 (1988), esp. 97–120. Cf. Landau (ed.), *ha-Migzar ha-ʿAravī bĕ-Isra'el wĕ-ha-bĕḥīrōt la-Knesset, 1988* (1989), esp. Avraham Diskin's paper, 'Heybetīm statistiyyīm shel ha-hatsbaʿa ba-migzar ha-ʿAravī', ibid. 22–33; Sara Ben-Hillel and Yĕhūda Tsūr, 'ha-Yaʿad: Mandaṭ me-ha-bōher ha-ʿAravī', *Hōtam*, 39 (23 Sept. 1988), 9–10; Johnny Gal, *ha-Bĕḥīrōt la-Knesset ha-12 ba-migzar ha-ʿAravī* (1989); Mifleget ha-ʿAvōda, *Tōtsĕ'ōt ha-bĕḥīrōt la-Knesset ha-12: nittūaḥ ri'shōnī* (1989); ʿIsām Abū Zahiyyā, 'Tarīqat al-intikhābāt al-Isrā'īliyya ilā ayna?', *al-Mujtamaʿ*, 18/5 (May 1990), 19–23; Asher Arian, 'The 1988 Elections—Questions of Identity', *Jerusalem Letter/Viewpoints*, 83 (15 Jan. 1989), 1–6.

of the *intifāḍa* in the Israeli-held territories, strengthening the nationalist camp among the Arabs in Israel.[19] Again, no Arab list allied to a Jewish one ran. Further, most of the Jewish parties registered proportionate losses in the Arab vote. This was true of the Alignment (on whose slate Nawāf Maṣālḥa entered the Knesset), the Likkūd, the NRP, and others. Indeed, the Alignment was reduced to the ILO, running without MAPAM, which independently obtained 4 per cent of the Arab vote; among MAPAM's three MKs, one was a Muslim Arab, Ḥusayn Fāris.[20] The Likkūd rose somewhat, proportionately, compared to 1984, for instance among the Druzes, perhaps in recognition of the Likkūd-led Cabinet's improving the economic status of several of their more important villages. The Movement for Citizens' Rights, a centrist Jewish party, also improved its vote in the Arab sector, thanks to its steady campaign for equalizing Arab civil rights.[21] Three nationalist Arab parties ran as well. RAQAḤ/ḤADASH improved its Arab vote only by less than 1 per cent compared to 1984, despite—or, perhaps, because of—its electoral alliance with the Jewish 'Black Panthers' and several other tiny groups. It obtained more electoral support among the Druzes, of whom approximately 20 per cent of those participating voted for it. RAQAḤ/ḤADASH gained, as in 1984, four MKs, who, after some personal changes (Tawfīq Ṭūbī and Meʾīr Wīlner resigned their seats), left two Arabs and two Jews representing the party in the Knesset. The former are Hāshim Maḥāmīd and Muḥammad Naffāʿ, both Muslims. The PLP retreated by about 4 per cent, probably owing to the absence of an appropriate organizational infrastructure, and inter-feuding just before the elections.[22] It received one seat only, for its leader, Muḥammad Mīʿārī. Most of

[19] This, notwithstanding the different opinion of Mājid al-Haj, ʿBĕḥīrōt ba-rĕḥōv ha-ʿAravī bĕ-tsel ha-intifāḍaʾ, in Landau (ed.), *ha-Migzar ha-ʿAravī bĕ-Israʾel wĕ-ha-bĕḥīrōt*, 35–49, who argues that the *intifāḍa* influenced more the electoral propaganda than the voting. However, various Arabs have explained their abstention by what they considered the harsh response of Rabin, then Minister of Defence, in the Israeli-held territories.

[20] About whom see Ben-Hillel and Tsūr (n. 18 above).

[21] When referring to the Arabs in Israel, there were obvious similarities in the electoral platforms of the Movement for Citizens' Rights, MAPAM and RAQAḤ/ḤADASH—which was, indeed, the most forceful and aggressive of all three.

[22] Kāmil Dāhir, ʿha-Rĕshīma ha-mitqaddemet ḥayya wĕ-qayyemet w-fĕʿīla mĕʿōdʾ, *ʿAl ha-Mishmar*, 14 June 1987, 8. The writer was the party's spokesman at the time. Cf. A. Dayyan, ʿSīʿat yaḥīdʾ, *Kol ha-ʿĪr*, 2 Dec. 1988, 35–8.

its voters were Muslims from the Little Triangle and Western Galilee. Other Muslims may have been less happy with the fact that the second on the PLP slate was a retired Jewish general, Matityahū Peled, while the third was an Anglican priest, Riyāḥ Abū al-ʿAsal. Some compensation for Muslim reservations can be found in Christian support, as about 11.5 per cent of the PLP's votes in 1988 originated in localities with a Christian majority (but only 0.6 per cent from Druze ones). A new all-Arab competitor, the DAP, received one seat, for its head, ʿAbd al-Wahhāb Darāwshe. Some DAP voters came from the PLP and others from the Alignment: In certain villages, a correlation exists between the votes gained by the DAP and those lost by the Alignment. Most DAP voters were Muslims, mainly from Eastern Galilee (Darāwshe's residence) and from several small villages in the Little Triangle, but also from not a few Bedouin (who seem to have thought, as already mentioned, that Darāwshe continued to represent the ILP). In contrast, Arab support for RAQAH/ḤADASH and the PLP originated especially in the towns. The three slates combined received almost 59 per cent of all Arab votes (although their Knesset representation remained unaltered, due to the absence of pre-election agreements, which resulted in a waste of votes). The propaganda of all three employed a clear-cut nationalist message, alluding to the PLO. It should be emphasized that, in addition to the continuing politicization of the Arabs in Israel, the 1988 elections revealed radical Palestinization, chiefly in the generation born and growing up during the forty years of the state. Palestinization, that is, the crystallizing of solidarity with Palestinians outside Israel, was expressed not merely in a readiness for oral and written confrontation, but in electoral behaviour as well. Almost 59 per cent of Arab votes indicated preference for nationalist demands, while only a little over 41 per cent tended to Israelization and the hope of improving the situation of the Arabs in Israel via the Israeli Establishment.[23] This parallels, to some extent, the division between hawks and doves in the Jewish sector.

---

[23] Joseph Ginat, 'Děfūsey hatsbaʿa wě-hitnahagūt pōlīṭīt ba-migzar ha-ʿAravī', in Landau (ed.), *ha-Migzar ha-ʿAravī bě-Israʾel wě-ha-běḥīrōt*, 3–21, concludes, however—on the basis of his participant observation—that the struggle for complete equality mattered more to the Arab voters than Palestinian nationalist subjects.

LOCAL ELECTIONS

The experience of local authorities in the Arab sector, including self-administration and elections, has been shorter than in the Jewish one. As early as the British Mandate in Palestine the Jewish population had developed a wide network of local government, on Western models. Decision-makers in the State of Israel, while maintaining the dependence of local on central government (mainly by control over financial allocations and budgets), have striven, via the Ministry of the Interior, to set up municipalities or local councils in the Arab localities, by secret universal ballot, as specified by law. This policy was largely designed to persuade the inhabitants to look after their own affairs, to inculcate notions of democracy, and to encourage modernization. Considering this, *post factum*, one may opine that in this context modernization may have been too swift, since it was no simple matter for the newly formed local councils to struggle with complex problems and wide-ranging relations with government offices, the Histadrut, and political parties. Nevertheless, despite the reservations of the village Elders, and most particularly of *hamula* heads, apprehensive of changes liable to diminish their traditional dominance, the number of local councils grew speedily. Further, to the two municipalities of Nazareth and Shafā ʿAmr others were added, namely Umm al-Faḥm (in 1990),[24] and subsequently Ṭaiyyba and Ṭīra. By the end of the 1980s, out of 151 Arab localities, two-thirds had acquired the status of municipalities, local councils, or regional councils. Only 56 had not attained such a status, and of these, 30 were small Bedouin encampments in the Negev; most of the other 26 localities were also tiny, usually with fewer than 1,000 inhabitants.

Over the years, most Arabs have tended to accept a situation in which such services as health, education, roads, running water, drainage, and collection of waste would be provided. Many *hamula* heads accepted these new circumstances as given, but none the less attempted to safeguard their power by watching developments closely and putting forward their preferred kinsmen for appointment in local government. In response, young people have increasingly demanded the reduction of *hamula* power and the basing of local elections on competing political slates instead of rival

---

[24] ʿAmōs Gilbōʿa, 'Ṭaiyyba—ʿīr kĕ-mashal', *Maʿarīv*, 22 June 1990, E4.

hamulas. For instance, an article by Dr Zuhayr al-Ṭībī, of Ṭaiyyba, in the weekly *al-Qindīl* published in Bāqa al-Gharbiyya, argues that the population will be able to control its representatives only if these are elected on political slates.[25] Indeed, a law determining direct elections for mayors and heads of local councils, put into practice since the 1978 local elections, has stirred new (but sometimes unfounded) expectations among younger Arabs.

According to research carried out by Dr al-Haj and Professor Rosenfeld, both of Haifa University, who have examined reports of meetings of Arab local councils,[26] the following main topics are of concern there: the collection of taxes, education, water supply, drainage, building permits, and organizing special events. Since the 1967 War, under the impact of increasing politicization, particularly among younger councillors, more general subjects began to be debated, such as problems relating to all Arabs in Israel and the Israeli-held territories. This process was accelerated by feelings of financial discrimination in allocations from the state budget to Arab localities. While the government and its agencies did improve conditions in the Arab local authorities, the budgets allocated to them remained small, in comparison with those earmarked for Jewish localities. Consequently, various services lagged behind.

In 1990, budgetary deficits in all Arab municipalities and local authorities reached 90 million New Shekels (about £22,500,000 at the time).[27] Demonstrations protesting against discrimination became more and more frequent.[28] A characteristic article by Nimr Murquṣ, head of the Kafr Yāsīf local council, in the Communist daily *al-Ittiḥād*, was entitled 'Facing a sky-shaking discrimination',[29] and stated (with some exaggeration) that 'in the local

---

[25] The article in *al-Qindīl* has been transl. in *Arabs in Israel*, 1/20 (29 Sept. 1991), 1, 6. For the local government of the Arabs in the first two decades of the state, see Elie Rekhess, *ha-Kěfar ha-ʿAravī bě-Israʾel—mōqed pōlīṭī lě'ūmī mithaddesh* (1985); Majid al-Haj and Henry Rosenfeld, *Arab Local Government in Israel* (1988), 24 ff.

[26] al-Haj and Rosenfeld, *Arab Local Government*, 30 ff; Mahmud Bayadsi, 'The Arab Local Authorities: Achievements and Problems', *New Outlook*, 18/160 (Oct.–Nov. 1975), 58–61.

[27] Smadar Perī, '38 Rěshūyōt ʿAraviyyōt—90 milyōn sheqel geraʿōn', *Yědīʿōt Aharōnōt*, 27 Feb. 1990, 7.

[28] ʿAṭallāh Manṣūr, 'Raʾshey ha-rěshūyōt ha-ʿAraviyyōt yafgīnū bě-meḥaʾa ʿal qīppūhan', *ha-Aretz*, 7 Mar. 1991, A5.

[29] Nimr Murquṣ, 'Fī muwājahat tamyīz yaṣraḵẖ ḥattā al-samāʾ', *al-Ittiḥād*, 23 Aug. 1991, Suppl., 1.

authorities, one Jewish citizen equals four Arab ones'. As a result of this trend and with increasing politicization in the Arab sector in the 1970s and 1980s, political affairs were increasingly discussed in its local councils, frequently in a nationalist vein. For instance, a debate on the lack of industrialization and the absence of a sound economic basis in the locality would turn into a more heated argument concerning country-wide matters.[30] Still, the Arabs, unsuccessful in exercising a far-reaching influence on national Israeli affairs, turned their attention to local matters, frequently in a nationalist spirit. Much of this is evident in their voting in local elections, which frequently reflects their more general political attitudes as well.

A number of trends are particularly noticeable in municipal and local voting:

1. One of the main differences between municipal and local elections and those to the Knesset is that in the former various political parties assisted *hamula*s and other local groups, while in the latter the same parties were aided, in return, by their local allies. Owing to a law which determined that Knesset and local elections were to be held on the same day, the above process had even more effect, for a good number of years; it still goes on, even though this law has been changed.

2. Until 1967, approximately, the focus in local election propaganda was on local demands, some of which emphasized the bias against Arab local authorities compared with Jewish ones in the allocation of development funds, completing village ordinance-plans, assistance in housing, education, health, sanitation, transport, and electricity. In those years, election pacts were agreed upon between various *hamula*s (especially from the same religious denomination), as well as between some *hamula*s (chiefly in the larger localities) and Jewish parties. Inter-*hamula* rivalry and the parties' commitment to carry out their undertakings always loomed in the background. In this multiple-choice situation, parts of the *hamula* which were at odds with one another would often seek alliances with various competing elements. All this caused visible fragmentation, expressed in a large number of competing groups in

---

[30] Sālim Jubrān, 'Taḥqīq al-maṭālib al-ḥayawiyya wa-'l-'ājila li-'l-suluṭāt al-maḥalliyya miftāḥ li-'l-taṭawwur al-ijtimā'ī li-'l-jamāhīr al-'Arabiyya', ibid. 27 Feb. 1990.

the local elections of the Arab sector and in the subsequent make-up of its local councils.

3. After 1967, along with advances in education, modernization, and growing politicization, expectations for the attainment of demands on the local level have been growing stronger; these demands have increasingly assumed a political nationalist character. In other words, local politics have been turning into country-wide politics, as already pointed out: thus, local demands were frequently combined with those for full equality with the Jewish population, and couched in a more and more aggressive style. This process was expressed not only in the violent contents and wording of local election propaganda, but also in the setting up of independent slates of younger candidates, sometimes without *hamula* patronage, indeed even against its explicit wishes. There have recently been fewer and fewer aged candidates and councillors aged 60 and over, and more and more younger ones (aged 30 to 50).[31] Slates of the latter kind, very unusual before 1967 (and, anyway, younger persons were very rarely elected as councillors), subsequently became almost the rule. For example, the Sons of the Village ran in the 1973 local elections in Umm al-Faḥm and won a seat on the local council, thanks to a platform which demanded the improvement of Arab localities, indeed, but also expressed loyalty to the PLO and its principles.[32] Other local slates took pains to ally themselves with the PLP, winning handsomely as a result. Such independent slates registered gains in the 1989 local elections (to be discussed below), after having allied themselves with—or having been initiated by—fundamentalist Islamic circles. In consequence, a growing number of political groups have grasped that setting up a country-wide power base first needs local support.

4. A few rare cases excepted, Arab participation in local elections has constantly been heavier than in parliamentary ones, generally moving from a low of 80 per cent to a high of 97.5 per cent of qualified voters. The main reason seems to be that Arab voters, no less than others, are well aware of the direct immediate significance of local issues in their daily life. When public debates in local elections assumed a political nationalist character, the

---

[31] Landau, 'A Note on the Leadership of the Israeli Arabs', *Il Politico*, 27/3 (1962), 625–35.
[32] Yechiel Harari, *ha-Bĕḥīrōt ba-migzar ha-ʿAravī 1973*, 23–8.

combined effect of local and country-wide interests continued to bring about heavy participation in local elections, even when that in Knesset elections declined.

5. Considering the absence of historical tradition in Arab local government, the scarcity of experienced officials (compared to a Jewish locality of the same size), reluctance to pay taxes, and the rather niggardly allocations by the government, it is easy to explain electoral alliances of local politicians with external factors, such as political parties. Also, one understands better how the heads and councillors of Arab local authorities have increasingly become politicized no less than Jewish ones. As already said, Jewish parties continue to obtain honours and funds for Arab mayors and councillors allied with them and then, on election days, hope to get their quid pro quo.

6. Although many political parties are intensively involved in Arab towns and local authority councils, their activity is mostly visible on election-eve and focuses on the larger localities, for obvious reasons. As a rule, the larger the locality, the more fragmented it is; equally, if it is inhabited by people of more than one denomination, fragmentation is greater than in homogeneously Muslim, Christian, or Druze places.

7. The main parties and groups involved in municipal and local elections in the Arab sector since 1967 have been RAQAH/ ḤADASH, the ILP/Alignment, MAPAM, the NRP, and the Likkūd; and, more recently, the Sons of the Village, the PLP, the DAP, and several Islamic groups.

i. RAQAH/ḤADASH ran in almost all localities, with the avowed aim of getting the post of mayor or head of the local council. In this it often succeeded, thanks to the 'democratic fronts' it established in many villages and to its continuous, all-year-round propaganda, well-planned and frequently seasoned with aggressive nationalist criticism of the state and its policies. As a result, in the local by-elections of 19 December 1990, its candidates won, among others, the position of head of the local council in Kafr Yāṣīf and Abū Sinān.

ii. The ILP/Alignment was the only party to compete with RAQAH/ḤADASH for the position of head of the local council, usually via *hamula* slates, to which it could offer aid in welfare, education, industrialization, employment, and the like—at least until 1977, when it lost its leading position in the Cabinet. Its propaganda was mainly directed at integrating the Arab population into Israeli state and society, thus frequently clashing with RAQAH/ḤADASH. Other parties generally concentrated their electoral efforts on winning a place on the municipal and local councils.

iii. MAPAM has consistently continued its activities in the Arab local authorities—at first as a middle-of-the-road party, somewhere between MAPAI/ILP and the Communists; then (after having joined an Alignment with the ILP in 1965), it went on presenting itself independently, to some extent, as the most trustworthy friend of the Arabs in Israel. Unlike MAPAI/ILP (which has only recently been seeking supporters among the younger people), MAPAM, like RAQAH, always addressed itself to the younger and better-educated. MAPAM's kibbutzim have maintained extensive relations with neighbouring Arab localities.

iv. The NRP, in its propaganda directed to Arab localities, argued that it was appealing to them in the name of religion. It seems, however, that it was assisted in its electoral campaigning—for the local authority no less than for the Knesset— by the fact that the Ministers of the Interior, Religious Affairs, Welfare, and Education often came from its ranks. These, of course, could influence local matters subsequently. Pragmatic voting for the NRP brought it modest, but steady, results in the councils of the Arab local authorities.

v. The Likkūd started its involvement in the Arab sector in earnest after it became the predominant element in the Cabinet in 1977. In its propaganda on the local level, it tried to soft-pedal its Zionist militancy and to emphasize local interests common to it and local voters, insinuating that, as the majority component of the Coalition Cabinet, it was best equipped to carry out its electoral promises. The Likkūd has registered some success, mostly among the Druzes.

vi. Other Jewish parties obtained but few votes.

vii. The Sons of the Village ran in Umm al-Faḥm and several other local authorities and obtained several seats on the local councils.

viii. The PLP and the DAP, also, achieved only modest results, owing to the competition of Muslim groups, particularly in 1989.

ix. Muslim groups, on the other hand, registered some notable achievements, mainly at the expense of RAQAH/ḤADASH and the PLP. In 1989, they won the mayoralties of Umm al-Faḥm and Ṭaiyyba and positions on various local councils, including even Rahaṭ, an important Bedouin permanent settlement.

8. Elections to Arab municipalities and local authorities during the 1970s and 1980s severally comprised all, or most, or some of the above parties and groups. This renders it difficult, perhaps impossible, to analyse the results comparatively. I shall focus therefore on the last country-wide local elections, held in 1989, attempting to assess their characteristics by comparing them with the preceding ones in 1983. They took place in 49 Arab localities (46 in 1983), on 28 February 1989; in 8 localities another round was needed, which took place on 14 March 1989.[33] Preceded by a very lively election campaign, voter participation among a population numbering 400,200 (324,900 in 1983) reached about 88 per cent (about 84 per cent in 1983) of qualified voters. The number of contested seats had risen from 430 to 516, and the competing slates from 340 to 440. All these were steep changes upward. Despite the large number of slates, in both 1983 and 1989, only 0.58 per cent of them obtained some representation; in many cases, they were the same ones, indicating a certain stability in the vote. Split voting for the mayor or the head of the local council, on the one hand, and the candidates for the municipal or local council itself, on the other, was rather common, probably indicating deals behind the scenes. Approximately 68 per cent of the slates were

---

[33] Details have been regularly published in the official *Yalqūṭ ha-Pirsūmīm*. See also E. El'ad, 'Mered ha-tsĕ'īrīm bĕ-Baqa al-Gharbiyya', *ha-Aretz*, 18 Oct. 1970; Nahman Fabian, 'Noṣrat—ha-ma'ōz shel RAQAH: mitqarvīm la-bĕhīrōt', ibid. 20 Nov. 1970, 17; Misrad ha-Pĕnīm, *ha-Bĕhīrōt bi-shĕmōneh rĕshūyōt mĕqōmiyyōt ba-seqṭōr ha-'Aravī ba-shanīm 1971, 1972* (1972); id., *Rĕshīmat ha-rĕshūyōt ha-mĕqōmiyyōt bĕ-yishshūvey ha-mī'ūṭim* (1973); id., *ha-Bĕhīrōt la-rĕshūyōt ha-mĕqōmiyyōt ba-seqṭōr ha-'Aravī 1973* (1974); Shā'ūl Hōn, 'Hafīkhat ḥatser bĕ-Qalansuwa', *Ma'arīv*, 17 Feb. 1974, 7; Tawfīq Ṭūbī, 'Liqr'at ha-bĕhīrōt la-rĕshūyōt ha-mĕqōmiyyōt', *'Arakhīm*, 69 (Feb. 1982), 12–25; 'al-Suluṭāt al-maḥalliyya azmat majālis wa-baḥbūḥat al-ru'asā'', *al-Sināra*, 24 Nov. 1983; Abū Sharīf, 'Ru'asā' judud wa-qudāmà wa-intimā'āt taṭhbut bi-'l-tajriba', ibid. 20 Dec. 1983, 2; 'al-Sulṭa al-maḥalliyya akthar qawmiyya!', ibid. 14 June 1985.

independent, many of these reserving their top places for teachers, physicians, engineers, and other educated candidates, with many traditionally elected notables left out.

9. The results of the 1989 local elections in the Arab sector were roughly as follows:[34] RAQAH/HADASH declined in strength, winning only 14 positions of heads of localities (19 in 1983); the PLP, 1; the DAP, 3; Movement for Citizens' Rights and Likkūd, 1 each; the Islamic Movement, an informal organization of separate groups, country-wide, won the top positions in 5 localities, including Umm al-Fahm and Kafr Qāsim;[35] the rest was divided between local slates, part of them allied to the ILP/Alignment.[36] The picture differs somewhat when the local councils (not their heads, dealt with above) are considered. In these, independent slates emerged first, followed (in descending order) by RAQAH/HADASH, the Islamic Movement, Jewish parties, the PLP, the DAP, and others. RAQAH/HADASH maintained its position in Nazareth, Galilee, and the towns, but candidates of the Islamic Movement obtained 6 seats (out of a total of 19) on the Nazareth municipal council.[37] In the mixed towns, also, Arab voting made itself felt. Generally speaking, Muslims supported RAQAH/HADASH, the Islamic Movement, the PLP, the DAP, and Jewish parties, besides independent slates. Christians voted mostly for independent slates and RAQAH/HADASH. Druzes voted for independent slates, Jewish parties, and to a lesser extent RAQAH/HADASH. The main surprise was the participation of the Islamic

[34] 'Ba-migzar ha-ʿAravī: hanhaga ḥadasha', *Maʿarīv*, 3 Mar. 1989, B1; ʿAṭallāh Manṣūr, 'HADASH kĕdey lishmōr yashan', *ha-Aretz*, 23 Dec. 1990, B3; Sālim Jubrān, 'al-Aḥammiyya al-quṭriyya li-'l-intikhābāt al-maḥalliyya', *al-Ittiḥād*, 24 Feb. 1989; 'Muqābala maʿa al-Shaykh Rāʾid Ṣāliḥ raʾīs baladiyyat Umm al-Faḥm al-muntakhab', *al-Ṣināra*, 3 Mar. 1989, 5; Rajāʾ Aghbariyya, 'Mulāhaẓāt awwaliyya ḥawl natāʾij al-intikhābāt al-baladiyya fī Umm al-Faḥm', *al-Rāya*, 8 (9 Mar. 1989), 5 (the writer is a leader of the Sons of the Village); Tawfīq Ṭūbī, 'al-Durūs wa-'l-ʿibar al-mustafāda min intikhābāt al-sulṭa al-maḥalliyya', *al-Ittiḥād*, 20 Mar. 1989, 3; 'Intikhābāt al-sulṭa al-maḥalliyya', *al-Rābiṭa*, 43/3 (Mar. 1989), 14–18; Munqidh al-Zuʿbī, 'al-Tajriba allatī fashilat', *al-Ṣināra*, 23 June 1989, 2; Marda Dunsky, 'A New Reality Sparks New Fears', *Jerusalem Post*, 10 Mar. 1989, Suppl., 9.

[35] On 6 Nov. 1989 local elections were also held in Kābūl, in Galilee, the Islamic Movement winning the vote for head of the local council—its first victory of the kind in Galilee.

[36] Jewish parties generally do not contest these local elections under their own names, but rather via alliances with local factors, which renders it difficult to assess their success precisely.

[37] Reactions in Munqidh al-Zuʿbī's 'Nāṣirat al-jamiʿ wa-baladiyyat al-jamiʿ', *al-Ṣināra*, 10 Mar. 1989.

Movement and its remarkable success.[38] Campaigning in 13 localities only, it thus concentrated its efforts and obtained the following results:[39] 8 seats out of 52 in Galilee, or 15.4 per cent; 25 seats out of 81 in the Little Triangle, or 30.8 per cent; 3 seats out of 13 among the Negev Bedouin, or 23 per cent. Besides all this, as mentioned, its candidates became heads of five municipalities and local councils. All in all, the Islamic Movement won 41 seats (or 28.08 per cent) out of a total of 146 in the exclusively Arab localities. In addition, it won 2 seats in the municipal council of Lydda, and 1 in Ramleh. Its most noteworthy gains were, understandably, in the all-Muslim Little Triangle, an area bordering on the West Bank and a centre of Islamic and nationalist activities.[40] In the local by-elections of 6 November 1990, a candidate of the Islamic Movement, Sheikh Muhammad Rayyān, was elected head of the local council in Kābūl. Hence the Movement now chairs six Arab municipalities and local councils.[41] It seems, indeed, that the Islamic Movement has contributed more than any other group to the changes in the current leadership of Arab local authorities— which is partly veteran and partly new.

HISTADRUT ELECTIONS

The Histadrut is the largest body in Israel (except fot the civil service) to have Arab members and deal with Arab affairs.[42] About 230,000 Arabs belong to it,[43] constituting about 14 per cent of the entire Histadrut membership—almost their ratio in the overall population. Together with their families, they number more than 450,000 people, or more than half the entire Arab population of Israel. The Histadrut has organized and maintains in the Arab sector 171 sports teams, 46 branches of the working-and-studying youth movement, and 115 medical clinics.[44] (See also Table 8.4.)

[38] For the reasons of its success, see Rāsim Ḥamāyisī, 'Tĕnū'at meha'a mi-sūg ḥadash', *Davar*, 3 May 1989, 7.
[39] Reuven Paz, *ha-Tĕnū'a ha-Islāmīt bĕ-Isra'el bĕ-'iqvōt ha-bĕḥirōt la-rĕshuyōt ha-mĕqōmiyyōt: sĕqīra wĕ-nittūah* (1989), 1–2.
[40] Avner Regev, 'Israeli Arabs and Islam', *Israeli Democracy*, Spring 1991, 30–1.
[41] *Arabs in Israel*, 1/3 (25 Nov. 1990), 5.
[42] For an outdated, but still useful, study, cf. E. L. Gutmann and H. Qlef, *ha-Histadrut w-fĕ'ūlōteyha ba-seqṭōr ha-'Aravī* (1970).
[43] Cf. *ha-Aretz*, 20 Jan. 1989, 3.
[44] *Pōlīṭīqa*, 21 (June 1988), 48; *Arabs in Israel*, 1/7 (15 Mar. 1991), 4–6.

TABLE 8.2. Jewish and non-Jewish* membership in the Histadrut, 1975–1989 (31 March of each year)

Year	Jews	Non-Jews	Total	% non-Jews
1975	1,193,283	92,830	1,286,113	7.22
1976	1,235,291	104,709	1,340,000	7.81
1977	1,275,174	119,158	1,394,332	8.55
1978	1,293,234	126,822	1,420,056	8.93
1979	1,317,378	134,219	1,451,597	9.25
1980	1,342,526	139,343	1,481,869	9.40
1981	1,371,956	146,289	1,518,245	9.64
1982	1,350,925	181,910	1,532,835	11.87
1983	1,356,952	191,728	1,548,680	12.38
1984	1,346,864	193,410	1,540,274	12.56
1985	1,359,152	196,910	1,556,062	12.65
1986	1,398,600	197,500	1,596,100	12.37
1989	1,402,033	243,395[†]	1,645,428	14.79

* The term 'non-Jew' includes non-Jews married to Jews, mainly among new immigrants. Their number is close to 30,000.
† The figure includes those who have ceased to pay their membership dues.

Source: Tsvī Ḥayeq (ed.), ha-Ḥaverīm ha-'Aravīm wě-ha-Děrūzīm ba-Histadrūt (1989), 12.

Relations between the Histadrut and the local Arabs began to be established during the period of British rule in Palestine. In 1953 it opened its trade unions to Arab membership. Five years later, a small number, 883 in all, mostly Druzes, were accepted for full Histadrut membership. Since 1959 others have also been registering as members with equal rights. An Arab Department paved the way for the full integration of the Arab sector into the various bodies of the Histadrut. In 1965, Arabs participated for the first time as delegates to the Histadrut convention and were placed in its various component bodies, chiefly the Arab Department. After Land Day in March 1976, and again subsequently, further steps were taken towards certain structural changes aiming at fully integrating the Arab population into the Histadrut on a basis of complete equality. None the less, some organizational difficulties have persisted, such as the fact that many people still inhabit tiny

TABLE 8.3. Main areas of Histadrut activity in the Arab sector

---

(*a*) Trade unions
(*b*) Medical services and clinics
(*c*) Enterprises and co-operatives
(*d*) Cultural activities and sport
(*e*) Vocational schooling
(*f*) Working and studying youth
(*g*) Women's groups
(*h*) The Jewish–Arab Institute and its publishing house

Source: Tsvī Ḥayeq (ed.), *ha-Ḥaverīm ha-ʿAravīm wĕ-ha-Dĕrūzīm ba-Histadrūt* (1989), 10.

villages and Bedouin encampments, which does not really permit the formation of workers' councils and the setting up of services. Hence, workers' councils and services have been located in nearby larger localities, a system which, however, does not allow continuous presence everywhere. In July 1991 the Arab Department of the Histadrut was disbanded, and all services were given directly to Arabs and Jews alike. Nevertheless, some Arab members of the Histadrut still complain of discrimination,[45] maintaining that they hold very few senior positions.

The number of Arabs joining the Histadrut, probably out of pragmatic considerations (medical services, employment, etc.) rather than ideological ones, has risen annually, as has their ratio in the overall membership in both absolute and relative figures (see Table 8.2).

One deduces from Tables 8.3 and 8.4 that the Histadrut has been paying particular attention, in the Arab sector, to working-and-studying youth, women's groups, and publishing, as well as to medical care. Its Arabic publishing house has continuously put out books and periodicals for adults, youth, and children; the latter are regularly sent to schools. Despite obvious difficulties, the Histadrut has dealt with similar topics among its members in East Jerusalem since late in 1967.

Due to various structural changes in its organization,[46] Arab

---

[45] ʿAṭallāh Manṣūr, 'Mĕnūddīm ba-histadrūt', *ha-Aretz*, 6 Aug. 1990, B3.
[46] Yosef Goell, 'Histadrut's Failure in the Arab Sector', *Jerusalem Post*, 30 Jan. 1987, 16, criticizes these changes.

TABLE 8.4. Medical services of the Histadrut in
the Arab sector, 1968–1988

Year	No. of clinics	No. of Arabs medically insured
1968	44	110,000
1974	65	210,000
1979	82	326,000
1983	92	398,000
1988	111	495,000

Note: The data do not include non-Jews in mixed towns.

Source: Tsvī Ḥayeq (ed.), ha-Haverīm ha-'Aravīm wĕ-
ha-Dĕrūzīm ba-Histadrūt (1989), 34.

representation in the Histadrut's decision-making bodies has
gradually increased, particularly after the so-called Har'el Com-
mission had investigated the relations between the Histadrut and
the Arabs and recommended that they should be reinforced. Two
years later, an Arab was co-opted to the Central Committee, the
decision-making body of the Histadrut, then two more were
invited. Subsequently, two Arab members joined the committee
directing the Histadrut's economic enterprises, an Arab woman
member its central women's association, and another Arab the
governing body of its health service network. In 1988, yet another
joined the secretariat of the agricultural centre. Although these
figures are notably lower than those implied by the ratio of Arab
Histadrut membership, even these appointments were an innovation denoting an improvement in status and functions. Many Arabs
see a positive value in the Histadrut, appreciating its contribution
to their sector.[47] Fewer, like the Sons of the Village, have attacked
it, describing it in their writings as 'an instrument of Zionist
oppression'.[48] The advancement of Arabs to important roles in the
Histadrut bureaucracy and the continuing improvement in the

[47] e.g. Samīr Kabhā, 'Khiṭaṭ Khālid Aghbariyya al-mustaqbaliyya li-'l-wasaṭ al-
'Arabī', Kull al-'Arab, 21 Dec. 1990.
[48] al-Lajna al-quṭriyya li-ḥarakat Abnā' al-balad—al-Idāra al-thaqāfiyya, al-
'Ummāl al-'Arab wa-'l-histadrūt.

TABLE 8.5. Participation in elections for the Histadrut convention, 1989

Type of Locality	Qualified voters	Votes	% participation
Three cities*	314,351	160,772	51.14
Jewish towns	824,729	468,806	56.84
Jewish villages	21,221	11,580	54.57
Moshavim†	60,984	34,177	56.04
Kibbutzim	69,359	53,241	76.76
Arab localities	150,992	98,231	65.06
Other localities	5,202	2,879	55.34

* Jerusalem, Tel-Aviv–Jaffa, and Haifa.
† The *moshavim* are co-operative settlements where possessions are not jointly owned.
Source: *Tōtsĕʾōt ha-bĕḥīrōt ba-histadrūt 13. 11. 1989*, 4.

services offered to them have influenced, *inter alia*, their participation in Histadrut elections.

A number of trends is noticeable in Arab voting for the Histadrut, although it should be remembered that fewer people are involved than in parliamentary or local elections.[49]

1. As shown in Table 8.5, the rate of Arab members' participating in the Histadrut conventions (its most important institution) has declined steadily: 90 per cent in 1965; 78 per cent in 1969; 76 per cent in 1973;[50] and, in the most recent ones, in 1989, a mere 65 per cent.[51] This repeats the pattern already observed, proportionately, in Arab voting for the Knesset (although, again, not all Arabs who vote for the Knesset vote for the Histadrut). However, it should be noted that the Jewish sector, also, displays low participation rates in voting for the Histadrut conventions. Indeed, barring the kibbutzim, Arab participation has been higher, proportionately, than the Jewish, at least recently.

2. The electoral contest in the Arab sector for the Histadrut

[49] Yechiel Harari, *ha-Bĕḥīrōt ba-migzar ha-ʿAravī bi-shĕnat 1973* (1975), 2–22; Sara Ōsetskī and Asʿad Ghānim, 'Nittūah tōtsĕʾot ha-bĕḥīrōt la-histadrūt ba-migzar ha-ʿAravī', *Sĕqīrōt ʿalʿArviyyey Israʾel*, 1 (18 Mar. 1990), 1–18.
[50] J. M. Landau, *The Arabs and the Histadrut* (1976), 15.
[51] Mashhūr Musṭafā misrepresents the situation in his 'Qirāʾa sarīʿa fī nataʾij intikhābāt al-histadrūt al-akhīra', *al-Maydān*, 1/1 (24 Nov. 1989), 5.

TABLE 8.6. Arab voting for ILP, MAPAM, and RAQAH in selected elections to the Histadrut conventions (% of valid votes)

	1965	1969	1973	1985	1989
MAPAI/ILP	60.0				41.8
		61.5	61.7	45.6	
MAPAM	13.4				9.3
RAQAH/HADASH*	19.8	31.5	26.9	43.2†	33.8

Note: In 1989, 8.3% of valid Arab votes went to the Movement for Citizens' Rights (3.8% in 1985) and 6.6% to the Likkūd (4.1% in 1985).

* In 1989, RAQAH/HADASH ran in a United List together with some other groups.

† In the 1985 elections to the Histadrut convention, RAQAH enjoyed the support of the PLP, established one year earlier, which did not run then.

Source: *Tōtsĕʾōt ha-bĕhīrōt ba-histadrūt 13. 11. 1989*, 4. See also Y. Cohen, 'ha-Bĕhīrōt la-histadrūt bĕ-qerev ha-ʿAravīm', *Leqeṭ Yĕdīʿōt*, 28 (Apr.–Dec. 1969), 3–8.

conventions has generally been beween the ILP/Alignment and RAQAH/HADASH, with MAPAM forming a third factor in the years in which it was not part of the Alignment. The changing ratio among the competing factors, shown in Table 8.6, already discussed in the context of parliamentary and local elections, is observable in the Histadrut elections as well, although not necessarily to an equal extent.

3. The ILP and MAPAM, with some 73 per cent of the Arab vote to their joint credit in the 1960s, declined in the 1970s and even more so subsequently, to about 54 per cent in 1981 and about 46 per cent in 1985, recovering somewhat to about 51 per cent in 1989 (see Table 8.6). The drop was, however, less marked than in their combined vote for the Knesset and the local authorities; indeed, together they more or less succeeded in getting half of the Arab delegates, or even a little more. The main party that profited from this decline was RAQAH/HADASH, which triumphantly proclaimed this achievement in the press, both locally and abroad.[52] The reservations indicated by Arab members of the Histadrut vis-à-

[52] 'Israel: Erfolg der Kommunisten bei Gewerkschaftswahlen', *Informations Bulletin: Materialien und Dokumente kommunistischer und Arbeiterparteien*, 19 (1969), 950–1.

TABLE 8.7. Vote distribution in Arab localities for the Histadrut convention, 1989 (%)

ILP	MAPAM	Likkūd	Movement for Citizens' Rights	RAQAḤ/ḤADASH (United List)
41.87	9.28	6.6	8.37	33.82

Source: Tōtseʾōt ha-běḥīrōt ba-histadrūt, 4. These data do not refer to Arab voting in the mixed towns.

vis the Alignment were probably similar to those expressed in Knesset and local elections; that its decline was more moderate in Histadrut voting was due to the fact that many Arab voters knew quite well that the Alignment, or at least the ILP, still remained the dominant factor in the Histadrut. The rise of RAQAḤ/ḤADASH was not too steady, owing (as in Knesset elections) to Arab reservations of a nationalist, religious, or pragmatic nature: indeed, as a minority factor in the Histadrut, it could benefit its supporters much less than the Alignment. In 1989, an obvious change occurred. Two-thirds of the Arab vote for the Histadrut convention went to Jewish/Zionist parties, apparently because of pragmatic considerations. Only a third went to a United List set up by RAQAḤ/ḤADASH together with the PLP and the DAP, a move which led some of their potential Arab supporters to express reservations concerning one or another of these components.

4. The Arab vote distribution among competing parties has started to create its patterns in the elections to the Histadrut conventions no less than to Knesset and local ones. An example may be found in the 13 November 1989 Arab vote to the Histadrut convention, shown in Table 8.7. It is interesting to compare this distribution with the voting results country-wide (in percentages): ILP, 55.07; MAPAM, 8.97; the Likkūd, 27.49; the Movement for Citizens' Rights, 3.98; RAQAḤ/ḤADASH (the United List), 4.49. In other words, the ILP and the Likkud obtained a higher ratio of the vote, country-wide, from Jewish members of the Histadrut than from Arab ones;[53] while RAQAḤ/ḤADASH (the United List), MAPAM, and the Movement for Citizens' Rights obtained less

[53] Shalōm Yĕrūshalmī, 'Nigrarīm la-qalpey', *Kol ha-ʿĪr*, 17 Nov. 1989, 14–16.

country-wide support and bolstered their overall vote by relatively broader backing from Arab voters. This is particularly true for RAQAH/HADASH, which received a third of the Arab vote, as in the 1984 and 1988 Knesset elections. Still, in the 1989 vote for the Histadrut convention, as already mentioned, RAQAH/HADASH ran together with two other partners, the PLP[54] and the DAP,[55] without thereby improving its electoral gains.[56] To the contrary, it seems that this tripartite electoral alliance dissuaded would-be supporters who were put off by RAQAH/HADASH.[57] The ILP, on the other hand, was stronger among the Bedouin, who may have transfered to it some of their 1988 DAP support, and maintained itself handsomely amongst the Druzes.[58]

5. Arab participation and vote distribution were somewhat different in the elections to the Histadrut's Workers' Councils, held on the same day in 1989 as its elections for the Convention. Indeed, Arab voting for the Workers' Councils was heavier, since it probably resembles their voting for local councils more than for the Knesset. After all, Workers' Councils are expected to determine immediate local matters, chiefly labour and employment. As well as the parties mentioned above in the convention elections, other Arab elements competed with one another in those to the Workers' Councils. The most prominent was the Islamic Movement, which had refrained from taking part in the electoral campaign for the convention. In several of the localities in which it ran for the Workers' Councils, the Islamic Movement attained impressive results. This was particularly so in the Nazareth Workers' Council, where it obtained 3,282 votes, or 26.9 per cent of the 12,177 valid votes cast (more than the ILP, which received only 2,717 votes, or 23.3 per cent). It is quite likely that a good part of the Islamic Movement's vote was at the expense of RAQAH/HADASH (the

---

[54] Cf. the analysis of Muḥammad Mīʿārī, 'Natījat al-intikhābāt laysat bi-'l-ḍarūra tuʿabbir ʿan al-mawqif al-waṭanī wa-'l-iltizām al-Filasṭīnī', *al-Ṣināra*, 24 Nov. 1989, 9–10.

[55] Sālim Jubrān, 'Naḥw intikhābāt al-histadrūt . . . wa-abʿad min intikhābāt al-histadrūt!', *al-Ittiḥād*, 30 June 1989; Khālid Badr, 'Tanqiyat al-jaww al-ijtimāʿi wa-taʿmīq al-taʿāmul al-dīmuqrāṭī', *al-Ṣināra*, 18 Aug. 1989; Tamīm Manṣūr, 'Qāʾima mushtaraka wa-lākin laysa bi-kull thaman', ibid. 25 Aug. 1989.

[56] See the debate among the representatives of the competing parties, *al-Ṣināra*, 10 Nov. 1989, 8–10.

[57] ʿAṭallāh Manṣūr, 'Meḥaʾa neged ha-ʿAvōda', *ha-Aretz*, 18 Sept. 1989.

[58] Yōram Katz, *Maʿarekhet ha-bĕḥīrōt la-histadrūt ba-migzar ha-ʿAravī/ha-Dĕrūzī* (1989).

United List). The Islamic Movement won 6 seats (out of 21) on the Nazareth Workers' Council,[59] thus serving as a pivot between RAQAH/HADASH (8 seats) and the Alignment (5 seats).[60] Spokesmen of the Islamic Movement have argued that it could have done better, had not RAQAH/HADASH (the United List) waged a particularly intensive campaign against it.[61]

[59] Ghassān Basūl, 'Da'ū al-qāfila tasīr', *al-Sināra*, 1 Sept. 1989; 'Natā'ij intikhābāt al-histadrūt fī jamī' al-mudun wa-'l-qurà al-'Arabiyya', ibid. 17 Nov. 1989, 7–9; Ibrāhīm al-Khatīb, 'Nadwa fī Dabbūriyya hawl natā'ij al-intikhābāt li-'l-histadrūt', *Sawt al-Haqq wa-'l-Hurriyya*, 1 Dec. 1989, 8.

[60] As well as one seat for MAPAM and another to a local group.

[61] 'Liqā' ma'a al-Shaykh Rā'id al-Sālih ra'īs baladiyyat Umm al-Fahm', *al-Usbū' al-Jadīd*, 15 Jan. 1990, 22–3.

9

Problems of Identity

INTRODUCTORY

If identity is defined as feelings of belonging that one has about oneself and one's group, it would seem that members of the minorities in Israel are not absolutely clear about their identity problems.[1] Arabs and Druzes do not quite agree among themselves in defining their own collective belonging and group relationship.[2] If asked 'Who and what is an Arab in Israel?' they would give differing—and probably incomplete—replies. This seems to be a more difficult question even than 'Who is a Palestinian?'[3] None the less, coping with problems of identity is a central and unavoidable facet of the modernization process, and of the politicization and radicalization that Arabs in Israel are undergoing; more particularly so as coping becomes increasingly complex. The main difficulty lies in the fact that Arabs are a minority within a state defined by its majority as Jewish and Zionist, which has long been at war with its neighbours. These, on their part, are kith and kin of Israel's minority groups in ethnic origins, culture, and language; moreover, these neighbours form a majority in the Middle East as a whole. Considering the complexity of the identity of the minorities in Israel, it is difficult to diagnose it, especially since it changes with time and situation.

---

[1] Ramzī Sulaymān, 'al-Hawiyya al-qawmiyya wa-'l-muwāṭana', al-Jadīd, 11–12 (Nov.–Dec. 1983), 15–19; id., 'al-Hawiyya al-Filasṭīniyya wa-'l-muwāṭana li-muthaqqafīn ʿArab fī Isrāʾīl', in Khālid Khalīfa (ed.), Filasṭīniyyūn 1948–1988 (1988), 83–106; Khālid Khalīfa, 'Aqalliyya ʿArabiyya fī Isrāʾīl am juzʾ' la yatajazzaʾ' min al-shaʿb al-Filasṭīnī', ibid. 30–7; Yochanan Peres, Yahasey ʿedōt bĕ-Israʾel (1976), 176–87; Mōshe Gabbay, ʿArviyyey Israʾel—shĕʾela shel zehūt (1984), ch. 2; ʿUmar Maṣālha, "ʿArviyyey Israʾel bi-mĕdīnat Israʾel", in Adam Dōrōn (ed.), Mĕdīnat Israʾel wĕ-Eretz Israʾel (1988), 315–25; Benyamin Neuberger, ha-Mīʿūṭ ha-ʿAravī: Nikkūr lĕʾūmī wĕ-hishtallĕvūt pōlīṭīt (1991), esp. 43–61. Nadim Rouhana, 'Collective Identity and Arab Voting Patterns', in A. Arian and M. Shamir (eds.), Elections in Israel—1984 (1986), 121–49.

[2] Bōʿaz Shapīra, 'ha-Intifāḍa ha-riʾshōna', ha-Aretz, 29 Mar. 1991, B7.

[3] Bernard Rosenberg, 'The Arabs of Israel', Dissent, 27 (Spring 1980), esp. 162.

Although it has been argued that the Arabs in Israel possess a collective identity,[4] it may be simpler to grasp its essentials by examining its components. Following the findings of Dr Rafi Israeli of the Hebrew University of Jerusalem, and others,[5] it may be convenient to discuss the identity of the Arabs in Israel in four concentric circles, which often intersect with one another, but are distinguishable in characteristics. None necessarily excludes the others; rather, they integrate with one another from various perspectives. Of course, this is an integral part of the difficulty in analysing the identity of the Arabs, both as perceived by themselves and by others. Classifying the circles, from the smallest to the largest, they may be labelled Israeli, Palestinian, Arab, and Islamic. The Arabs in Israel nowadays perceive their identity as a mixture of most—possibly all—these circles, or perhaps as a delicate balance between them. This situation is responsible for the Arabs' identity crisis, which has been going on, in one form or another, since the establishment of the State of Israel.

IDENTITY PROBLEMS BEFORE 1967: ISRAELISM VERSUS ARABISM

In 1948 the Arab sector in the State of Israel was in shock, having almost overnight become a minority, following the defeat of the Arab states and the loss of a large part of their community. Cut off from their relatives beyond the closed borders, influenced by the Jewish sector in several domains, the Arabs remaining inside Israel tended to see in their Jewish neighbours a role model to be imitated (chiefly in matters relating to modernization),[6] and to reconcile themselves to the State of Israel and its society, generally accepting its existence.[7] One of the reasons for these attitudes is the fact that minorities (particularly in a situation of weakness) are generally

[4] Khalil Nakhleh, 'Cultural Determinants of Palestinian Collective Identity: The Case of the Arabs in Israel', *New Outlook*, 18/160 (Oct.–Nov. 1975), 31–40.

[5] Yochanan Peres and Nira Davis, "Al zehūtō ha-lě'ūmīt shel ha-'Aravī ha-Isrě'elī', *ha-Mizrah he-Hadash*, 18/1–2 (1968), 6–13; R. Israeli, 'Arabs in Israel: The Surge of A New Identity', *Plural Societies*, 11/4 (Winter 1980), 21–9.

[6] Yochanan Peres, 'Modernization and Nationalism in the Identity of the Israeli Arabs', *Middle East Journal*, 24/4 (Autumn 1970), 479–92.

[7] Ellen Geffner, 'An Israeli Arab View of Israel', 134–41.

inclined to imitate the majority and identify with it.[8] Official policies indeed insisted on non-assimilation. However, the curricula in the state schools persistently strove to strengthen the Israeli identity of all Arabs—true enough, without seeking to turn them into Zionists. Since the language of instruction in these schools was Arabic from the first and the core curriculum was made up of Arabic and Islamic literature and history, pupils were simultaneously attracted to the Arabic circle as well, although of course less trenchantly so than in the Arab states.[9] At all events, it seems that in those early years the bonds of tradition and *hamula* loyalty provided the bulk of the sentiments of Arabism, perhaps as an alternative to the wider circle of Arab identity. It also seems more than likely that *hamula* loyalty assisted the strengthening of the circle of Israeli identity by discouraging tendencies towards other circles.[10]

However, owing to the development of Arab education in Israel and the resulting exposure to modernization, the attraction to the Arab circle grew, especially during the presidency of Jamāl ʿAbd al-Nāṣir in Egypt, with its nationalist and Pan-Arab slogans. The Egyptian media, particularly the radio, fostered the Arab circle among the Arabs in Israel, thus bringing about a conflict between Israelism and Arabism—especially since the Arab circle, in ʿAbd al-Nāṣir's interpretation, obviously meant the annihilation of Israel. This had a powerful appeal to the emotions; but by then the Arabs were already fairly well integrated in the state and its economic life, and were apprehensive of charges of double loyalty. The Arabs in Israel have constantly had to seek a balance between opposing forces by compartmentalizing the norms of pragmatic individual daily behaviour and the ideological trends of the Arab sector. In other words, they suppressed the inner conflict between Israeli and Arab identities, with most of them giving priority to the Israeli circle, at least in their daily behaviour. All this was to change visibly, however, after the 1967 War.

---

[8] Sharif Kanaana, *Socio-Cultural and Psychological Adjustment of the Arab Minority in Israel* (1976).

[9] Jalāl Abū Tuʿma, "Arviyyey Israʾel mitkaḥashīm lĕ-zīqqatam ha-lĕʾūmīt', *ha-Aretz*, 26 May 1972, 12.

[10] Mahmoud Miʿari, 'Traditionalism and Political Identity of Arabs in Israel', *Journal of Asian and African Studies*, 22/1–2 (1987), 33–44.

IMPACT OF THE ARABS IN THE ISRAELI-HELD TERRITORIES

Modernization, openness, secularism, and democratic values which the Arabs in Israel absorbed from Jewish society in the state's first twenty years led to the strengthening of the Israeli circle among them.[11] However, various factors, to be considered immediately, brought about conditions in which Arabs felt that they ought to redefine their relations with the state. Some of this is reflected in the words of Samīr Darwīsh, head of the local council in Bāqa al-Gharbiyya, who was invited to be one of the twelve people to light the ceremonial torches on Independence Day in 1986. He explained his feelings at the time as follows: 'Some Jews do not grasp—and perhaps find it difficult to believe—that there are in this state Arabs who are proud of their Arabism, culture, and heritage, and simultaneously wish to be a part of the state.'[12] At all events, since the 1967 War Arabs in Israel have enlarged the circles of their identity, by giving first consideration to their new direct relationship with the Arabs in the Israeli-held territories—the West Bank and the Gaza Strip,[13] and through these with the residents of Jordan and Arabs in neighbouring states.

The direct impact of the inhabitants of the Israeli-held territories on the Arabs in Israel since 1967 has not yet been exhaustively investigated.[14] Still, what is known is enough to prompt some tentative remarks about its contribution to the creation of a dif-

[11] Mark A. Tessler, 'The Identity of Religious Minorities in Non-Secular States: Jews in Tunisia and Morocco and Arabs in Israel', *Comparative Studies in History and Society*, 20/3 (July 1978), 359–73; Jalāl Abū Ṭuʿma, ''Arviyyey Israʾel měʿunyanīm bě-shillūv', *ha-Aretz*, 22 Apr. 1982, 10.

[12] Samīr Darwīsh, 'Lihyōt ʿAravī bě-Israʾel: maddūaʿ hidlaqtī et massūʾat yōm ha-ʿatsmaʾūt', *ha-Aretz*, 17 June 1986, 14.

[13] Elie Rekhess, ''Arviyyey Israʾel lě-aḥar 1967 (1976), 11 ff; id., 'ha-ʿAravīm bě-Israʾel wě-ʿArviyyey ha-Shěṭaḥīm: zīqqa pōlīṭīt wě-sōlīdariyyūt lěʾūmīt (1967–1988)', *ha-Mizraḥ he-Hadash*, 32/125–8 (1989), 165–91; S. Smooha, *The Orientation and Politicization of the Arab Minority in Israel* (1984); Mark A. Tessler, 'Israel's Arabs and the Palestinian Problem', *Middle East Journal*, 31/3 (Summer 1977), 313–29; Elie Rekhess, 'Israeli Arabs and the Arabs of the West Bank and Gaza: Political Affinity and National Solidarity', *Asian and African Studies*, 23/2–3 (Nov. 1989), 119–54.

[14] See, however, Riyāḍ Kabhà, *Barṭaʿa* (1986); Raʿanan Cohen, *Bi-Sěvakh ha-neʾemanūyōt: ḥevra w-pōlīṭīqa ba-migzar ha-ʿAravī* (1990), 51 ff; Alexander Schölch, 'Die Beziehungen zwischen den Palestinensern in Israel und auf dem Westufer seit 1967', *Orient*, 24/3 (Sept. 1983), 422–7.

ferent, more complex identity among the Arabs in Israel. Upon renewing contact with the inhabitants of the Israeli-held territories, people soon felt that, although they were economically better off, they had fallen behind as regards higher education and status in government service. Arabs in Israel were also the butt of suspicion and mockery on the part of nationalist elements in the Israeli-held territories, who accused relatives and acquaintances in Israel of betraying Arab nationalism and selling themselves for material benefits. Doubts arose among the Arabs in Israel, who found it more and more difficult to continue avoiding confrontation with the new realities. Alienation from the state of Israel increased,[15] and the road was paved for the strengthening of the Palestinian circle at the expense of the Israeli, with tensions increasing between the two.[16]

The Arabs in the West Bank and the Gaza Strip were able to influence those in Israel more than be influenced by them by virtue of being better educated in Arabic and Islamic studies; further, they comprised many more graduates of higher institutions of education and were imbued with a sharper sense of Arab nationalism. The latter, by contrast, were confused and split in their identity. The differences became even more striking against the background of intensive political activity in the Israeli-held territories, especially the West Bank, as compared to the limited political involvement of the Arabs in Israel. It can also be argued that ancient, time-honoured, cultural ties proved stronger than differences (for the Arabs in Israel are Israeli citizens, as well as being bilingual and even bicultural). Various channels of communication exist between the Arabs in Israel and those in the Israeli-held territories, such as the seeking of employment in Israel, encounters with Druze and Bedouin soldiers, family and business contacts, and so forth.[17] Among the factors bringing the Arabs in Israel and those in the Israeli-held territories closer, the following may be mentioned: (1) the 1973 War, interpreted as an Israeli defeat, as against the increase in Arab power due to the oil boycott;[18] (2) the improvement in the PLO's standing since Yāsir

---

[15] Hayyīm Misgav, 'Ezrahīm mĕnūkkarīm', *ha-Aretz*, 12 Mar. 1991, B4.

[16] Landau, *The Arabs in Israel* (1969), 231–6.

[17] Sharif Kanaana, *Channels of Communication and Mutual Images Between the West Bank and Areas in Israel* (1976).

[18] D. Rubinstein, 'Simhat ha-gĕvūra wĕ-ha-tsĕlīha', *Davar*, 24 Mar. 1974, 7.

ʿArafāt's speech at the United Nations, in 1974;[19] (3) Land Day in 1976, perceived as a landmark in the rise of nationalist awareness amongst the Arabs in Israel; (4) the 1982 War, seen as an Israeli failure to liquidate the Palestinians in Lebanon; and (5) the 1991 Gulf War, which revealed a new indecision concerning Arab identity in Israel. Accordingly, a 1985 study found that 68 per cent of the Arabs in Israel defined themselves as Palestinians, versus 46 per cent only nine years previously.[20]

New patterns of contact were created between the Arabs in Israel and those in the Israeli-held territories, which one may perhaps perceive as élite relationships—that is, between intellectuals, journalists, politicians, men of letters, religious leaders, and businessmen. In this context, some Arab graduates of Israeli universities, unable to find appropriate employment at home, have been teaching at universities and colleges in the territories. Over the years, numerous ties have been forged, in the domains of politics and journalism, between inhabitants of the territories and RAQAH/HADASH and the PLP. Although close social ties have not been easy to establish, still the political influence of the Arabs in the territories on those in Israel and their contribution to the latter's Palestinization cannot be doubted.[21] There have been cases where Arabs in Israel felt that Israeli action against inhabitants in the territories concerned them as well.[22] Radical groups and movements in Israel like the Sons of the Village, and others, responded to the political inspiration of the speeches, writings, and activities of the Arabs in the Israeli-held territories, as well as to the propaganda directed by the PLO at the Arabs in Israel.[23] In addition, political and social relations developed amongst students from both sides.

Various studies have indicated, however, that only a minority among the Arabs in Israel have been radicalized perceptibly against

---

[19] The prestige of the PLO rose among Israel's Arabs even earlier, in 1971, when its National Council co-opted three of those Arabs as representatives of 'the Arabs of Palestine under Israeli occupation'.

[20] Līlī Galīlī, 'Seqer haṣḥwaʾatī ṣhel ḥōqer bĕ-ūnīversītat Ḥeyfa', *ha-Aretz*, 23 Dec. 1985, 2.

[21] Mājid al-Ḥaj, 'ha-Haṣḥlakhōt ha-pōlīṭiyyōt wĕ-ha-ḥevratiyyōt ṣhel ha-mifgaṣḥīm ha-Pàlesṭīniyyīm mi-ṣḥĕney ʿevrey ha-qaw ha-yārōq', in Arnon Soffer (ed.), *ʿEsrīm ṣhanah lĕ-milḥemet ṣḥeshet ha-yamīm* (1987), 20–89.

[22] Ian Lustick, 'Israel's Arab Minority in the Begin Era', in R. O. Freedman (ed.), *Israel in the Begin Era* (1982), 135 ff.

[23] Gideon Shīlō, *ʿArviyyey Israʾel bĕ-ʿeyney mĕdīnōt ʿArav wĕ-Aṣḥaf* (1982), ch. 3.

the state as a result of those influences, at least until the start of the *intifaḍa* in December 1987.[24] None the less, the removal of some Palestinian bases from the Lebanon in the 1982 War and the weakened position of those remaining turned the Arabs in Israel and the territories into the chief target of those wishing to strengthen PLO influence—this being one of the main reasons for the emergence in 1984 and the early electoral success of the PLP (which warmly recommended the PLO). The bitter competition between RAQAḤ/ḤADASH and the PLP to obtain PLO recognition is further evidence of PLO influence on the Arabs in Israel. Since 1967, Arab literature in Israel, also, has increasingly expressed its joy at the reunion of the Palestinian people and appealed for a joint struggle of all its segments. In Ṭaiyyba and other large population centres in Israel, various institutions for the fostering, study, and encouragement of the Palestinian heritage have been set up, and several conventions of intellectuals have been devoted to this topic.[25] In the literary domain, Communist writers and poets have set an example. Prominent among these are Emile Ḥabībī, Tawfīq Ziyād, Samīḥ al-Qāsim, with others joining in.[26] In Professor George Qanāziʿ's view, Arabic literature in Israel shows tendencies towards increasing Palestinization (in his view, at the expense of Arabism) in the identity of the Arabs in Israel.[27]

The journalist Luṭfī Mashʿūr, editor of the Nazareth weekly *al-Ṣināra*, has attempted to summarize the problems of identity perception on the eve of the *intifāḍa* and during its course. He quotes the opinion of Dr Sāmī al-Marʿī, of Haifa University, writing in 1985, as follows: 'The Arabs in Israel have completed their search for an identity, deciding that they are Palestinians (by peoplehood), Arabs (by nation), and Israelis (by citizenship)—in this order.' Mashʿūr goes on to say,

In past times, we have deceived ourselves that it is possible to balance our national appurtenance with our civic one. We have even opined that when

---

[24] Schölch (n. 14 above), 422–7.
[25] See e.g. 'Ilà al-liqāʾ fī al-muʾtamar al-qādim', *al-Ṣināra*, 17 May 1985.
[26] George Qanāziʿ, 'Yĕsōdōt ideyʾōlōgiyyīm' (Ch. 6 n. 17 above), 129 ff.
[27] Id., 'al-Hawiyya al-qawmiyya fī adabinā al-mahallī', *al-Mawākib*, 2/3–4 (Mar.–Apr. 1985), 19–20; ʿAṭallāh Manṣūr, "Aravīm, Palesṭīnaʾīm, Kĕnaʿanīm', *ha-Aretz*, 12 Jan. 1986, 9; Suhaila Haddad, R. D. McLaurin, and Emile A. Nakhleh, 'Minorities in Containment: The Arabs of Israel', in R. D. McLaurin (ed.), *The Political Role of Minority Groups in the Middle East* (1979), esp. 82–3, 107.

one of these feels 'threatened' by the other, the latter is broadened at its expense. Perhaps we have succeeded in this. However, our national belonging has always been more threatened and hence the balance was upset. Nevertheless, we have found difficult and complex formulae to maintain both loyalties together. True, we are first and foremost Palestinians, then Arabs, and only then Israelis. This has deeper and special significance, however: not a new people, but also not one of total and absolute identification with our folk, the Palestinians. We differ from them in mentality, in our perception of the future and many other issues. Our future and our fate are different.[28]

THE INTIFĀḌA AND THE STRENGTHENING OF THE PALESTINIAN CIRCLE

The *intifāḍa* (or uprising) in the Israeli-held territories, beginning in December 1987, has by and large confirmed the hypothesis of Professor Sammy Smooha, of Haifa University, that the so-called 'Green Line' still exists between the Arabs in Israel and those in the territories.[29] True enough, the Arabs in Israel have not massively joined the *intifāḍa*. However, hostile activities among them have increased substantially. According to a report in the Knesset, presented on 6 December 1989 by Ehūd Ōlmert, the Minister responsible for Arab affairs, 69 armed attacks by Arabs in Israel occurred in 1987, rising to 187 in 1989; in addition, there were 101 subversive events in 1987 and 353 in 1989. The *intifāḍa* must have hastened certain processes and given an important impetus to the Palestinization of Arabs in Israel, adding another dimension to the complexity of their identity.[30] They showed a great interest in the *intifāḍa*, felt pride in its developments, sympathized with its dead and wounded, collected money for the needy, raised PLO banners, wrote articles, stories and poems, even demonstrated and

---

[28] Luṭfī Mashʿūr, 'Palestīnaʾī, ʿAravī, Isrěʾelīʾ, *ha-Aretz*, 26 Oct. 1990, B2; Mashʿūr expressed similar views in *al-Ṣināra*, 3 Aug. 1990.

[29] Sammy Smooha, 'Hashwaʾa beyn ha-Palestīnīm ba-Shětahīm w-vě-Israʾel kěmivḥan lě-teyzat ha-sippūaḥ ha-zōhel ha-loʾ-hafīkh', in Arnon Soffer (ed.), *ʿEsrīm shanah lě-milḥemet sheshet ha-yamīm*, 37–56. Cf. Asʿad Ghānim and Sara Osetski-Lazar, 'Qaw yarōq, qawīm adūmmīm, ʿArviyyey Israʾel nōkhaḥ ha-intifāḍa', *Sěqīrōt ʿal ʿArviyey Israʾel*, 3 (May 1990), 1–23; Rekhess, 'Israeli Arabs and the Arabs of the West Bank' (n. 13 above), 148–58; Joseph Ginat, 'Israeli Arabs: Some Recent Social and Political Trends', *Asian and African Studies*, 23/2–3 (Nov. 1989), 183–204.

[30] ʿAzmī Bishāra, 'ha-Hevra ha-ʿAravīt be-Israʾel—mi-něqūdat rěʾūt aḥeret', *Mědīna, Mimshal wě-Yěhasim Beynleʾūmiyyīm*, 32 (Spring 1990), 81–6.

went on strike—but practically always within the limits of the law, ably using the legal openings available in Israeli democracy; all this is very different from what has been happening in the Israeli-held territories.[31] In East Jerusalem the intifāḍa has been proceeding as in the territories, sometimes even more intensively. In Arab localities in Israel, violent clashes occasionally occurred, for instance on the so-called Peace Day of 21 December 1987. On 21 May 1990, after seven Arabs from the territories had been shot by a mentally unbalanced young Jew in Rishōn lĕ-Zion (in Israel), not only did Arabs organize demonstrations with black banners, but some of them, masked, stoned Israeli policemen, while others blocked roads and set fire to car tyres—all on the intifāḍa pattern.[32] This identification of the Arabs in Israel is conditioned by the course of events in the Israeli-held territories as well as in Israel itself.

Thus, the solidarity of Arabs in Israel with their kinsfolk in the territories has been expressed on two levels, the emotional-ideological and the pragmatic-behavioural, the latter being low in tone in comparison with the former, that is, without any direct active involvement in the intifāḍa. The Arabs in the Israeli-held territories have expected effective participation, not just expressions of solidarity with the intifāḍa. The Arabs in Israel, for their part, are aware of these expectations, to which they do not really respond—all of which heightens the tensions in their own identity problems. It seems that one of the main consequences of the intifāḍa in Israel is the predominance of the Palestinian over the Israeli circle,[33] which, however, has not been abandoned by most

---

[31] Majid al-Haj, 'Standing on the Green Line', Israeli Democracy, Winter 1988, 39–41; Yitzhak Reiter, 'Forming their Identity', ibid. Fall 1989, esp. 33. There are varying opinions among Jewish observers regarding the degree to which the Arabs in Israel have been carried away by the intifāḍa. See examples in Maʿarīv, 1 May 1989, A7.

[32] A. Ringel-Hofman, 'ha-Intifāḍa zōḥelet la-Galīl', Yĕdīʿōt Aharōnōt, 28 July 1989, Suppl., 8–11.

[33] Z. Schiff and E. Yaari, Intifāḍa (1990), 205–21; Muḥsin Yūsuf, al-Filasṭīniyyūn fī Isrāʾīl wa-ʾl-intifāḍa (1990); ʿAmōs Gilbōʿa, 'ha-Im higgīʿa ha-intifāḍa lĕ-ʿArviyyey Israʾel', Maʿarīv, 8 June 1989, B3; Adar Avīsar and Gideon Marōn, 'Intifāḍa zōḥelet lĕ-Ṭaiyyba', Maʿarīv, 4 Apr. 1990. D1; Khālid ʿĀyid, al-Intifāḍa al-thawriyya fī Filasṭīn: al-abʿād al-dākhiliyya (1988), esp. 77–89; ʿAzīz Shahāda, 'al-Intifāḍa muḥāwala li-baḥth al-asbāb waʾ-l-taʾthīr wa-rudūd al-fiʿl', al-Mawākib, 5/1–2 (Jan.–Feb. 1988), 7–13; Munqidh al-Zuʿbī, 'Naḥnu maʿa al-intifāḍa, yā Ehūd Ōlmerṭ!', al-Ṣināra, 6 Oct. 1989; Taysīr Jabbāra, al-Intifāḍa al-shaʿbiyya al-Filasṭīniyya min al-nawāḥī al-siyāsiyya waʾ-l-iʿlāmiyya (1989), 103–25;

Arabs in Israel. Echoes of the perplexity which they have been experiencing can be recognized in an article by Dr Fārūq Muwāsī, entitled 'The Arabs in Israel—Where To?' This opens with the following passage:

We have been called, crazily, 'Israeli Arabs'. We have named ourselves 'Arabs in Israel' and, later, 'Palestinians in Israel'. Most Israelis oppose our self-rooting in Palestinianism, just as most of the Arabs whom we meet abroad refuse to let us mention Israel's name. When we say, 'We are Palestinians', they ask us, 'Why do you not start your own *intifāḍa*?' And when we say, 'We are Israeli citizens', they enquire, 'What do you care about what happens in the West Bank and the Gaza Strip?'[34]

The impact of the *intifāḍa* in strengthening the Palestinian circle among the Arabs in Israel since 1987 has been expressed, with ups and downs, not only in the number of strikes and disturbances, but also in their character. During those years, public demonstrations have become more numerous, larger, and more vociferous. Damage to roads, attack on cars, and the like, imitate the patterns of the *intifāḍa* in the Israeli-held territories. Arab leadership in Israel is divided within itself in its perceptions of identity, and attempts—not always successfully—to restrain the younger people and extremists who opt for Palestinization and perceive the PLO as their leader. Considering the fact that most of the assistance offered by the Arabs in Israel to those in the territories dates from the first four months of the *intifāḍa* and that all their attempts to put pressure on the Israeli government in the matter have failed, it is not surprising that the younger and more extreme Arabs identifying with the Palestinian circle have become more radical. Some signs of this were noticeable in the 1988 Knesset elections, then in the 1989 local ones, as shown above (in Chapter 8).

There are still signs, however, within the Israeli circle of identity, that certain Arabs prefer to integrate fully into Israeli society and state. One such testimony is an article by Asʿad Ghānim, entitled 'the Future of the Arabs in Israel Remains in Integration'

Nazīr Majallī, 'Naḥnu wa-'l-dhikrà al-thāniya li-indilāʿ al-intifāḍa', *al-Ittiḥād*, 4 Dec. 1989, 3; id., 'Hal taqūm intifāḍa Isrāʾīliyya', ibid. 8 Dec. 1989, Suppl., 6–9; special issue of *al-Mujtamaʿ*, 19/1 (Jan. 1990); Asʿad Ghānim, 'al-Intifāḍa wa-'l-ʿArab fī Isrāʾīl', *al-Aswār*, 6 (Winter 1990), 55–71.

[34] Fārūq Muwāsī, 'al-ʿArab fī Isrāʾīl ilà ayna?', *al-Nadwa*, 16 Mar. 1990, 1. Translation mine.

(that is, in conditions of full equality within a state belonging to all its citizens).[35] In contrast, in a poll conducted by the newspaper *al-Nadwa*, in August 1990 (that is, immediately after the Iraqi invasion of Kuwait), among the Arabs in Israel, including references to Ṣaddām Ḥusayn's personality, 62 per cent of the 208 interviewees replied that they supported the take-over of Kuwait, while 69 per cent responded that they perceived Ṣaddām Ḥusayn as 'a national Arab hero'.[36] By implication, this could mean that they identified both with his support for the Palestinians and his threats against Israel. Anyway, at the moment of writing there are no clear signs of the *intifāḍa* physically overflowing in any significant way to radical circles in Galilee and the Little Triangle. There is still the possibility, however, that the *intifāḍa* may act as a catalyst to cause such groups to imitate the methods used in the Israeli-held territories more closely, and indeed there are already indications of the mythologization of the heroism of the *intifāḍa*, of its martyrs, and of its stones.[37]

Some interesting bits of evidence exist as to the general mood, in at least a part of the Arab sector in Israel, and how it affects self-identification. In an interview published in March 1988, Nawāl, an Arab woman living in Tel-Aviv, said, 'It is clear to me that living side by side with you has influenced us. We speak Hebrew and there exists a measure of assimilation. However, all in all, this state does not represent us. It is not my state, nor is its flag mine. This is a sort of game which we have to play.'[38] Ilhām Abū Nimr, a woman from a Galilee village who had moved to Jerusalem, added, 'As a woman I can say that I was positively influenced by Jews, in my social status; but as a Palestinian, I cannot express myself nationalistically in this state. Consequently, I cannot define myself as an Israeli. I can explain what my being a Palestinian means; but I cannot tell even myself what my being an Israeli signifies.'[39]

Further, a 1989 survey among 508 Arab students, all Israeli citizens, at the Hebrew University of Jerusalem, concluded that a large majority (88.7 per cent) supported the establishment of a

[35] Asʿad Ghānim, 'Mustaqbal al-ʿArab fī Isrāʾīl al-indimāj faqaṭ', *al-Ṣināra*, 9 Feb. 1990, 10.

[36] *al-Nadwa*, 10 Aug. 1990.

[37] Mike Levin, 'Tĕfīsōt qitsōniyyōt qibbĕlū legīṭīmatsiyya', *ha-Ūnīversīṭa*, 5 (Winter 1991), 18–21 (interview with Dr Avraham Selaʿ).

[38] 'Sīḥa bĕ-veyt Abū Nimr', *Kōteret Raʾshīt*, 277 (23 Mar. 1988), 18.

[39] Ibid.

Palestinian state side by side with Israel, but an even greater
majority wished to continue living in Israel even after the foundation of such a state.[40] In other words, they are ready to continue to
live with the ambiguity in their self-identification. Tactically, at
least, they seem ready to live inside the Green Line, reserving their
option of joining the *intifāḍa* and using this option to speed up the
dynamics of their struggle for full civil equality in Israel—an
equality which would (so they argue) dispense them from joining
the *intifāḍa*. Hence, it becomes clearer that ideology and behaviour
are disparate among many Arabs in Israel. Ideologically, emo-
tionally, and declaratively, the Palestinian element has been
strengthened in its identity; however, behaviourally and pragmatically, the Israeli component still exists, although apparently in
retreat; it seems, indeed, that their alienation from the State of
Israel, its institutions, and Jewish society, is on the increase.[41]

THE ISLAMIC CIRCLE

Another element in the identity of the Arabs in Israel is the religious circle, which for most means Islam (Christians and Druzes
will be discussed below). Religion has been a prime Middle East
identity-maker for centuries. It is hardly surprising that Israel, set
up as a Jewish state, should encounter identification problems in its
Arab population, with their various religions, more particularly
since the legal systems of the different denominations, and separate
education, were indeed likely to sharpen the disparateness of
identity.[42] The Islamic circle is naturally much wider than the
Israeli, the Palestinian, or the Arab, and fosters a sense of belonging to hundreds of millions of believers. Yearning for this
union is one of the explanations for the deepening of religious
sentiment among Israel's Muslims and the resulting political
implications (as discussed above); all this despite the fact that most
Arabs in Israel—like the Jews—are secularly minded.[43] Increas-

[40] Report in *Yĕdīʿōt Aharōnōt*, 5 Dec. 1989, and other newspapers.
[41] J. M. Landau, 'Nikkūr w-mĕtahīm ba-hitnahagūt ha-pōlīṭīt', in A. Layish
(ed.), *ha-ʿAravīm bĕ-Israʾel* (1981), 197–212.
[42] W. M. Brinner, 'The Arabs of Israel: The Past Twenty Years', *Middle East
Review*, 20/1 (Fall 1987), esp. 15.
[43] Mark Tessler, 'Secularism and Nationalism in the Israeli–Palestinian Conflict',
UFSI Reports, 9 (1982), Asia, pp. 1–12.

ingly close relations between Muslim leaders in the Israeli-held territories and in Israel have affected the politicization of the latter. In this process, the intense Islamic life manifested in the territories and the establishment of political organizations by Islamic zealots (al-Ḥamās, Muslim Brethren, al-Jihād al-Islāmī, and others) also had considerable influence. The contents and tone of Muslim activism in Israel are no less nationalistic than those of their peers in the West Bank and the Gaza Strip, and both are pervaded by an ardent belief in Islam. Identification with Islam, on the nationalist level, created a sort of nationalist Islam, based on more extreme political premises than those of other nationalist Arab leaders in Israel, some of whom have been declaring—within Arab and Palestinian circles—that they strive for a Palestinian State side by side with Israel; while Islamic zealots have unwaveringly demanded a Muslim state in the entire area of Western Palestine, as part of a Muslim state in the whole of the Middle East, and later of global dimensions. Some of them have pointed out that, at least in Iran, the notion of an Islamic state has proved feasible.

The Islamic Movement in Israel struggles against what it perceives as the over-intervention of the Jewish state in the affairs of Muslim institutions, on the one hand, and against secularism among Muslims, on the other. To strengthen the impact of the Islamic circle, spokesmen of the Islamic Movement take steps such as preaching for a return to Islam, appealing for political activism, and calling for increased awareness of the significance of Islam and for the preservation of its innate rights. According to reports in the Movement's weekly, *al-Ṣirāṭ*, the preachers move about from place to place and intensify the consciousness of Islamic identity, meanwhile attacking secularism. Their perception is that a religious war is being waged between orthodox Muslims and Jews in the Israeli-held territories; naturally, this approach bears both on the future of their movement and on the situation in Israel.[44] Indeed, there are Arabs in Israel who, disappointed by the lack of any effective assistance from the Arab states, trust that belief in Allah and Islam—which would not accept the existence of the Jewish state—might help them materially.[45] When in demonstrations activists of

---

[44] ʿAṭallāh Manṣūr, 'Milḥemet ha-těnūʿa ha-Islāmīt ba-ḥilōniyyūt', *ha-Aretz*, 5 May 1983.

[45] ʿAmōs Gilbōʿa, 'Eyn ʿArviyyey Israʾel; yesh Palesṭīnīm', *Maʿarīv*, 25 May 1990, B1.

the Islamic Movement raise green banners (the colour of Islam), side by side with others who wave PLO flags, the Palestinian and Islamic circles are joined.

Luṭfī Mashʿūr has suggested that two approaches may be found among Muslims in Israel concerning their understanding of their Islamic identity. The first holds that the innermost circle is Palestinian, surrounded by an Arab one, which again is encircled by the largest, the Islamic. A second view has it that Islam is the core of the issue and the decisive identity circle in any case.[46] The latter interpretation is preferred by Sheikh ʿAbdallāh Nimr Darwīsh, of Kafr Qāsim, a prominent leader of the Islamic Movement and the editor of *al-Ṣirāṭ*. Avoiding militant slogans, Darwīsh maintains that once upon a time he would have defined himself as Arab-Israeli-Palestinian, but now he prefers to be Muslim-Palestinian-Israeli, in this order and without acknowledging any conflict among the various identities.[47] According to Darwīsh, the Islamic circle is the most important one in defining identity, since it provides both a grass-roots basis and strategic depth; it is a stage on which many peoples and states play a part, with the Islamic Movement in Israel being one component of the world Islamic Movement.[48]

The Bedouin,[49] all Muslims, have been experiencing a serious identity crisis, originating in their passing from nomadism and pasturing to sedentarization in townlets with the resulting occupational changes. This is a group generally loyal to the state and ready to integrate into the Israeli circle of identity, so much so that a number of Bedouin have volunteered for service in the Defence Forces (160 in 1990).[50] However, certain Bedouin have adopted the Arab and Palestinian circles, in response to increasing modernization and better education, as well as discontent with sedentarization, changes in life patterns, and expropriation of land. The participation of Bedouin youths in religious seminars held in Galilee or the Little Triangle hastened their politicization and their

[46] Luṭfī Mashʿūr, 'al-Jamāhīr al-ʿArabiyya ḥasamat hawiyyatahā al-Filasṭīniyya allatī saqqalathā al-intifāḍa', *al-Ṣināra*, 3 Aug. 1990.

[47] 'Anaḥnū lōʾ jihād Islāmī', *Kōteret Raʾshīt*, 277 (23 Mar. 1988), 20–3.

[48] Ibrāhīm Mālik, 'al-Bunya al-ijtimāʿiyya' (Ch. 4 n. 12 above), 3–4.

[49] Liora Moriel, 'Negev Bedouin: Don't Separate Us from Other Israeli Arabs', *Jerusalem Post*, 25 Oct. 1985, 3.

[50] Acc. to *al-Ittiḥād*, 9 Aug. 1991, quoted by *Arabs in Israel*, 1/18 (25 Aug. 1991), 2.

growing integration into the Islamic circle—not instead of, but rather in addition to, the other circles, in varying proportions. The events of the *intifāḍa* left their mark also on the Bedouin, who, in quite a few cases, erected blocks on roads, threw stones, damaged Israeli cars, burned Israeli flags, and raised the PLO ones instead; there were also some instances of more aggressive attacks. In their voting for the Knesset, too, the Bedouins' support for Jewish parties diminished, as part of a process in the entire Arab sector in Israel.

THE CHRISTIAN CIRCLE

Identification is much less definite within the Christian circle, perhaps because Christian Arabs comprise a mosaic of denominations, so that many of them feel that their identity is Greek Orthodox, Greek Catholic, and so on, not merely Christian. True, the ecumenical spirit fostered by important Christian communities world-wide has already led some to consider themselves as Christians, first and foremost. The Christian-Arab press, also, does not offer hard answers regarding questions of identity. Neither do such answers emerge from the bulletin published by the Ministry of Religious Affairs,[51] which has tended to emphasize the points that Christians in Israel have in common with the state. So far as their own national identity is concerned, empirical research indicates that Christians in Israel identify themselves as Arabs, while Muslims incline to see themselves as Palestinians.[52] In addition, the process of Arab identification influences the call for indigenization, that is, the demand of various Christian groups throughout the Middle East that all holders of church positions should be local people, that is, Arabs and not foreigners such as Greeks and Italians. In this context, a cleavage is noticeable between various parts of the Christian community: an increasing number of locally born church dignitaries have deviated from traditional policies of political non-involvement, and have responded directly to the expectations of many members of their respective congregations, including the more politicized and

---

[51] *Christian News from Israel*, published in Jerusalem.
[52] Yochanan Hofman, *Dīmmuyīm wĕ-zehūt shel nō'ar 'Aravī bĕ-Isra'el* (1977), 20 ff; Lustick, 'Israel's Arab Minority' (n. 22 above), 135.

radicalized. None the less, various Christians perceive their identity in different ways, sometimes attempting to 'insure' themselves in a geographical area permeated by strong Arab nationalism; this is all the more applicable to many of their expressed attitudes in Israel and the Israeli-held territories. One example of these attitudes was given by that Christian Arab in Israel who defined himself (in this order) Palestinian, Arab, Christian, and citizen of Israel.[53] Other Christians, of course, might have listed their circles of identification in a different order.

THE DRUZE CIRCLE

Muslims in Israel are attracted, not just to their own religious circle, but to the Palestinian; likewise the Christians to the Arab circle. In the same way for numerous years the Druze have inclined, outside their own Druze circle, to the Israeli one, their men serving with distinction in Israel's Defence Forces.[54] More recently, matters have changed somewhat, again owing to modernization and education as well as feelings of economic and social discrimination. I have already discussed two Druze organizations set up in the 1970s—the pro-Israeli Zionist Druze circle and the RAQAH/HADASH-inspired Druze Initiative Committee,[55] close to Arab and Palestinian groups. Both enjoy a limited adherence,[56] but are symptomatic of the identity crisis within the Druze community, with Druzism, Arabism, and Israelism sharply competing with one another.[57] This situation was taken into consideration by the Ministry of Education and Culture when preparing a curriculum for Druze schools, largely orientated towards their own

[53] Julia Slater, 'Palestinians in Israel: Who are They?', *Middle East International*, 329 (8 July 1988), 16–17.
[54] Qays Farw, 'Hawiyyat al-Durūz—naẓra ta'rīkhiyya', in Salmān Fallāḥ (ed.), *al-Durūz fī Isrā'īl* (1989), 49–60; Oppenheimer, 'ha-Dĕrūzīm bĕ-Isra'el' (Ch. 3 n. 36 above); Sharīf Abū Rukn, 'Shĕ'ela shel zehūt', *al-Hudà*, Feb. 1976, 39–40; Yĕhūda Olīva, 'ha-Dĕrūzīm bĕ-Isra'el—be'ayat zehūt 'atsmīt we-hishtayykhūt pōlīṭīt', *Mĕdīna w-Mimshal*, 2/1 (1972), 98–109; Ela Barqat, 'ha-Dĕrūzīm bĕ-Isra'el: shĕ'ela shel zehūt', *ha-Aretz*, 8 Oct. 1976, Suppl., 12–13.
[55] *Arabs in Israel*, 1/5 (6 Jan. 1991), 2.
[56] Shakīb Ṣāliḥ, *Tōlĕdōt ha-Dĕrūzīm* (1989), 251. Cf. McLaurin (ed.), *Political Role of Minority Groups* (1979), 94–6.
[57] Salmān Nāṭūr, 'al-Durūz fī Isrā'īl', in Khālid Khalīfa (ed.), *Filasṭīniyyūn 1948–1988* (1988), 164–76. The writer is a member of the Druze Initiative Committee.

heritage (as discussed above, in Chapter 5).[58] This decision has encouraged the separate identity awareness of the Druzes, as distinct from the Arabs.

From the vantage-point of their secular culture, language, and socio-economic conditions, the Druzes are close to the Arab minority in Israel and by and large form a part of it; however, from that of their legal, political, and military status, their situation is ambiguous. Events in the Israeli-held territories (where, indeed, no Druzes live), and the *intifāḍa*, attract them to the Arab circle (and lately to the Palestinian one as well, apparently). The 1982 War in Lebanon (where there is a large Druze community) disconcerted the Druzes in Israel and rendered their identity problems even more acute. Leaders of the Druzes in Syria have been urging their kinsmen in Israel—chiefly on the Golan Heights—to adopt anti-Israeli attitudes. At times, they have been quite successful in this. An example may be found in a book by Usāma Ḥalabī (born in Dāliyat al-Karmil in 1959), a Druze lawyer. His work, entitled *The Druzes in Israel: From A Denomination to A People?*, was published in Arabic in 1989 by the Association of University Graduates on the Golan Heights.[59] The entire work consists of an attack on the State of Israel and its authorities, which are accused, on the one hand, of discrimination against the Druzes, and, on the other, of attempting to fashion a separate identity for them, different from their natural Arab one.

All this said and done, one should remember, however, that for many generations the Druzes have been accustomed to behave loyally towards the authorities in every land of their diaspora, and lately in Israel as well. Still, some of the identity dilemmas that face them are also expressed in their voting in various Knesset elections, where their support is no longer offered to Jewish parties only, but also to RAQAḤ/ḤADA<u>SH</u>, in patterns which are as yet fluid.

ARAB–JEWISH RELATIONS IN ISRAEL

Much has been said and written about the complex relationships between Arabs and Jews in the State of Israel.[60] A large part of this

---

[58] Shakīb Sāliḥ, *Tōlĕdōt ha-Dĕrūzīm*, 232–3.
[59] Usāma Ḥalabī, *al-Durūz fī Isrā'īl: min ṭā'ifa ilà sha'b?* (1989).
[60] The most recent study of these issues seems to be Smooha's *Arabs and Jews in Israel*, i (1989).

is controversial, chiefly because the two sides comprise elements that exhibit different stages of readiness to accept or reject others, and to struggle with stereotypes and prejudices.[61] The topic will be discussed briefly in this chapter, mainly in an attempt to see how these relationships have influenced the various identity circles of the minorities in Israel,[62] paying due attention to the asymmetry usually innate in majority–minority relations and to the conflictual relationship between the two in Israel.[63]

The fact that Israeli Cabinets have not perceived the problems of the minorities as a primary issue, but rather as a secondary one,[64] has frequently caused postponement in dealing with matters that irritated the Arabs and the Druzes, apparently on the assumption that such problems would somehow solve themselves. The view expressed by certain authors, such as Ṣabrī Jiryis, Ian Lustick, and Sammy Smooha, that successive Israeli governments have concocted a well-planned policy of suppressing[65] and controlling[66] the Arabs in Israel can hardly be considered as anchored in reality. There is no proof, anyway, that a policy of control, intended to keep the Arabs in a lowly position—economically, educationally, or politically—was ever adopted and carried out. On the contrary, not

[61] Edward Robins, 'Attitudes, Stereotypes, and Prejudices among Arabs and Jews in Israel', *New Outlook*, 15/136 (Nov.–Dec. 1972), 36–48.

[62] Peres, *Yaḥasey ʿedōt bĕ-Isra'el* (n. 1 above), 56–76, 91–6; Sammy Smooha, 'A Typology of Jewish Orientations toward the Arab Minority in Israel', *Asian and African Studies*, 23/2–3 (Nov. 1989), 155–82; id., *Orientation and Politicization* (n. 13 above) part i.

[63] Sami Khalil Marʿi, 'Sources of Conflict in Arab–Jewish Relations in Israel', in John E. Hofman *et al.*, *Arab–Jewish Relations in Israel* (1988), 1–20; Ofira Seliktar, 'National Integration of a Minority in an Acute Conflict Situation: The Case of Israeli Arabs', *Plural Societies*, 12/3–4 (Autumn–Winter 1981), 25–40; Don Peretz, 'Israeli Jews and Arabs in the Ethnic Numbers Game', *Ethnicity*, 8 (1981), 233–55; Sammy Smooha and Don Peretz, 'The Arabs in Israel', *Journal of Conflict Resolution*, 26/3 (Sept. 1982), 451–84.

[64] Sammy Smooha, 'Mĕdiniyyūt qayyemet wĕ-alternaṭīvīt kĕlappey ha-ʿAravīm bĕ-Isra'el', *Mĕgammōt*, 26/1 (Sept. 1980), 12–14. See, however, Amnon Rubinstein, "ʿArviyyey Isra'el: gīsha mĕtsī'ūtīt', *Kalkala wĕ-Ḥevra*, June 1966, 29–31.

[65] Ṣabrī Jiryis, *ha-ʿAravīm bĕ-Isra'el* (1966).

[66] Ian Lustick, *Arabs in the Jewish State* (1980). Even Lustick acknowledges, however, that, at least in the early years of the state, government policy was absent in important domains. See his 'Zionism and the State of Israel: Regime Objectives of the Arab Minority in the First Years of Statehood', *Middle Eastern Studies*, 16/1 (Jan. 1980), 127–46. Cf. Sammy Smooha, 'Control of Minorities in Israel and Northern Ireland', *Comparative Studies in History and Society*, 22/2 (Apr. 1980), 256–80; Ofira Seliktar, 'The Arabs in Israel: Some Observations on the Psychology of the System of Controls', *Journal of Conflict Resolution*, 28/2 (June 1984), 247–69.

one Cabinet meeting is known to have been devoted to reaching practical decisions regarding the Arabs in Israel.[67] On 23 May 1976, indeed, the Cabinet debated the trends then evident in the Arab sector and decided to encourage its full integration into public life, while recognizing its special religious and cultural characteristics. Three new bodies were set up as a result: (1) a ministerial-level committee, presided over by the Prime Minister, to co-ordinate the relevant activities of the government offices; (2) a committee of director-generals of ministries, headed by the Prime Minister's Adviser for Arab Affairs, to implement the decisions of the ministerial-level committee; and (3) a Public Board, made up of Jews and Arabs, to advise the two committees and recommend courses of action. On 4 August 1976, two and a half months after the Cabinet decision, the Public Board was nominated, with forty Arab and forty Jewish members, and the Prime Minister as its president. The committee of director-generals was appointed only on 29 May 1985 (that is, nine years later!). So far as is known, none of the three bodies has achieved anything, if indeed they met at all. Another two years later, on 21 April 1987, the Cabinet resolved unanimously 'to advance the Druze and Circassian population in order to ensure their equality in both theory and practice', listing incentives for industry, education, vocational guidance, and welfare services, and proposing increased development budgets. Even in such an important matter as bringing the budgets allocated to Arab local authorities up to the level of the Jewish ones, a decision was reached not in a regular Cabinet meeting, but by a telephone poll of all the ministers, on 26 August 1991.

It may safely be said that official policy towards the Arabs in Israel has been non-policy. While most of the officials who have served as Advisers for Arab affairs to the Prime Minister performed their duties conscientiously, their main brief was to co-ordinate the relevant functions dispersed among the various ministers (the Advisers have no powers or budgets of their own) rather than to decide on policies or implement them.[68] Various public and other

---

[67] A Cabinet meeting, on 29 July 1973, ended without any practical decisions being taken. Another, in 1986, did not complete its discussion in the matter and reached no conclusions.

[68] Sh. Toledano, 'Israel's Arabs—A Unique National Minority', *International Problems*, 12/23 (June 1973), 39–43; ʿAṭallāh Manṣūr, 'Memshelet Peres—sikkūm', *ha-Aretz*, 19 Oct. 1986, 3; Giōra Eylōn, 'Le-mī ikhpat she-hithallef yōʿets rōʾsh ha-memshala lĕ-ʿinyĕnei ʿAravīm', *Yĕdīʿōt Aharōnōt*, 16 Nov. 1990, 23–4.

committees were set up, but either they did not meet at all, or their recommendations were mostly ignored. It seems that the civil administration's main perception of its role was to deal with problems as they arose, often without consulting anybody else. In consequence, much of the regularization of relations between the Arab and Jewish sectors has been left to non-governmental bodies, such as the Histadrut, political parties, and others, and to the inhabitants themselves.[69]

Certain other Israeli institutions are closely concerned with Jewish–Arab relations and are active in attempting to improve them. Among the more prominent are the Jewish–Arab Centre at the Givʿat Havīva kibbutz (of MAPAM), the Jewish–Arab Centre at Beyt Berl in Tsōfīt (ILO), the Harry S Truman Institute for Peace Research at the Hebrew University of Jerusalem, the Van Leer Institute in Jerusalem, the Jewish–Arab Centre at Haifa University, the Moshe Dayyan Centre at Tel-Aviv University, and others. In addition to the meetings they organize, these bodies publish various works in this area, to some of which I have alluded. For instance, in 1988 the Van Leer Institute prepared a study in Hebrew, entitled *The Arabs, Citizens of Israel*, which was adopted by the Ministry of Education and Culture as a textbook in teaching civics in the higher grades of Jewish secondary schools.

Further, public figures have, time and again, taken a personal initiative by proposing overall policy guidelines for the Arab sector—with their well-meant proposals usually remaining fruitless. Among these were Mōshe Qōl, then Minister of Tourism, in 1976;[70] MK Amnōn Līn, in 1980; and MK Raʿanan Cohen, who in 1989 wrote and widely distributed an interesting pamphlet in Hebrew, entitled *A New Approach to Israel's Arabs: Policy Guidelines*.[71] The heterogeneous approach of the system in establishing norms in this area has left its mark on the minorities' feelings of identity, chiefly in their attitudes towards the Israeli circle. I do not intend to survey the entire network of Jewish–Arab

---

[69] An example: a Jewish and an Arab girl, residing together in the students' dormitories of the Hebrew University of Jerusalem. For this rare case, see Avītal Elqayyam, 'Ḥeder qĕtsat aḥer', *Pī ha-Atōn*, 31/4 (Jan. 1989), 7. For another example, an attempt to organize a joint forum of both Jewish and Arab heads of local authorities in Galilee, cf. ʿAṭallāh Manṣūr, 'Daf ḥadash ba-Galīl', *ha-Aretz*, 5 Oct. 1989, 11.

[70] Mōshe Qōl, 'Pĕraqīm mi-yōman mĕdīnī', *Tĕmūrōt*, 9 (June 1976), 3–4.

[71] Raʿanan Cohen, *Gīsha ḥadasha lĕ-ʿArviyyey Israʾel: Qawey mĕdīniyyūt* (1989).

relations in Israel, but rather to point out several aspects which may have a bearing on Arab identity.

Conceptually, relations are much affected by mutual stereotypes—those relatively simple images which attribute certain characteristics to entire groups of people, whether ethnic, religious, or social. Many of the generalizations employing stereotypes derive from prejudice. Both before and after the establishment of the State of Israel, many people thought and still think in categories of generalizations, frequently as 'we' and 'them'. This is reflected in language as well: in Israeli Hebrew, the term 'Arab' has several pejorative connotations.[72] Even though not every Jew, nor every Arab, has adopted the sum total of stereotypes in use, they have influenced perceptions of identity of the opposite side and, by way of response, self-identity as well. Again, many—possibly most—stereotypes are pejorative, as is obvious from both Hebrew and Arab-Israeli literature. A recent book by Professor Gila Ramras-Rauch, of Boston,[73] has demonstrated the frequency of such stereotypes in Israeli Hebrew literature since 1948—and Arabs who write in Hebrew are included in the analysis. She concludes that the image of the Arabs in Israeli Hebrew literature is complex.

Should one examine the image of the Israeli Jew in Arabic literature written in Israel, one would find in it, too, that Jews are often perceived in pejorative stereotypes—as arrogant, uncouth, and responsible for all Arab misfortunes. This is also often the Jewish image in Arabic dailies and periodicals, which reach a wider readership; sometimes general radio and television programmes, owing to the brief time allotted, are pushed to employ generalizations based on stereotypes. It is difficult to avoid the strong emphasis, in both literatures, on the negative characteristics of the other side. Besides, literature and the press do not merely reflect attitudes; they frequently shape public opinion. It is likely that a part of what is written—probably, a large part—reflects everyday relations, both public and private, between the two sectors. The tendency of many groups all over the world to attribute positive features to themselves and negative ones to others applies here as well.[74] This affects relations between Jews and Arabs, with

---

[72] Examples in D. Rubinstein's 'Kĕvar lŏ' maḵhnīsīm ōrḥīm', *ha-Aretz*, 7 Sept. 1990, B5.

[73] Gila Ramras-Rauch, *The Arab in Israeli Literature* (1989).

[74] Aharōn Bīzman and Yĕhūda Amīr, 'Dīmmūyīm lĕ'ūmiyyīm hadadiyyīm shel

the entire system involved being influenced by political, social, economic, and cultural tendencies. Although much has been written on Jewish–Arab relations in Israel, only a part is based on research.[75] However, one can learn something from impressionistic reports. The ethnocentrism characterizing both sectors, constrained by their rival objectives, has a clear impact on interpersonal relations, which occur chiefly at work and, to a lesser extent, in education, as in joint courses for Hebrew and Arabic in the Centre for Adult Education at the Hebrew University of Jerusalem.[76] Non-structured meetings outside working and business hours, based on personal friendship, are still an exception,[77] a situation which seems to breed mutual suspicion and alienation,[78] at least in extreme cases. Seldom are relations equal, spontaneous, and intimate; more often they are authoritarian.[79] The conditions which prompted the Van Leer Institute to prepare and publish, in 1985, a pamphlet in Hebrew by Alouph Hareven, entitled *How to Deal with Questions Regarding*

Yĕhūdīm wa-ʿAravīm bĕ-Israʾel', *Mĕgammōt*, 28/1 (June 1983), 100–5; Sammy Smooha, 'Jewish and Arab Ethnocentrism in Israel', *Ethnic and Racial Studies*, 10/1 (Jan. 1987), 1–26.

[75] Yochanan Hofman (ed.), *Kenes ʿal matsav ha-mehqar bĕ-nōseʾ yahasey enōsh beyn ʿAravīm lĕ-Yĕhūdīm* (1971); H. M. Rosen, *ha-Yĕhasim beyn Yĕhūdīm la-ʿAravīm bĕ-Israʾel wĕ-ha-irgūnīm ha-tsibbūriyyīm ha-shōqdīm ʿal ṭippūham* (1971); Mina Tsemaḥ, *ʿEmdōt ha-rōv ha-Yĕhūdī bĕ-Israʾel kĕlappey ha-mīʿūt ha-ʿAravī* (1980); M. A. Seligson and Dan Caspi, 'Iyyūm, mōtsaʾ ʿadatī wĕ-haskala', *Kiwwūnīm*, 15 (May 1982), 37–53; John Hofman *et al.*, *Arab–Jewish Relations* (1988); Ernest Stock, *From Conflict to Understanding: Relations between Jews and Arabs in Israel since 1948* (1968); Baheej Khleif *et al.*, 'The Arab–Israeli Encounter', *Sociologia Internationalis*, 9 (1971), 167–78; E. A. Robins, 'Pluralism in Israel: Relations between Arabs and Jews', Ph.D. dissertation, Tulane University, 1972; Shmuel Toledano, *Jewish–Arab Relations during the Yom Kippur War* (1974); Sammy Smooha and J. E. Hofman, 'Some Problems of Arab–Jewish Coexistence in Israel', *Middle East Review*, 9/2 (Winter 1976–7), 5–14; J. J. Zogby, *Perspectives on Palestinian Arabs and Israeli Jews* (1977); Franz Ansprenger, *Juden und Araber in Einem Land* (1978).

[76] Qalman Yarōn and Ōra Grabelskī (eds.), *ha-Mifgash ha-hevratī-tarbūtī beyn Yĕhūdīm wĕ-ʿAravīm bĕ-ʿiqvōt sympōziōn* (1968); *Aḥawa bit̄ʾōn talmīdey ha-ūlpan ha-ʿIvrī-ʿAravī* (1971).

[77] 'It is absurd that there are Jews in Israel who have already hosted at their homes guests from Egypt even before they invited there even one Israeli Arab.' Review of Alouph Hareven, *Eḥad mi-kol shishsha Isrĕʾelīm wĕ-anaḥnū, Maʿarīv*, 11 Dec. 1980, 5.

[78] Qāsim Zayd, 'Hasīrū et ha-tawīt', *ha-Aretz*, 25 July 1971, B4.

[79] Sammy Smooha, "ʿAravīm wĕ-Yĕhūdīm bĕ-Israʾel—yahasey mīʿūṭ wĕ-rōv', *Mĕgammōt*, 22 (Sept. 1976), 397–423; Avraham Peleg, 'ha-Im atta mūkhan lĕhityadded ʿim ʿAravī?', *Maʿarīv*, 3 Sept. 1971, 16.

Jewish–Arab and Israeli–Arab Relations, and Democracy,[80] indicate the need to do away with mutual suspicion and the resulting anxieties. Jerusalem, reunited since 1967, may serve as an example of the situation. Physical and administrative union exists, but daily relations between Jews and Arabs are largely dictated by political considerations. Most contacts are made, therefore, in the domains of employment and commerce, few in the cultural and social ones, with economic connections occupying a grey area in between, also beating a retreat since the start of the *intifāda,*[81] together with an increase in the suspicion pointed out by Hareven.

However, among the few places in which more frequent mutual contacts exist, in addition to Galilee[82] and, sometimes, the Little Triangle,[83] there are still the mixed towns.[84] In these, certain groups lead their own particular ways of life, Arab or Jewish, while others, especially amongst the Arabs, have their own transitional life patterns—chiefly among the younger people and during their free time. Contributions have been made by certain cultural institutions which strive to bring Arabs and Jews together, such as Beyt ha-Gefen in Haifa, Beyt-Qedem in Acre, the Nazareth Peace Centre,[85] and others, founded by various voluntary associations. It is natural that political and economic relations influence social and personal ones and are also influenced by them. Thus, in

---

[80] This refers to the revised experimental edition, edited by A. Hareven and entitled in Hebrew *ma lĕ-hashīv*.

[81] Michael Romann, *Yaḥasey ha-gōmĕlīn beyn ha-migzar ha-Yĕhūdī wĕ-ha-ʿAravī bĕ-Yĕrūshalayim* (1984).

[82] ʿAmōs Ayyalōn, 'Galīl shel ʿAravīm wĕ-Yĕhūdīm', *ha-Aretz*, 30 Nov. 1979, 2–3 Dec. 1979.

[83] Etty Hasīd, 'Īdīliyya bĕ-Tīra', ibid. 21 Dec. 1990, Suppl., 17.

[84] For the relations in the mixed towns, see, *inter alia*: Arnon Soffer *et al.*, *Leqeṭ bibliyōgrafī*; *shĕkhūnōt mĕʿōravōt shel Yĕhūdīm wĕ-ʿAravīm bĕ-Isra'el* (1988); Ilan Shĕhōrī, "Arviyyey Yafō 1981: hitˀargĕnūt lĕˀūmanīt', *ha-Aretz*, 28 May 1981, 1; D. Rubinstein, 'Noṣrat liqrāt tĕlat-qiyyūm', ibid. 29 Nov. 1990, 2; *al-Ṣināra*, 9 Sept. 1983, comprises several articles on crises between neighbours in Nazareth. Erik Cohen, *Integration vs. Separation in the Planning of a Mixed Jewish–Arab City in Israel* (1973); Gerald Caplan, *Arab and Jew in Jerusalem* (1980); Michael Romann, 'Jews and Arabs in Jerusalem', *Jerusalem Quarterly*, 19 (Spring 1981), 23–46; David Rudge, 'Close Encounters of Another Kind', *Jerusalem Post Magazine*, 20 Oct. 1988, 8.

[85] D. Rabīnōvīts, 'Ḥalōm shel shĕnayim ʿal tselaʿ ha-har', *ha-Aretz*, 9 Aug. 1991, B2; Ernest Stock, 'Israel—A Jewish Polity with a Multi-Ethnic Population', *Patterns of Prejudice*, 15/4 (1981), 34–41; Helen Kaye, 'Beit Hagefen's 25 Years of Activity', *Jerusalem Post*, 18 Jan. 1991, 11.

Jerusalem,[86] tensions are felt between the two sectors; the municipality has been striving constantly to encourage coexistence (and, in
so far as feasible, a dialogue) between both. In Acre, there is
competition for the limited resources available, but in the Wolfsohn
Quarter, in the new part of the town, Jews and Arabs inhabit the
same neighbourhood, occasional tension notwithstanding.[87] In the
mixed towns with a sizeable Jewish majority, Jews regularly dictate
relationships, but in the combined area of Nazareth and Upper
Nazareth, in which they form a minority, they appear afraid of
being swallowed up in an Arab majority.[88] A study of Knesset
elections, carried out by MK Dr Raʿanan Cohen, comes to the
conclusion that Arabs inhabiting the mixed towns tend to be more
strongly nationalist than others.[89] Arabs in those towns have
protested against what they consider as arrogant behaviour by the
Jews,[90] while Jews in those same localities have been known to
express their apprehension lest the growing number of Arabs turn
them into a majority, as for instance in Ramleh.[91]

THE IDENTITY STRUGGLE

Summing up, a struggle has been going on, consciously or not,
since the establishment of the state, towards determining the

---

[86] For the relevant statistics, see Ziva Wainshal and Dafna Pelli (eds.),
Yĕrūshalayim nĕtūnīm statīstiyyīm (1983); Shimon Bigelman (ed.), *Shĕnatōn statīstī
lĕ-Yĕrūshalayim*, 6 (1987). Further details in Gideon Weigert's *Israel's Presence in
East Jerusalem* (1973).

[87] ʿAmalya Argaman-Barneʿa, 'Yaḥasey shĕkhenūt bi-shĕkhūna mĕʿōrevet',
Yĕdīʿōt Aharōnōt, 20 Oct. 1982, 23. During the 1991 Gulf War, young Arab people
in Acre offered to visit lonely elderly Jews and to help them, see *ha-Aretz*, 21 Jan.
1991, A6.

[88] Matityahū Peled, 'Maʿamad ha-mīʿūt ha-ʿAravī bĕ-Israʾel', *Maʿarīv*, 1 Aug.
1975, 20; Mazzal Muʿallim, 'Noṣrat—Mĕnassīm lĕhatsīl et ha-dū-qiyyūm', ibid. 25
May 1990, B2; A. Ringel-Hofman, 'Be-Noṣrat ʿĪllīt mĕdabbĕrīm, ʿal kĕvīsh ʿōqef
Noṣrat', *Yĕdīʿōt Aharōnōt*, 19 Oct. 1990, 12–13; 'al-Taʿāyush al-Yahūdī—al-ʿArabī
yaḥtall makān al-ṣadāra fī al-nadwa al-ṣuḥufiyya fī al-Nāṣira', *Kull al-ʿArab*, 30 Oct.
1990, 8.

[89] 'Dōqṭōr Cohen wĕ-ʿArviyyey Israʾel', *ha-Aretz*, 3 Aug. 1990. B3.

[90] e.g. Aḥmad Darwīsh, 'Marra ukhrà maʿa al-yasār al-Ṣahyūnī', *al-Ṣināra*, 24
Aug. 1990.

[91] Aḥmad al-Tawrī, 'Raʾīs al-baladiyya qaliqa min tazāyud al-sukkān al-ʿArab',
Kull al-ʿArab, 5 Oct. 1990, 10. On the feelings of being threatened, in both sectors,
see Michal Shamir and J. L. Sullivan, 'Jews and Arabs in Israel', *Journal of Conflict
Resolution* 29/2 (June 1985), 283–305.

identity of the Arabs living in it. During the first nineteen years, new realities created conditions for the Israeli circle (to continue to use this analogy) to penetrate. However, in those years mutual stereotypical perceptions grew in both sectors, owing to continued more or less voluntary separation in residence, education, and business. Readiness to enter into mutual personal relationships was slight and has apparently even decreased since 1967.[92] Before that date, external propaganda encouraging people to identify themselves as Arabs influenced them only peripherally, as in the case of groups like al-Arḍ. After 1967, however, the Palestinian circle exercised increasing impact on identity, largely owing to renewed relations with kinsfolk in the Israeli-held territories. Not-a few Arabs in Israel have complained of being perceived as Arabs by the Jews, and as Jews by neighbouring Arabs.[93] In 1987, this was characteristically expressed by ʿĀdil Mannāʿ, then a lecturer in Middle Eastern history at the Hebrew University in Jerusalem and now at Bīr-Zeyt University in the West Bank, as follows: '[I am] a Palestinian, a citizen of Israel.'[94] It is no accident that some Arab homes maintain two living-rooms, one furnished traditionally in Arab style and the other in more modern, Jewish.[95]

The reinforcement of the Palestinian circle in the identity of the Arabs in Israel, together with diminution of the Israeli one, to some extent due to the non-resolution of their problems by the authorities and the aloofness of Jewish society, as well as to the impact of Arab and Palestinian propaganda, have brought about increasing alienation. This was expressed by ʿUmar ʿUthmān, the principal of the school at Abū Ghōsh, near Jerusalem, as early as 1972, as follows: 'I am not against the state: I believe in it. However, the state has failed to let the Arab feel that he is part of it.'[96] Fifteen years later, another Arab, Nādir Qadrī, from Shafā ʿAmr, put this more pungently: 'Being an Arab in Israel means feeling that one is a stranger in one's own country.'[97] Most important, of course, is the younger Arabs' and Druzes' perception

[92] J. E. Hofman, 'Social Identity and the Readiness for Social Relations Between Jews and Arabs in Israel', *Human Relations*, 35/9 (1982), 727–41.

[93] Linda Gradstein, 'Just a little In-Between', *Jerusalem Post*, 15 July 1987, 5.

[94] In an interview with Ran Kislev, reported in his *Hem wĕ-anaḥnū: ʿAravīm bĕ-Israʾel* (1987), 6.

[95] Ibid. 8.

[96] *Maʿarīv*, 25 Dec. 1972, quoted by Mōshe Gabbay (n. 1 above), 25.

[97] 'All We Want Is to Be Treated As Equals', *Jerusalem Post*, 26 June 1987, 5.

of their own identity—since it is they who, in due course, will determine relations with the state and its Jewish inhabitants. In sample interviews, held in 1989 with twenty-four of these young people, most saw themselves as Palestinian Arabs, living in Israel; even those who declared their Israelism, mentioned it only at the end of the list of their identity circles.[98]

Such feelings of deep alienation from the state and its Jewish society seem to prevail among at least a part of the Arabs in Israel, and are probably at the basis of their frequently emotional and distrustful reactions towards the state authorities. Thus when in 1976 the Koenig Report (mentioned above, in Chapter 8), recommending harsh measures against the Arabs in Israel, was leaked to the press, a wave of fury swept the Arabs—although Prime Minister Rabin rejected the report and would have nothing to do with it.[99] In addition, a certain parallelism exists in that, side by side with sharp Arab reactions, similar ones are noticeable in the Jewish sector. Every violent event or utterance, on either side, adds a drop to the cup of hostility.

I have discussed the reduction in the Israeli circle and the strengthening of the Arab and even more the Palestinian and Islamic ones in the identity perceptions of many Arabs in Israel. The subject has not been determined statistically, and satisfactory quantitative analysis is probably impossible. Empirical investigations have not agreed in their conclusions. So far as can be ascertained at this stage, the Israeli circle still seems significant in the identity perceptions of the Arabs in Israel; probably more among the Druzes, certainly much less, if at all, in East Jerusalem.[100] However, the other circles—chiefly the Palestinian and the Islamic—more and more determine Arab perceptions of identity and acts of identification. Many feel, as the journalist ʿAṭallāh Manṣūr phrased it, that 'only Arabs care about Arabs'.[101] True, the disappointment of quite a few people with Ṣaddām Ḥusayn and his promises of support caused a re-examination of nationalist strategy, which is continuing at the time of writing.[102] If it is correct, as we

[98] Yitzhak Platek and Muḥammad Mahāmīd, *Ōt shel peḥam: ʿŌlamam shel tsěʿīrīm ʿAraviyyīm bě-Israʾel* (1989).

[99] e.g. 'Hawl mudhakkirat Koenig', *al-Rābiṭa*, Nov. 1976, 8–16.

[100] Abraham Ashkenasi, *Opinion Trends among Jerusalem Palestinians* (1990).

[101] ʿAṭallāh Manṣūr, 'Raq la-ʿAravīm ikhpat me-ʿAravīm', *ha-Aretz*, 2 Nov. 1986, 9.

[102] Yizhar Běʾer, 'Naʿalayim reyqōt ba-ḥōl', ibid. 22 Mar. 1991, Suppl., 27, 30.

assume, that in the identity perceptions of the younger generation—and, chiefly, of the better-educated—Palestinization is
radically advancing at the expense of Israelization, as a mirror
reaction to growing extremism among some Jewish groups,[103] this
is a phenomenon which ought to give cause for concern to anyone
caring for the peaceful coexistence of all components of Israeli
society.

[103] Cf. the sharp reactions in Umm al-Faḥm to the activities of the KAKH group,
Ṣawt al-Ḥaqq wa-'l-Ḥuriyya, 9 Aug. 1991.

Conclusion

It is impossible to arrive at finite conclusions in a situation in which processes relating to the Arabs in Israel are continually changing under local, regional, and international impact. I shall attempt, none the less, to reply to a question which has seemed crucial throughout, about the essence and scope of political radicalization in the Arab sector; then I shall outline possible avenues of its future course; and, lastly, suggest some ways of coping with it.

Public opinion research in Israel has indicated that the Arab sector is politically divided between moderates and extremists, differing in expression and activity. It is not always a simple matter to distinguish between them. In general, the moderates consider full equality as a worthwhile and achievable objective. While not a few became enthusiastic over Ṣaddām Ḥusayn and his promises, all remained loyal to the state, many sympathizing with Jewish friends and acquaintances after the missile attacks early in 1991. The methods of political protest increasingly resemble those of the Jews—meetings, demonstrations, and strikes—and manifest a low level of violence. Research carried out by Dr Sam Lehman-Wilzig of the Department of Political Science at Bar-Ilan University has indicated that, in 1982, public protests by the Arabs constituted 15.4 per cent of all protest activities in Israel, that is, approximately proportionate to their ratio in the overall population.[1] This permits us to deduce that the Arab sector in Israel, or at least its moderate element, has adopted the democratic norms of Israeli society. However, there is no guarantee that this will continue so indefinitely, should this sector continue to suffer feelings of discrimination.

On the other hand, extremists in the Arab sector are debating their attitudes towards the state and its Jewish majority. A poll among Arabs in Israel, carried out by the East Jerusalem weekly al-Nadwa,[2] has shown that 69 per cent of the interviewees unequivocally supported Iraq's invasion of Kuwait in 1990. This position was confirmed not only at meetings called by a peripheral group

---

[1] Sam Lehman-Wilzig, *Stiff-Necked People, Bottle-Necked System: The Evolution and Roots of Israeli Public Protest, 1946–1986* (1991), ch. 4.
[2] *al-Nadwa*, 10 Aug. 1990.

such as the Sons of the Village, but also by the pronouncements of political parties like the PLP and the DAP, both of which have seats in the Knesset. All of them associated their approval with the resolving of the Palestinian problem—without condemning Saddām Husayn's threats to destroy Israel. This attitude continued to be manifested, chiefly by the PLP leader Muḥammad Mī'ārī, even after missiles landed in Israel. The Islamic Movement at first had reservations regarding Iraq's annexation of Kuwait, considering the former anti-religious stand of Saddām Husayn, but gradually its criticism mellowed, thanks to its opposition to the increasing United States involvement in the Gulf.

These extremist positions indicate that politically organized groups of Arabs in Israel have not hesitated to adopt positions hostile to the interests of the state, as the great majority of its citizens perceive them. Most probably, this stance was influenced by the PLO and the Palestinians in the Israeli-held territories, who strongly supported Saddām Husayn's intentions against both Kuwait and Israel. Such expressions, in this and other cases, have reflected nationalist views whose spokesmen have apparently given up hope of attaining their aspirations gradually and peacefully. The radicals do talk, certainly, about the need to achieve full equality for the Arabs in Israel, as one part of their general nationalist demands. However, their spokesmen are more militant and prone to confrontation, although not yet to an outright combat in which they cannot hope to get the upper hand—within the rule of law and democracy—at least not until the demographic ratio changes in their favour.[3]

The relative strength of the two Arab camps is difficult to assess. Even Professor Sammy Smooha, author of several important empirical studies on this issue, who thinks that the Arabs in Israel have been politicized rather than radicalized, has acknowledged that probably half of them reject the right of the state to exist, or at least have reservations on this matter.[4] The movement towards radicalization is not less obvious in Arab voting for the Knesset. In recent elections, the trend towards an ideological rather than

---

[3] A. Soffer, 'Yĕḥasīm mishtannīm shel rōv w-mī'ūt w-vīṭṭūyyam ha-merḥavī—ha-miqreh shel 'Arviyyey Isra'el', Ōfaqīm bĕ-Geyōgrafiyya, 9–10 (1984), 69–80.

[4] Sammy Smooha, Orientation and Politicization of the Arab Minority (1984), 166. See also Neuberger, ha-Mī'ūt ha-'Aravī (1991), 59–60.

pragmatic vote has been increasingly evident. As shown above (in Chapter 8), the combined Arab vote for nationalist parties reached 38 per cent in 1981 (for RAQAH/HADASH), 51 per cent in 1984 (for RAQAH/HADASH and the PLP), and 58.3 per cent in 1988 (RAQAH/HADASH, the PLP, and the DAP). If one adds that among those who did not vote at all were supporters of the Sons of the Village, a small group, and the Islamic Movement, a much larger (and growing) one, it is obvious that the radical camp, even if disunited, is growing.

One notes also that those inclined to radicalism are better organized than the moderates and more popular in their constituency, thanks to external nationalist support. The moderates, on the other hand, are on the defensive, and the Israeli authorities do not seem to have assisted them very effectively (anyway, not openly). One result is that many moderates have adopted the strongly worded nationalist slogans of the extremists, so that the most obvious difference between the two camps is that the former are less prone to confrontation with the Jewish majority and the state authorities. Briefly, many moderates have adopted the politically nationalist views of the extremists, since they feel that their own demands for full equality (their main argument, until recently) have not met with a sufficiently substantial and rapid response—at least, not in light of their own expectations.[5] Thus even among those considered moderate, there is a certain retreat from what I have called the Israeli circle of identity and an advance towards Palestinization.[6]

Moreover, radicalism among Arabs in Israel has not merely recruited more support, nor has it merely become more prominent among the politically aware and the better-organized, penetrating the ranks of the moderate (or formerly moderate) as well. There is also a significant change in the content and style of the demands presented by the extremists. This applies both to the nationalists (whose increasing hostility may well have been prompted by modernization[7]) and those active in the Islamic Movement. The bluntest attacks of the former are directed against the Jewish character of Israel as a Jewish state and, even more so, as a Zionist

---

[5] For the basic arguments, see Roselle Tekiner, 'On the Inequality of Israel's Citizens', *Without Prejudice*, 1/1 (Fall 1987), 48–57.

[6] Rekhess, *'Arviyyey Isra'el lĕ-ahar 1967* (1976), 43.

[7] Yochanan Peres, 'Modernization and Nationalism in the Identity of the Israeli Arabs' (ch. 9 n. 6).

192   *Conclusion*

one, since the more radical Arabs consider this character non-democratic (views expressed at a meeting of 200 Arab intellectuals in Nazareth in 1990)[8] or even fascist.[9] The solutions voiced in those circles are usually 'a state for all its citizens, changing its symbols [meaning the flag and national anthem] and its contents [abolishing the Law of Return, which favours Jewish over Arab immigration]'.

A minority among the radicals canvasses a 'democratic secular state', PLO-style (that is, in which an Arab majority will rule over a Jewish minority), while certain other groups have been airing, cautiously as yet, proposals for autonomy for the Arab minority in Israel—cultural, administrative, territorial, or political.[10] The adherents of the Islamic Movement are even more radical than the secular nationalists; while paying lip-service to Israel's existence as a state, they often imply that an Islamic state ought to take its place. More moderate Arabs tend to support a status of cultural minority with well-defined links to the central authority, while the more extremist demand a status of national minority with its own political and other institutions and minimal links to the Jewish centre; as I have demonstrated, Arab political institution-building for this purpose has been proceeding apace. For example, at the third national convention of the PLP, a motion was introduced (though not adopted) that the Arab population in Israel ought to administer its own internal affairs autonomously, via separate cultural, social, and political institutions.[11] (Something to this purpose, but more moderately phrased, is embodied in the party's platform.)

Although the number of those demanding autonomy is still tiny,[12] it may well grow, in direct ratio to dashed hopes of obtaining equality in status or opportunities, and the erosion of the Israeli circle in their identity. In other places, time and again, autonomy has led to the separation of a minority from its home country; modern states are well aware of this and appropriately

---

[8] Gideon Levi, 'Kĕ-shetaqīmū mĕdīna demŏqraṭīt—talpĕnū', *ha-Aretz*, 1 June 1990, Suppl., 13–14.
[9] ʿAbd al-Ḥalīm Muḥammad Maṣālḥa, 'al-Fāshiyya fī Isrāʾīl asbābuhā wa-muwājahatuhāʾ, *al-Mawākib*, 2/3–4 (Mar.–Apr. 1985), 32–40.
[10] Cf. Gideon Levi (n. 8 above).
[11] Kahbà Sufyān, 'Sismat ha-shiwyŏn nŏtēra kĕ-shehayta', *ha-Aretz*, 10 Oct. 1990, 47.
[12] Sara Osetski-Lazar and Asʿad Ghānim, *Ŏtŏnŏmiyya la-ʿAravīm bĕ-Israʾel—diyyūn bĕ-reʾshītŏ* (1990), 21.

cautious. Israel is in a particularly delicate situation in the matter, since its two largest Arab population centres are in Galilee and the Little Triangle, that is, at Israel's frontiers on the Green Line. Should the inhabitants of the Israeli-held territories, all or in part, get an autonomous status of their own, it is more than plausible to assume that the more extremist among the Arabs in Israel would intensify their demands for self-determination on an identical or similar pattern. Should a Palestinian state be founded in all or part of the above territories, a separatist movement may arise among the Arabs in Israel to demand a state of their own. Those supporting such a concept potentially constitute a critical mass, numerically, and they are busy establishing appropriate institutions for such a contingency. It is likely, also, that in such circumstances their nationalism would adopt an irredentist character, striving to strengthen relations with Arabs across the Green Line and then, perhaps, to join them, in population and territory, in a common Palestinian state. There are already some signs pointing that way,[13] so far few in number; but it has already happened—and it may happen again—that moderates are dragged along by political radicals. It seems that growing alienation among the Arabs in Israel, already symptomatic of anomie, contains a time-bomb, with a steadily ticking clock.[14]

In recent years, the Arabs in Israel have been passing through two opposing processes, both influenced by speedy modernization; acquiring wider experience in the rules of the game, while amassing political power (for example, in voting),[15] their alienation has increased,[16] along with a rise in nationalism. Not all are able to withstand the pressures thus resulting.[17] Hence the growth in

[13] R. Israeli, 'Arabs in Israel (ch. 9 n. 5), 24; ʿAmōs Gilbōʿa, 'Lōʾ lĕhatmīn et ha-rōʾsh ba-ḥōl', Maʿarīv, 15 Dec. 1989, 4; Avner Regev, ʿArviyyey Israʾel (1989), 25–6. Many instances are mentioned by Ūrī Guṭmann, 'Gillūyey badlanūt lĕʾumīt bĕ-qerev ha-ḥūgīm ha-radīqaliyyīm shel ʿArviyyey Israʾel bi-shĕnōt ha-shivʿīm wĕ-ha-shĕmōnīm', MA thesis, Hebrew University of Jerusalem, 1990. See also Arnon Soffer, "Arviyyey Israʾel, mi-kĕfar lĕ-meṭrōpōlīn w-ma halʾa?', ha-Mizraḥ he-Ḥadash, 32/125–8 (1989), esp. 98–9.
[14] Arnon Soffer, ʿAl ha-matsav ha-demōgrafī wĕ-ha-geyʾōgrafī bĕ-Eretz-Israʾel: ha-omnam sōf he-ḥazōn ha-Tsiyyōnī? (1988); Sandra Anderson García, 'Israeli Arabs: Partners in Pluralism or Ticking Time Bomb?', Ethnicity, 7 (1980), 15–26.
[15] Ian Lustick, 'Creeping Binationalism within the Green Line', New Outlook, 31/283 (July 1988), 14–19.
[16] ʿAṭallāh Manṣūr, 'Lōʾ mizdahīm ʿim ha-mĕdīna', ha-Aretz, 19 June 1988, 11.
[17] S. Khalil Marʿi and Avraham M. Levi, 'Modernization or Minority Status', Journal of Cross-Cultural Psychology, 10/3 (Sept. 1979), 375–89.

radicalism, chiefly among the younger people and the better-educated, who will constitute a major share in any future leadership. Well-meant suggestions have been made, occasionally, to improve the situation of the Arabs and thereby secure a better future both for them and for the whole state.[18] Some of these ideas are useful, but they seem to have touched on certain parts of the issue only, ignoring the core of the problem.

However one may assess the degree of radicalization of the Arabs in Israel, it is obvious that they already find themselves in a conflictual situation with the Jewish majority. Perhaps the conflict was unavoidable; at all events, nothing would be gained by pointing an accusing finger in one direction or another. However, as the literature dealing with conflicts tells us, a conflict, if unattended, tends to become ever more aggravated. At the time of writing, most Jewish public opinion in Israel is focused on the Israeli–Arab conflict outside the Green Line rather than on the one developing between Jews and Arabs inside it. Perhaps justifiably, most Jews consider the former issue more immediate to Israel's survival. Nevertheless, the Jewish–Arab confrontation within the State of Israel is increasingly displaying more overt conflictual symptoms and may well affect the future of both sectors in the coming years. It is, therefore, in the interest of both to see this conflict as a continuous challenge and to strive for its accommodation, speedily and methodically—most particularly so since the matter is much more within the power of decision of Israel's citizens than is ending the conflict with their neighbours beyond the Green Line. While nobody can offer a magic panacea for resolving this internal conflict rapidly and painlessly, various options may be pointed out, on the personal, institutional, and governmental levels, which, if integrated in one common effort, could moderate this conflict and perhaps control it up to its resolution.

Since no attempts at repressing minorities have ever succeeded for very long, but, on the contrary, have embittered the conflict between them and the majority, one may start from the premise that this would not be attempted in Israel, either. On the contrary,

---

[18] Sammy Smooha, 'Mĕdīniyyūt qayyemet wĕ-alternatīvīt' (ch. 9 n. 64), 7–36; ʿAdnān Abū Rabīʿ, 'al-Tafkīr hawl mustaqbal al-jamāhīr al-ʿArabiyya', *al-Ittihād*, 22 Jan. 1990; Raʿanan Cohen, *Bi-Sĕvakh ha-neʾemanūyōt* (ch. 9 n. 14), 143–7; 'What Future for the Palestine Arabs?', *War and Peace*, 10/6 (June–July 1970), 3–11; Mark Tessler, *Arabs in Israel* (1980), 23–4.

it is certain that a great majority of Israel's citizens have opted for a state with a dominant Jewish majority, but also for a democratic, liberal, and pluralistic one. I shall refer, therefore, to necessary activities within such a context (in addition, naturally, to intensive education for coexistence), on the three levels suggested—assuming that for the institutional and governmental ones well-defined laws would be needed.

1. On the personal level, Arabs have complained, again and again, in speech and in writing, that they feel insulted in their relations with the Jews. One may suggest that if all citizens, Jew or Arab, would strive to relate to people in the other sector with the same good manners and reciprocal respect that they would employ in their own families, at work, or in their social environment, very probably at least one important cause for friction might be removed.

2. On the institutional level, one hears frequent allegations of discrimination. Should every institution, private or public, attempt to relate to both sectors equally, in all matters of employment and promotion,[19] the attitude of many Arabs towards Jewish society might change and their economic complaints diminish or disappear altogether.

3. There is a general feeling, however, that major intervention could and ought to come on the governmental level. Should master-plans be drawn up in everything connected with the Arab sector, from the perspective of an overall policy directed towards achieving both theoretical and practical equality, in rights and in duties, the share of the Israeli circle would increase in the awareness of the identity of Arabs, citizens of Israel, and possibly their desire to create extra-state structures of their own might become less intense.

I mean a well-planned policy, applicable to the short, medium, and long range. This ought to recognize the right of the Arab to be

---

[19] A rare example is provided by a body, calling itself the Centre for Jewish–Arab Economic Development, which in 1988–9 strove to obtain low-interest loans for Arab business projects and instructed their initiators in administration, marketing, and sales. See Haggay Fōrshner, 'ha-Merkaz yamlīts wĕ-ye'ashsher', *Davar*, 22 Sept. 1991, 14.

different,[20] within the purview of the law[21]—with both Jews and Arabs participating in shaping this policy and implementing it. Its planning and execution should start immediately, with the objective of creating conditions where the Arabs in Israel could develop their own road towards a high culture of their own, and also ensuring equal opportunities for employment and economic and political advancement. This in exchange for equal duties in every domain, including national service, as an alternative to service in the Defence Forces, at least until a secure peace is signed between Israel and the Arabs states.

Obviously, such a policy would not be easy to implement. It would necessitate changes in attitudes as well as concessions on both sides. On the one hand, the Arabs in Israel should recognize Israel as a state with a Jewish majority, eager to preserve its dominant national identity. After all, a minority cannot seriously expect a state and society to change its own nature, thus imposing the minority will on the majority. On the other hand, Israeli Jews would have to acknowledge that if the Arab share of the country's resources is increased by standards of equal conditions and opportunities, the Jewish share would be accordingly diminished, if only temporarily. None the less, if all Israel's citizens aspire to a better and safer future, this is the only feasible way to encourage the minorities in the State of Israel to see themselves committed to it and to being full partners with its Jewish citizens.

---

[20] Ōrī Ṣṭendel, 'Zekḥūt ha-shōnī shel ʿArviyyey Isra'el—heybeṭīm mishpatiyyīm', *ha-Mizraḥ he-Ḥadash*, 32/125–8 (1989), 192–207.

[21] Cf. Menachem Hofnung, *Isra'el—biṭĕhōn ha-mĕdīna mūl shilṭōn ha-ḥōq 1948–1991*, index, s.v. ''Aravīm'.

Select Bibliography

The bibliography comprises only works mentioned in the book, arranged by language—Arabic, Hebrew, and others; the definite article has not been considered in the alphabetical sequence. For fuller reference, the following are useful: Erik Cohen (ed.), *Bibliography of Arabs and Other Minorities in Israel* (Givat-Haviva: Centre for Arab and Afro-Asian Studies, 1974); Sammy Smooha and Ora Cibulski (eds.), *Social Research on Arabs in Israel, 1948–1976: An Annotated Bibliography* (Ramat-Gan: Turtledove, 1978); Sammy Smooha (ed.), *Social Research on Arabs in Israel, 1977–1982* (Haifa: Haifa University—Jewish–Arab Centre, 1984).

1. Arabic

(a) Books

ʿĀyid, Khālid, *al-Intifāḍa al-thawriyya fī Filasṭīn: al-abʿād al-dākhiliyya* (Amman: Dār al-Sharq li-ʾl-nashr wa-ʾl-tawzīʿ, 1988).

al-ʿAwdāt, Ḥusayn, *al-Sīnimā wa-ʾl-qaḍiyya al-Filasṭīniyya*² (Acre: Dār al-Aswār, 1989).

al-Barnāmaj al-siyāsī li-ʾl-ḥaraka al-waṭaniyya al-taqaddumiyya—Abnāʾ al-balad fī al-jāmiʿāt (n.p., n.d. [1988–9]).

Fallāḥ, Salmān (ed.), *al-Durūz fī Isrāʾīl* (Shafā ʿAmr: Dār al-Mashriq li-ʾl-Tarjama wa-ʾl-Nashr, 1989).

Ghazzāwī, ʿUmar, *al-Ṣahyūniyya wa-ʾl-aqalliyya al-qawmiyya al-ʿArabiyya fī Isrāʾīl* (Acre: al-Aswār, 1979).

Ḥalabī, Usāma, *al-Durūz fī Isrāʾīl: min ṭāʾifa ilà shaʿb?* (n.p., 1989).

Ḥarakat Abnāʾ al-balad mawāqif wa-munṭalaqāt (Haifa, 1989). *Ittiḥād al-Kuttāb al-ʿArab* (n.p., 1988).

Jabbāra, Taysīr, *al-Intifāḍa al-shaʿbiyya al-Filasṭīniyya min al-nawāḥī al-siyāsiyya wa-ʾl-iʿlāmiyya* (Nablus: Jāmiʿat al-Najāḥ al-waṭaniyya, 1989).

Kanafānī, Ghassān, *Adab al-muqawama fī Filasṭīn al-muḥtalla* (Beirut: Dār al-Ādāb, 1968).

Khalīfa, Khālid (ed.), *Filasṭīniyyūn 1948–1988* (Shafā ʿAmr: Maṭbaʿat al-Sharq, 1988).

al-Lajna al-quṭriyya li-Ḥarakat Abnāʾ al-balad—al-Idāra al-thaqāfiyya, *al-ʿUmmāl al-ʿArab wa-ʾl-histadrūt* (n.p., 1989).

Muḥārib, Maḥmūd, *al-Ḥizb al-shuyūʿī al-Isrāʾīlī wa-ʾl-qaḍiyya al-Filasṭīniyya 1948–1981: dirāsāt naqdiyya* (Jerusalem: 1989).

Taqrīr ʿan aʿmāl al-lajna li-dawrat 1988–1989 (n.p. [Jerusalem], n.d. [1989]).

Yĕhōshūʿa, Jacob, *Taʾrīkh al-ṣiḥāfa al-ʿArabiyya fī Filasṭīn fī al-ʿahd al-ʿUthmānī (1908–1918)* (Jerusalem: Maṭbaʿat al-Maʿārif, 1978).

—— *Taʾrīkh al-ṣiḥāfa al-ʿArabiyya al-Filasṭīniyya 1919–1929* (Haifa: Jāmiʿat Ḥayfā, 1981).

—— *Taʾrīkh al-ṣiḥāfa al-ʿArabiyya al-Filasṭīniyya fī nihāyat ʿahd al-intidāb al-Brītānī ʿalà Filasṭīn 1930–1948* (Jerusalem: Dār al-Mashriq wa-Maʿhad Truman, 1983).

Yūsuf, Muḥsin, *al-Filasṭīniyyūn fī Isrāʾīl wa-ʾl-intifāḍa* (Jerusalem: al-Jāmiʿa al-Filasṭīniyya al-Akādīmiyya li-ʾl-shuʾūn al-Dawliyya, 1990).

(*b*) *Articles*

ʿAbd al-Fattāḥ, ʿAwaḍ, ʿLi-naʿmal ʿalà khalq ṣiḥāfa mawḍūʿiyya wa-multazamaʾ, *al-Maydān*, 1/1 (24 Nov. 1989), 3.

Abū Ḥannā, Anīs Rāshid, ʿal-Ṭālib al-ʿArabī fī al-jāmiʿāt al-ʿIbriyyaʾ, *al-Ṣināra*, 27 Jan. 1989, 13.

Abū Ḥannā, Ḥannā, ʿal-Arḍ wa-ʾl-lughaʾ, *al-Ṣināra*, 29 Mar. 1990.

Abū Khayṭ, Nasīm, ʿal-Kulliyya al-Urthūdhuksiyya fī Ḥayfāʾ, *al-Ittiḥād*, 1 Nov. 1978.

Abū Maʿādh, ʿHunāk man yaḥtāj ilà tarbiya dīmuqrāṭiyya wa-tarbiya waṭaniyyaʾ, *al-Maydān*, 6 Apr. 1990, 3.

Abū Rabīʿ, ʿAdnān, ʿal-Tafkīr ḥawl mustaqbal al-jamāhīr al-ʿArabiyyaʾ, *al-Ittiḥād*, 22 Jan. 1990.

Abū Sharīf, ʿRuʾasāʾ judud wa-qudāmà wa-intimāʾāt tathbut bi-ʾl-tajribaʾ, *al-Ṣināra*, 20 Dec. 1983.

Abū Zahiyyā, ʿIṣām, ʿTarīqat al-intikhābāt al-Isrāʾīliyya ilà aynaʾ?ʾ, *al-Mujtamaʿ*, 18/5 (May 1990), 19–23.

Aghbāriyya, Rajāʾ, ʿMulāḥaẓāt awwaliyya ḥawl natāʾij al-intikhābāt al-baladiyya fī Umm al-Faḥmʾ, *al-Rāya*, 8 (9 Mar. 1989), 5.

ʿʿArab al-mudun al-mukhtalaṭa yarfuḍūn al-iqtilāʿ wa-yurīdūn al-musāwāhʾ, *al-Ittiḥād*, 21 Nov. 1990, 2.

Ashqar, Ṭaha, ʿMustaqbal al-tanẓīm al-siyāsī ʿind al-ʿArab fī Isrāʾīlʾ, *al-Ṣināra*, 1 Dec. 1989, 7.

ʿAwda, Ibrāhīm, ʿTaṭwīr al-taʿlīm al-tiknūlūjīʾ, *al-Mawākib*, 2/9–10 (Sept.–Oct. 1985), 80–2.

Badr, Khālid, ʿTanqiyat al-jaww al-ijtimāʿī wa-taʿmīq al-taʿammul al-dīmuqrāṭīʾ, *al-Ṣināra*, 18 Aug. 1989.

Basūl, Ghassān, ʿDaʿū al-qāfila tasīrʾ, *al-Ṣināra*, 1 Sept. 1989.

Daḥlān, Jamīl, 'al-Sayyid Ibrāhīm Nimr Ḥusayn ra'īs al-majlis al-baladī Shafā 'Amr fī ḥadīth ṣarīḥ wa-muthīr', *al-Qasam*, 22 Mar. 1989.

Darwīsh, Aḥmad, 'Marra ukhrà ma'a al-yasār al-Ṣahyūnī', *al-Ṣināra*, 24 Aug. 1990.

Fallāḥ, Ghāzī, 'al-Awjuh al-jughrāfiyya li-inmāṭ istiqrār al-badw fī Isrā'īl', in Khālid Khalīfa (ed.), *Filasṭīniyyūn 1948-1988* (Shafā 'Amr: Maṭba'at al-Sharq, 1988), 177-95.

Faraj, Yūsuf, 'Kayfa tastaqbil madārisunā al-sana al-dirāsiyya al-jadīda?', *al-Ittiḥād*, 30 Aug. 1991, Suppl. 1, 5.

Fāris, Ḥusayn, 'Lā narà amalan kabīran fī al-ḥall al-silmī ṭālamā baqiya al-Līkūd fī al-ḥukm', *al-Usbū' al-Jadīd*, 1 Mar. 1990, 20-1.

Farw, Qays, 'Hawiyyat al-Durūz—naẓra ta'rīkhiyya', in Salmān Fallāḥ (ed.), *al-Durūz fī Isrā'īl* (Shafā 'Amr: Dār al-Mashriq li-'l-Tarjama wa-'l-Nashr, 1989), 49-60.

'Fi istiṭlā' taḥlīlī li-'l-ra'y al-'āmm al-'Arabī al-Filasṭīnī dākhil al-khaṭṭ al-akhḍar tawaqqu'āt al-ra'y fī intikhābāt al-Knesset al-muqbila', *al-Usbū' al-Jadīd*, 1 July 1990, 33-9.

Ghanāim, Maḥmūd, 'Namādhij min qaṣaṣinā al-maḥallī fī al-sab'īnāt wa-al-thamānīnāt', *al-Ittiḥād*, 6 July 1990.

Ghanāim, Muhammad Ḥamza, 'Riwāya 'Arabiyya Filasṭīniyya bi-ḥurūf 'Ibriyya', *al-Jadīd*, 35/6 (June 1986), 57-9.

Ghānim, As'ad, 'al-Intifāḍa wa-al-'Arab fī Isrā'īl', *al-Aswār*, 6 (Winter 1990), 55-71.

—— Mustaqbal al-'Arab fī Isrā'īl al-indimāj faqaṭ', *al-Ṣināra*, 9 Feb. 1990, 10.

—— 'al-Jabha al-'Arabiyya al-sha'biyya wa-al-ṣirā' ḍidd muṣādarat al-arāḍī 1958-1961', *Qaḍāyā*, 3 (May 1990), 50-8.

Gharīb, Mundhir, 'al-Ta'līm al-'Arabī fī Isrā'īl fī iṭār taqārīr al-lijān al-dirāsiyya al-mukhtalifa', *al-Jadīd*, 7 (July 1978), 19-28.

Ḥabashī, Amīra, 'al-Ra'y mattà tu'addī al-mar'a al-Filasṭīniyya dawrahā al-thaqāfī wa-'l-ijtimā'ī fī Isrā'īl wa-Filasṭīn al-muḥtalla', *al-Mujtama'*, 18/5 (May 1990), 38-46.

Ḥabīb, Shafīq, 'al-Riqāba ḥarrafat tarjamat qaṣā'idī', *al-Ṣināra*, 22 June 1990, 3.

Ḥabībī, Emile, 'Ta'thīr ḥarb 1967 'alà al-adab al-Filasṭīnī fī Isrā'īl', *al-Jadīd*, 1-2 (Jan.-Feb. 1976), 51-65.

—— 'Istimrār al-thaqāfa al-'Arabiyya al-Filasṭīniyya fī Isrā'īl', *al-Jadīd*, 3 (Mar. 1984), 13-18.

Ḥaddād, Mun'im, 'al-Liqā' bayn al-thaqāfa al-Filasṭīniyya al-taqlīdiyya wa-bayn al-thaqāfa al-gharbiyya fī Isrā'īl', *al-Aswār*, 9 (Spring 1991), 119-31.

al-Ḥāj, Mājid, 'al-Ḥamūla al-'Arabiyya fī Isrā'il', *Āfāq*, 1/2 (Apr. 1981), 17-28.

al-Ḥāj, Mājid, 'al-Ḥamūla al-ʿArabiyya bayna al-tafakkuk wa-ʾl-tarābuṭ', *al-Mawākib*, 2/7–8 (July–Aug. 1985), 60–8.

—— 'al-Akādīmiyyūn al-ʿArab fī Isrāʾīl: mumayyizāt raʾīsiyya wa-ḍāʾiqat al-ʿamal', *al-Aswār*, 2 (Summer 1988), 41–58.

—— al-Lājiʾūn al-ʿArab fī Isrāʾīl', *al-Mawākib*, 5/5–6 (May–June 1988), 12–22.

Ḥakīm, Ramzī, 'Anẓimat al-ṭawāriʾ fī dawlat al-ṭawāriʾ', *al-Ittiḥād*, 6 July 1970, 6.

'Hal al-ḥadīth ḥawl tashkīl ḥizb ʿArabī muwaḥḥad huwa mujarrad kalām?', *al-Nadwa*, 23 Mar. 1990.

'Hal taḥūḍ al-ḥaraka al-Islāmiyya intikhābāt al-Knesset?', *al-Nadwa*, 16 Mar. 1990.

Ḥalabī, Majdī, "Usfiyya janna fī aʿālī al-Karmil', *Kull al-ʿArab*, 8 Mar. 1991, 6.

—— 'Jafrā', *Kull al-ʿArab*, 3 May 1991.

Ḥalabī, Usāma, 'Ḥurriyyat al-taʿbīr dākhil al-madrasa wa-khārijahā', *al-Jadīd*, 9 (Sept. 1983), 17–19, 45.

Ḥasan, Shākir Farīd, 'Naqd dhātī li-masīrat ḥizbinā al-shuyūʿī', *al-Ittiḥād*, 27 Feb. 1990.

'Ḥawl mudhakkirat Koenig', *al-Rābiṭa*, Nov. 1976, 8–16.

Ḥaydar, ʿAzīz, 'Maẓāhir al-faqr bayn al-ʿArab fī Isrāʾīl', *al-Aswār*, 1 (Spring 1988), 39–55.

Ḥaydar, Yūsuf, 'al-Ḥaraka al-masraḥiyya fī al-bilād', in Khālid Khalīfa (ed.), *Filasṭīniyyūn 1948–1988* (Shafā ʿAmr: Maṭabʿat al-Sharq, 1988), 228–64.

al-Hindāwī, ʿAlī, 'Khudh al-ḥikma min afwāh . . . al-ḥaṭṭābīn,' *al-Ṣināra*, 1 Dec. 1989, 7.

Ḥusayn, Ibrāhīm Nimr, 'Lam nafqud quwwat taʾthīrinā wa-lākin yajib an nughayyir al-taktīk', *al-Ṣināra*, 20 June 1989, 7, 10.

'Ilā al-liqāʾ fī al-muʾtamar al-qādim', *al-Ṣināra*, 17 May 1985.

"Iṣmat, Riyāḍ, 'Taʾṣīl al-masraḥ al-ʿArabī', *al-Shaʿb*, 15 Nov. 1978.

'al-Iʿtidāʾ ʿalā ʿAwnī Ḥannā Rūk min al-Nāṣira', *al-Rābiṭa*, 39 (Feb. 1985), 27–30.

Jadʿūn, Nihād, 'al-Marʾa al-ʿāmila mustaghalla min ṣāhib al-ʿamal wa-min al-zawj', *al-Ṣināra*, 20 Apr. 1990.

Jubrān, Sālim, 'al-Aḥammiyya al-quṭriyya li-ʾl-intikhābāt al-maḥalliyya', *al-Ittiḥād*, 24 Feb. 1989.

—— 'Qaḍiyyatunā al-ʿādila, kayfa naksib al-raʾy al-ʿāmm taʾyīdan lahā?', *al-Ittiḥād*, 31 Mar. 1989.

—— 'Naḥw intikhābāt al-histadrūt . . . wa-abʿad min intikhābāt al-histadrūt!', *al-Ittiḥād*, 30 June 1989.

—— 'Taḥqīq al-maṭālib al-ḥayawiyya wa-ʾl-ʿājila li-ʾl-suluṭāt al-maḥalliyya miftāḥ li-ʾl-taṭawwur al-ijtimāʿī li-ʾl-jamāhīr al-ʿArabiyya', *al-Ittiḥād*, 27 Feb. 1990.

—— 'al-Dawr al-siyāsī li-'l-jamāhīr al-ʿArabiyya—baʿīdan ʿan al-adhnāb wa-'l-muzāyada!', *al-Ittiḥād*, 31 May 1991, 6.

Kabhā, Samīr, 'Khiṭaṭ Khālid Aghbāriyya al-mustaqbaliyya li-'l-wasaṭ al-ʿArabī', *Kull al-ʿArab*, 21 Dec. 1990.

Katz, Yōram, '10% min aʿdāʾ ḥizb al-ʿamal ʿArab', *Kull al-ʿArab*, 5 July 1991.

Khalīfa, Khālid, 'Aqalliyya ʿArabiyya fī Isrāʾīl am juzʾ lā yatajjaza' min al-shaʿb al-Filasṭīnī', in Khālid Khalīfa (ed.), *Filasṭīniyyūn 1948–1988* (Shafā ʿAmr: Maṭbaʿat al-Sharq, 1988), 30–7.

—— 'al-Majāl al-ṣuḥufī—al-ṣiḥāfa al-Filasṭīniyya ilà ayna?', in Khālid Khalīfa (ed.), *Filasṭīniyyūn 1948–1988* (Shafā ʿAmr: Maṭbaʿat al-Sharq, 1988), 317–20.

Khamāyisī, Rāsim, 'al-Mubādara al-dhātiyya wa-taṣnīʿ al-qarya al-ʿArabiyya', *al-Mawākib*, 2/9–10 (Sept.–Oct. 1985), 16–24.

al-Khaṭīb, Ibrāhīm, 'Nadwa fī Dabbūriyya ḥawl natāʾij al-intikhābāt li-'l-histadrūt', *Ṣawt al-Ḥaqq wa-'l-Ḥurriyya*, 1 Dec. 1989, 8.

Khūrī, Muwaffaq, 'Bi-Imkān kull adīb wa-kātib an yaṭlub al-daʿm wa-lan nataraddad fī al-musāʿada', *al-Ṣināra*, 24 May 1991.

'Khuṭṭat tashwīshāt wa-khuṭuwāt kifāḥiyya ibtidāʾan min al-usbūʿ al-qādim tashhaduhā al-madāris al-ʿArabiyya', *Kull al-ʿArab*, 24 Aug. 1990, 15.

'Liqāʾ maʿa al-Shaykh Rāʾid al-Ṣāliḥ raʾīs baladiyyat Umm al-Faḥm', *al-Usbūʿ al-Jadīd*, 15 Jan. 1990, 22–3.

Majallī, Naẓīr, 'Hal taqūm intifāḍa Isrāʾīliyya', *al-Ittiḥād*, 8 Dec. 1989, Suppl., 6–9.

—— 'Naḥnu wa-'l-dhikrà al-thāniya li-indilāʿ al-intifāḍa', *al-Ittiḥād*, 4 Dec. 1989, 3.

—— 'Yawm al-arḍ 1990', *al-Ittiḥād*, 23 Mar. 1990, 6–7.

Makhūl, Najwà, 'al-Marʾa al-Filasṭīniyya fī Isrāʾīl bayn wāqiʿ al-ikhḍāʿ wa-imkānāt al-taḥarrur', *al-Jadīd*, 3 (Mar. 1982), 26–31.

Mālik, Ibrāhīm, 'al-Zirāʿa al-ʿArabiyya fī Isrāʾīl—muʿālaja awwaliyya', *al-Jadīd*, 3–4 (Mar.–Apr. 1976), 100–11.

—— 'al-Bunya al-ijtimāʿiyya al-ṭabaqiyya li-'l-jamāhīr al-ʿArabiyya fī Isrāʾīl', *al-Jadīd*, 2 (Mar. 1990), 4–7.

Manṣūr, Shawqiyya ʿUrūq, 'Liqāʾ maʿa ʿAbd al-ʿAzīz Abū Iṣbaʿ sekreter ḥarakat al-nahḍa', *al-Ṣināra*, 26 Jan. 1990.

—— 'al-Shaykh Ibrāhīm Ṣarṣūr', *al-Ṣināra*, 2 Feb. 1990.

Manṣūr, Tamīm, 'Qāʾima mushtaraka wa-lākin laysa bi-kull thaman', *al-Ṣināra*, 25 Aug. 1989.

Marʿī, Maryam, 'al-Ḥarakāt al-nisāʾiyya fī al-wasaṭ al-ʿArabī aydan rukkizat ʿalà al-buʿd al-siyāsī awwalan', *al-Ṣināra*, 9 Aug. 1991, 25.

Marʿī, Sāmī, 'al-Taʿlīm al-ʿArabī al-ibtidāʾī fī Isrāʾīl', *al-Mawākib*, 2/11–12 (Nov.–Dec. 1985), 16–39.

—— 'al-Madrasa wa-'l-ijtimāʿ fī al-qarya al-ʿArabiyya fī Isrāʾīl', *Āfāq*, 1/1

202　　　　　　　　　　　*Select Bibliography*

(July 1980), 3–29.
Maṣālḥa, ʿAbd al-Ḥalīm Muḥammad, ʿal-Fāshiyya fī Isrāʾīl asbābuhā wa-muwājahatuhāʾ, *al-Mawākib*, 2/3–4 (Mar.–Apr. 1985), 32–40.
Mashʿūr, Luṭfī, ʿal-Jamāhīr al-ʿArabiyya ḥasamat hawiyyatahā al-Filasṭīniyya allatī ṣaqalathā al-intifāḍaʾ, *al-Ṣināra*, 3 Aug. 1990.
Mīʿārī, Muḥammad, ʿNatījat al-intikhābāt laysat bi-ʾl-ḍarūra tuʿabbir ʿan al-mawqif al-waṭanī wa-ʾl-iltizām al-Filasṭīnīʾ, *al-Ṣināra*, 24 Nov. 1989, 9–10.
ʿMuqabala maʿa al-Shaykh Rāʾid Ṣāliḥ raʾīs baladiyyat Umm al-Faḥm al-muntakhabʾ, *al-Ṣināra*, 3 Mar. 1989, 5.
ʿal-Murāhana al-khāsira li-ḥarakat Abnāʾ al-baladʾ, *al-Ittiḥād*, 3 Apr. 1990.
Murquṣ, Nimr, ʿFī muwājahat tamyīz yaṣrakh ḥattà al-samāʾʾ, *al-Ittiḥād*, 23 Aug. 1991, Suppl., 1.
Muṣṭafà, Mashhūr, ʿQirāʾa sarīʿa fī natāʾij initikhābāt al-histadrūt al-akhīraʾ, *al-Maydān*, 1/1 (24 Nov. 1989), 5.
Muwāsī, Fārūq, ʿal-ʿArab fī Isrāʾīl ilà ayna?ʾ, *al-Nadwa*, 16 Mar. 1990, 1.
—— ʿZāhirat al-tadayyun fī al-shabāb al-ʿArabīʾ, *Āfāq* 1/1 (July 1980), 65–6.
ʿNadwat al-Quds ḥawl al-adab al-Filasṭīnī fī Isrāʾīlʾ, *al-Jadīd*, 11–12 (Nov.–Dec. 1983), 6–11.
ʿNadwat yawm al-arḍʾ, *Nidāʾ al-Aswār*, 30 Mar. 1990, 4–5.
ʿal-Nāʾib Muḥammad Mīʿārī fī ḥadīth maʿa al-Usbūʿ al-Jadīdʾ, *al-Usbūʿ al-Jadīd*, 15 Apr. 1989, 16–18.
ʿNatāʾij intikhābāt al-histadrūt fi jamīʿ al-mudun wa-ʾl-qurà al-ʿArabiyyaʾ, *al-Ṣināra*, 17 Nov. 1989, 7–9.
Nāṭūr, Salmān, ʿal-Durūz fī Isrāʾīlʾ, in Khālid Khalīfa (ed.), *Filasṭīniyyūn 1948–1988* (Shafā ʿAmr: Maṭbaʿat al-Sharq, 1988), 164–76.
Qabalān, Suhayl, ʿTasāquṭ al-ṭullāb wa-ʾl-qaḍāyā al-ijtimāʿiyyaʾ, *al-Ittiḥād*, 16 June 1989.
Qanāziʿ, George, ʿal-Hawiyya al-qawmiyya fī adabinā al-maḥallīʾ, *al-Mawākib*, 2/3–4 (Mar.–Apr. 1985), 6–21.
Qāsim, ʿAbd al-Sattār, ʿal-Qiyāda al-Filasṭīniyya qabl ʿām 1948 wa-atharuhā fī al-nakbaʾ, *al-Mawākib*, 4/11–12 (Nov.–Dec. 1987), 4–25; 5/1–2 (Jan.–Feb. 1988), 14–28; 5/5–6 (May–June 1988), 57–68.
Rouhana, Nadim, ʿBaʿḍ al-mumayyizāt li-ʾl-ṭullāb al-khirrījīn al-Jāmiʿiyyīn al-Filasṭīniyyīn min Isrāʾīlʾ, *al-Jadīd*, 5 (May 1984), 24–31.
Saʿd, Aḥmad, ʿal-Awḍāʿ al-iqtiṣādiyya li-ʾl-jamāhīr al-ʿArabiyya fī Isrāʾilʾ, in Khālid Khalīfa (ed.), *Filasṭīniyyūn 1948–1988* (Shafā ʿAmr: Maṭbaʿat al-Sharq, 1988), 107–25.
—— ʿHal tūjad azmat qiyāda ladà al-jamāhīr al-ʿArabiyya fī Isrāʾīl?ʾ, *al-Ittiḥād*, 1 Feb. 1990, 4 Feb. 1990.
Saʿdī, Aḥmad Ḥusayn, ʿal-Faqr fī al-wasaṭ al-ʿArabī: al-ʿArab aqalliyya bayn al-sukkān wa-akthariyya bayn al-fuqarāʾʾ, *al-Jadīd*, 2 (Mar. 1990), 39–51.

Salīm, Rashīd, 'al-Ḥaraka al-taqaddumiyya bi-ḥaja ilà intifāḍa li-isqāṭ al-qiyāda wa-mumārasatihā', *al-Ṣināra*, 9 Feb. 1990, 4.

Samʿān, Samʿān, 'al-Tarbiya al-siyāsiyya fī al-madāris al-ʿArabiyya', *al-Mawākib*, 3/7–8 (July–Aug. 1986), 78–83.

al-Samra, Maḥmūd, 'Dawāwīn shiʿr min al-arḍ al-muḥtalla', *al-Adīb* (Beirut), Nov. 1969, 12–14.

al-Sawāfīrī, Kāmil, 'al-Adab fī Filasṭīn fī ẓill al-intidāb', *al-Ufq al-Jadīd*, 4/1 (Jan. 1965), 23–4.

Shaḥāda, ʿAzīz, 'al-Intifāḍa muḥāwala li-baḥth al-asbāb wa-ʾl-taʾthīr warudūd al-fiʿl', *al-Mawākib*, 5/1–2 (Jan.–Feb. 1988), 7–13.

Shannān, ʿAbd al-Bāqī, 'Bidāyat al-ṣiḥāfa al-Filasṭīniyya', *al-Mawākib*, 4/7–8 (July–Aug. 1987), 42–6.

Sharāra, Riyāḍ, 'Adab al-muqāwama fī Filasṭīn al-muḥtalla', *al-Ḥawādith* (Beirut), 10/507 (29 July 1966), 24.

Sharīf, Sharīf Muḥammad, 'Nidāʾ al-judhūr—waqfa maʿa al-turāth al-Filasṭīnī fī al-dākhil', *al-Aswār*, 3 (Spring 1989), 76–82.

'al-Shaykh Rāʾid Ṣalāḥ raʾīs baladiyyat Umm al-Faḥm yarudd ʿalà al-hajma al-iʿlāmiyya al-mukaththafa', *Ṣawt al-Ḥaqq wa-ʾl-Ḥurriyya*, 9 Mar. 1990, 7.

al-Shihābī, Luṭfiyya, 'Dīwān al-waṭan al-muḥtall', *al-Adīb* (Beirut), June 1969, 39–40.

'Shuʾūn al-madāris wa-ʾl-taʿlīm fī al-wasaṭ al-ʿArabī', *al-Ṣināra*, 7 July 1989, 8–9.

Sulaymān, Ramzī, 'al-Hawiyya al-qawmiyya wa-ʾl-muwāṭana', *al-Jadīd*, 11–12 (Nov.–Dec. 1983), 15–19.

—— 'al-Hawiyya al-Filasṭīniyya wa-ʾl-muwāṭana li-muthaqqafīn ʿArab fī Isrāʾīl', in Khālid Khalīfa (ed.), *Filasṭīniyyūn 1948–1988* (Shafā ʿAmr: Maṭbaʿat al-Sharq, 1988), 83–106.

'al-Sulṭa al-maḥalliyya akthar qawmiyya!', *al-Ṣināra*, 14 June 1985.

'al-Suluṭāt al-maḥalliyya azmat majālis wa-baḥbūḥat al-ruʾasāʾ", *al-Ṣināra*, 24 Nov. 1983.

'al-Taʿāyush al-Yahūdī—al-ʿArabī yaḥtall makān al-ṣadāra fī al-nadwa al-ṣuḥufiyya fī al-Nāṣira', *Kull al-ʿArab*, 30 Oct. 1990, 8.

'Taḥrīk qaḍiyyat Iqrit wa-Kafr Barʿam', *al-Rābiṭa*, 40 (Mar. 1986), 32–5.

al-Ṭawrī, Aḥmad, 'Raʾīs al-baladiyya qaliqa min tazāyud al-sukkān al-ʿArab', *Kull al-ʿArab*, 5 Oct. 1990, 10.

Ṭubī, Tawfīq, 'al-Durūs wa-ʾl-ʿibar al-mustafāda min intikhābāt al-sulṭa al-maḥalliyya', *al-Ittiḥād*, 20 Mar. 1989, 3.

Zaḥāliqa, ʿAlī Ḥaydar, 'Mashākil al-taʿlīm al-ʿArabī fī al-waqt al-ḥāḍir wa-ʾl-sanawāt al-2000', *Kull al-ʿArab*, 7 Dec. 1990, 10.

Zaydānī, Saʿīd, 'al-Muwāṭana al-dīmuqrāṭiyya fī·Isrāʾīl', *Qaḍāyā*, 4 (Aug. 1990), 3–18.

al-Zuʿbī, Munqidh, 'Nāṣirat al-jamīʿ wa-baladiyyat al-jamīʿ,' *al-Ṣināra*, 10

Mar. 1989.

al-Zuʿbī, Munqidh, 'al-Tajriba allatī fashilat', *al-Ṣināra*, 23 June 1989, 2.

—— 'Naḥnu maʿa al-intifāḍa, yā Ehūd Ōlmerṭ!', *al-Ṣināra*, 6 Oct. 1989.

2. Hebrew

(a) Books

Aḥawa biṭʾōn talmīdey ha-ūlpan ha-ʿIvrī-ʿAravī (n.p., 1971).

Assaf, Michael, *Hitʿōrērūt ha-ʿAravīm bě-Eretz-Israʾel w-věrīḥatam* (Tel-Aviv: Tarbūt wě-Ḥīnnūkh, 1967).

—— *ha-Yěḥasīm beyn ʿAravīm wě-Yěhūdīm bě-Eretz-Israʾel (1860–1948)* (Tel-Aviv: Tarbūt wě-Ḥīnnūkh, 1970).

Balas, Shimʿōn (trans.), *Sīppūrīm Palesṭinaʾiyyīm* (Tel-Aviv: ʿEqed, 1970).

Bar-Gal, Yōram, and Soffer, Arnon, *Těmūrōt bi-khěfarey ha-mīʿūṭīm* (Haifa: Haifa University, 1976).

Ben-Gurion, David, *Pěgīshōt ʿim manhīgīm ʿAraviyyīm* (Tel-Aviv: ʿAm ʿŌved, 1967).

Ben-Porat, Yoram, *Kōakh ha-ʿavōda ha-ʿAravī bě-Israʾel* (Jerusalem: Falk Institute, 1966).

Ber, Ḥavīva, and ʿAsāqila, Jābir, *Mifgěshey nōʿar Yěhūdī-ʿAravī bě-Givʿat-Ḥavīva* (Jerusalem: Měkhōn Israʾel lě-Meḥqar Ḥevratī wě-shīmmūshī, 1988).

Bien, Yehuda, *Beyt ha-sefer ha-ʿAravī: ʿiyyūn bě-veʿayōtav ha-enōshiyyōt* (Givʿat-Haviva: Givʿat-Haviva Publications, 1976).

Bigelman, Shimʿōn (ed.), *Shěnatōn sṭaṭīsṭī lě-Yěrūshalayim*, 6 (Jerusalem: Měkhōn Yěrūshalayim lě-Ḥeqer Israʾel, 1987).

Binyamin, Avraham, and Peleg, Rahel, *Shěʾīfōt lě-ʿatīd shel talmīdey shěmīniyyōt ʿAraviyyīm wě-mashmaʿūtan ha-ḥevratīt* (Haifa: Haifa University, 1976).

Brodnitz, M. M., and Chemansky, Daniel, *Piqqūaḥ kalkalī ba-migzar ha-ʿAravī bě-Israʾel* (Haifa: Technion, 1986).

Cohen, Avraham, *ʿArviyyey Israʾel: heybeṭīm kalkaliyyīm* (Givʿat Haviva: ha-Makhōn le-Līmmūdīm ʿAraviyyīm, 1986).

Cohen, Erīk, and Grūnau, Ḥermōna, *Seqer ha-mīʿūṭīm bě-Israʾel* (Jerusalem: Hebrew University, Truman Institute, 1972).

Cohen, Raʿanan, *Gīsha ḥadasha lě-ʿArviyyey Israʾel: Qawey mědīniyyūt* (n.p.: January 1989).

—— *Bi-Sěvakh ha-neʾemanūyōt: ḥevra w-pōlīṭiqa ba-migzar ha-ʿAravī* (Tel-Aviv: ʿAm ʿŌved, 1990).

Dana, Nissim, *ha-Děrūzīm ʿeda w-massōret* (Jerusalem: Ministry of Religious Affairs, 1974).

Diskin, Avraham, *Běḥīrōt w-vōḥarīm bě-Israʾel* (Tel-Aviv: ʿAm ʿŌved, 1988).

Dōrōn, Adam (ed.), *Mĕdīnat Isra'el wĕ-Eretz-Isra'el* (Tsōfīt: Beyt Berl, 1988).

Enden, A., and Soffer, A., *Degem shĕkhūnōt ḥadashōt bi-khĕfarīm 'Araviyyīm bi-tsĕfōn Isra'el* (Haifa: Technological Institute, 1986).

Fallāḥ, Salmān, *Tōlĕdōt ha-Dĕrūzīm bĕ-Isra'el* (Jerusalem: Prime Minister's Office, 1974).

Gabbay, Moshe, *'Arviyyey Isra'el—shĕ'ela shel zehūt* (Giv'at Haviva: ha-Makhōn lĕ-Līmmūdīm 'Araviyyīm, 1984).

Gal, Johnny, *ha-Bĕḥīrōt la-Knesset ha-12 ba-migzar ha-'Aravī* (Giv'at Haviva: ha-Makhōn lĕ-Līmmūdīm 'Araviyyīm, 1989).

Gilbar, Gad, *Mĕgammōt ba-hitpattĕḥūt ha-demōgrafīt shel ha-Palesṭīnīm, 1870–1987* (Tel-Aviv: Tel-Aviv University, Dayyan Centre, 1989).

Ginat, Joseph, *Tĕmūrōt bĕ-mivne ha-mishpaḥa ba-kĕfar ha-'Aravī* (Tel-Aviv: Tel-Aviv University, Shiloah Centre, 1976).

—— *Ta'asūqa kĕ-gōrem lĕ-shinnūy ḥevratī ba-kĕfar ha-'Aravī* (Tel-Aviv: Tel-Aviv University, Sapir Centre, 1980).

Gutmann, E. L., and Qalf, Ḥayyīm, *ha-Histadrūt w-fĕ'ūlōteyha ba-seqṭōr ha-'Aravī: Meḥqar 'al 'amadōt, de'ōt we-hitnahagūt shel kafriyyīm 'Araviyyīm bĕ-Isra'el* (Jerusalem: ha-Makhōn lĕ-Meḥqar Ḥevratī Shīmmūshī, 1970).

al-Ḥaj, Mājid, *ha-Ḥinnūkh lĕ-demōqraṭiyya bĕ-veyt ha-sefer ha-'Aravī bĕ-Isra'el: be'ayōt wĕ-mĕsīmōt* (Giv'at Haviva: ha-Makhōn lĕ-Līmmūdīm 'Araviyyīm, 1989).

Ḥalabī, Muṣbāḥ, *ha-Dĕrūzīm bĕ-Isra'el: tōlĕdōt, massōret wĕ-ōrḥōt ḥayyīm* (Tel-Aviv: Millō', 1973).

Ḥamāyisī, Rāsim, *Tikhnūn wĕ-shikkūn bĕ-qerev ha-'Aravīm bĕ-Isra'el* (Tel-Aviv: International Centre for Peace in the Middle East, 1990).

Harari, Yechiel, *ha-Bĕḥīrōt ba-migzar ha-'Aravī 1973* (Giv'at Haviva: Semīnar ha-Kībbūtz ha-Artsī, 1975).

Hareven, Alouph (ed.), *Eḥad mi-kol shīshsha Isrĕ'elīm: Yaḥasey gōmĕlīn beyn ha-mī'ūt ha-'Aravī wĕ-ha-rōv ha-Yĕhūdī bĕ-Isra'el* (Jerusalem: Van Leer Institute, 1981).

—— (ed.), *Ma lĕhashīv? Keytsad lĕhitmōded 'im shĕ'elōt 'al yaḥasey Yĕhūdīm-'Aravīm, yaḥasey Isra'el-'Arav wĕ-demōqraṭiyya* (Jerusalem: Van Leer Institute, 1985).

Hatsa'at tsevet lĕ-tikhnūn ha-ḥīnnūkh li-shĕnōt ha-80 (Jerusalem: Ministry of Education and Culture, 1976).

Ḥaydar, 'Azīz, *ha-Ḥinnūkh ha-miqtsō'ī-tekhnōlōgī ba-migzar ha-'Aravī bĕ-Isra'el* (Jerusalem and Tel-Aviv: International Centre for Peace in the Middle East, 1985).

—— Rosenfeld, Henry, and Kahana, Reuven (eds.), *ha-Ḥevra ha-'Aravīt bĕ-Isra'el: miqra'a* (Jerusalem: Hebrew University, Faculty of Social Sciences, 1983).

Ḥayek, Tsvī (ed.), *ha-Ḥaverīm ha-'Aravīm wĕ-ha-Dĕrūzīm ba-histadrūt* (Tel-

Aviv: Histadrut, July 1989).

Hofman, Yochanan (ed.), *Kenes ʿal matsav ha-mehqar bĕ-nōseʾ yaḥasey enōsh beyn ʿAravīm lĕ-Yĕhūdīm* (Haifa: Haifa University, 1971).

—— *Dīmmūyīm wĕ-zehūt shel nōʿar ʿAravī bĕ-Israʾel* (Haifa: ha-Makhōn lĕ-Ḥeqer ha-Ḥīnnūkh ha-ʿAravī w-lĕ-Fīttūḥō, 1977).

Hofnung, Menachem, *Israʾel—biṭĕḥōn ha-mĕdīna mūl shilṭōn ha-ḥōq 1948–1991* (Jerusalem: Nĕvō, 1991).

Jiryis, Ṣabrī, *ha-ʿAravīm bĕ-Israʾel* (Haifa: al-Ittiḥād Press, 1966).

Kabhā, Riyāḍ, *Barṭaʿa* (Givʿat Haviva: ha-Makhōn lĕ-Līmmūdīm ʿAraviyyīm, 1986).

Katz, Yoram, *Maʿarekhet ha-bĕḥīrōt la-histadrūt ba-migzar ha-ʿAravī/ha-Dĕrūzī* (Tel-Aviv: Mifleget ha-ʿAvōda ha-Isrĕʾelīt, 1989).

Kislev, Ran, *Hem wĕ-anaḥnū: ʿAravīm bĕ-Israʾel* (Givʿat Haviva: ha-Makhōn lĕ-Līmmūdīm ʿAraviyyīm, 1987).

Landau, J. M. (ed.), *ha-Migzar ha-ʿAravī bĕ-Israʾel wĕ-ha-bĕḥīrōt la-Knesset, 1988* (Jerusalem: Mĕkhōn Yĕrūshalayim lĕ-Ḥeqer Israʾel, 1989).

Lavīʾ, Tsvī, *ha-Mahpekha ha-shĕqeṭa ba-rĕḥōv ha-ʿAravī* (Jerusalem: Ministry of Education and Culture, 1970).

Layish, Aharon (ed.), *ha-ʿAravīm bĕ-Israʾel: rĕtsīfūt w-tĕmūra* (Jerusalem: Magnes Press, 1981).

Makhōn Isrĕʾelī lĕ-mehqar w-meydaʿ, *ha-Qōʾōperatsiyya ha-ʿAravīt: mehqar hevratī-kalkalī* (Tel-Aviv, 1972).

Mayer, Thomas, *Hitʿōrĕrūt ha-Mūslĕmīm bĕ-Israʾel* (Givʿat Haviva: ha-Makhōn lĕ-Līmmūdīm ʿAraviyyīm, 1988).

Mĕdīnat Israʾel—Misrad ha-Pĕnīm, *Dīn wĕ-heshbōn ha-vĕʿada ha-beyn-misradīt li-vĕniyya biltī-ḥūqqīt ba-migzar ha-ʿAravī* (Jerusalem, 1986).

Mifleget ha-ʿAvōda ha-Isrĕʾelīt—ha-Merkaz. Agaf ha-Bĕḥīrōt, *Tōtsĕʾōt ha-bĕḥīrōt la-Kenesset ha-12: nīttūaḥ riʾshōnī* (n.p. [Tel-Aviv], 1989).

Mifqedet Ezōr Rĕtsūʿat ʿAzza—Ṣṭaṭīsṭīqa, *Muʿassaqīm bĕ-Israʾel: mĕtsīʾūt w-pōṭentsyal* (Gaza, April 1972).

Misrad ha-Pĕnīm [Ministry of the Interior], Agaf lĕ-Shilṭōn Mĕqōmī—ha-Maḥlaqa lĕ-Mīʿūṭīm, *ha-Bĕḥīrōt bi-shĕmōneh rĕshūyōt mĕqōmiyyōt ba-seqṭōr ha-ʿAravī ba-shanīm 1971, 1972* (Jerusalem, June 1972).

—— *Rĕshīmat ha-rĕshūyōt ha-mĕqōmiyyōt bĕ-yishshūvey ha-mīʿūṭīm* (Jerusalem, Mar. 1973).

—— *ha-Bĕḥīrōt la-rĕshūyōt ha-mĕqōmiyyōt ba-seqṭōr ha-ʿAravī 1973* (Jerusalem, Mar. 1974).

Netzer, Yĕhōshafat, and Raz, Tamar, *Tĕnūʿat ha-nōʿar ha-ʿAravī ha-ḥalūtzī* (Tel-Aviv: Tel-Aviv University, Shiloah Centre, 1976).

Neuberger, Benyamin, *ha-Mīʿūṭ ha-ʿAravī: Nīkkūr lĕʾūmī wĕ-hishtallĕvūt pōlīṭīt* (Tel-Aviv: Open University, 1991).

Ōsetzkī-Lazar, Sara, and Ghānim, Asʿad, *Ōṭōnōmiyya la-ʿAravīm bĕ-Israʾel—diyyūn bĕ-reʾshītō* (Givʿat Haviva: ha-Makhōn lĕ-Līmmūdīm ʿAraviyyīm, 1990).

Paz, Rĕʾūven, *ha-Tĕnūʿa ha-Islāmīt bĕ-Israʾel bĕ-ʿiqvōt ha-bĕḥīrōt la-rĕs̲h̲ūyōt ha-mĕqōmiyyōt: sĕqīra wĕ-nīttūaḥ* (Tel-Aviv: Tel-Aviv University, Dayyan and Shiloah Centres, 1989).

Peled, Matityahū, *ha-Ḥīnnūk̲h̲ ha-ʿAravī bĕ-Israʾel w-mĕgammōt hitpattĕḥūtō* (Tel-Aviv: Tel-Aviv University, Shiloah Centre, 1976).

Peres, Yochanan, *Yaḥasey ʿedōt bĕ-Israʾel* (Tel-Aviv: Sifriyyat ha-Pōʿalīm, 1976).

Platek, Yitzhak, and Maḥāmīd, Muḥammad, *Ōt s̲h̲el peḥam: ʿŌlamam s̲h̲el tsĕʾīrīm ʿAraviyyīm bĕ-Israʾel* (Givʿat Haviva: ha-Mak̲h̲ōn lĕ-Līmmūdīm ʿAraviyyīm, 1989).

Qamā, Blanche, *Maʿamad ha-is̲h̲s̲h̲a ha-ʿAraviyya bĕ-Israʾel* (Jerusalem: Prime Minister's Office, 1984).

Rappōpōrṭ, H., *et al.*, *Tĕnūʿat ha-nōʿar ha-ʿAravī bĕ-Israʾel: Yedaʿ, ʿarak̲h̲īm wĕ-hitnahagūyōt bĕ-nōseʾ ḥevra w-mĕdīna* (Jerusalem: Szold Institute, 1978).

Regev, Avner, *ʿArviyyey Israʾel: Sūgiyyōt pōlīṭiyyōt* (Jerusalem: Mĕk̲h̲on Yĕrūs̲h̲alayim lĕ-Ḥeqer Israʾel, 1989).

Rekhess, Elie, *ʿArviyyey Israʾel lĕ-aḥar 1967: haḥrafata s̲h̲el beʿayat ha-ōriyenṭatsiyya* (Tel-Aviv: Tel-Aviv University, Shiloah Centre, 1976).

—— *ʿArviyyey Israʾel wĕ-hafqaʿat ha-qarqaʿōt ba-Galīl* (Tel-Aviv: Tel-Aviv University, Shiloah Centre, 1977).

—— *ha-Kĕfar ha-ʿAravī bĕ-Israʾel—mōqed pōlīṭī lĕʾūmī mitḥaddes̲h̲* (Tel-Aviv: Tel-Aviv University, Dayyan Centre, 1985).

ha-Rĕs̲h̲īma ha-Mitqaddemet lĕ-S̲h̲alōm, *Hodaʿat ha-yissūd* (n.p., 1984).

Romann, Michael, *Yaḥasey ha-gōmĕlīn beyn ha-migzar ha-Yĕhūdī wĕ-ha-ʿAravī bĕ-Yĕrūs̲h̲alayim* (Jerusalem: Mĕk̲h̲ōn Yĕrūs̲h̲alayim lĕ-Ḥeqer Israʾel, 1984).

Rosen, H. M., *ha-Yĕḥasīm beyn Yĕhūdīm la-ʿAravīm bĕ-Israʾel wĕ-ha-irgūnīm ha-tsībbūriyyīm ha-s̲h̲ōqĕdim ʿal ṭippūḥam* (Jerusalem: American Jewish Committee, 1971).

Rosenfeld, Henry, *Hem hayū fallaḥīm* (n.p.: ha-Kibbūts ha-Mĕʾūḥad, 1964).

Ṣāliḥ, S̲h̲akīb, *Tōlĕdōt ha-Dĕrūzīm* (Ramat-Gan: Bar-Ilan University, 1989).

Schiff, Aryeh, and Yaari, Ehud, *Intifāḍa* (Jerusalem and Tel-Aviv: Schocken, 1990).

Shamir, Shimon, *ha-Perspeqṭīva ha-hīsṭōrīt—divrey mavōʾ* (Tel-Aviv: Tel-Aviv University, Shiloah Centre, 1976).

Shammās, Anṭūn, *ha-Sifrūt ha-ʿAravīt bĕ-Israʾel aḥarey 1967* (Tel-Aviv: Tel-Aviv University, Shiloah Centre, 1976).

Shilo, Gideon, *ʿArviyyey Israʾel bĕ-ʿeyney mĕdīnōt ʿArav wĕ-As̲h̲af* (Jerusalem: Magnes Press and Truman Institute, 1982).

Shimʿōnī, Yaʿaqōv, *ʿArviyyey Eretz-Israʾel* (Tel-Aviv: ʿAm ʿŌved, 1947).

S̲h̲mūʾelī, A., *et al.*, *Gilgūlō s̲h̲el ezōr: ha-Mĕs̲h̲ūllas̲h̲ ha-Qaṭan* (Haifa: Haifa University, Jewish–Arab Centre, 1985).

Soffer, Arnon (ed.), ʿEsrīm _shana_ lĕ-milḥemet _sheshet_ ha-yamīm = ʿIyyūnīm bĕ-Ḥeqer ha-Mizraḥ ha-Tīkhōn, NS 7 (June 1987).

—— ʿAl ha-matsav ha-demōgrafī wĕ-ha-geyʾōgrafī bĕ-Eretz-Israʾel: ha-omnam sōf he-ḥazōn ha-Tsiyyōnī? (Haifa: Gestelit, 1988).

—— et al., Leqeṭ bībliyografī: _shĕkhūnōt_ mĕʿōravōt _shel_ Yĕhūdīm wa-ʿAravīm bĕ-Israʾel (Haifa: Haifa University, Jewish-Arab Centre, 1988).

Sṭendel, Ōrī, ha-Cherkesīm bĕ-Israʾel (Tel-Aviv: ʿAm ʿŌved, 1973).

—— and ha-Rĕʾūvenī, E., ha-Mīʿūṭīm bĕ-Israʾel (n.p.: ha-Kībbūtz ha-Mĕʾūḥad, 1973).

Tōtsĕʾōt ha-bĕḥīrōt ba-histadrūt 13. 11. 1989 (Tel-Aviv: Histadrut, n.d. [1990]).

Tōtsĕʾōt ha-bĕḥīrōt la-Knesset (Jerusalem: Central Bureau of Statistics, various years).

Tsemaḥ, Mīna, ʿEmdōt ha-rōv ha-Yĕhūdī bĕ-Israʾel kĕlappey ha-mīʿūṭ ha-ʿAravī (Jerusalem: Van Leer Institute, 1980).

Vīlnāy, Zeʾev, ha-Mīʿūṭīm bĕ-Israʾel: Mūslĕmīm-Nōtsĕrīm-Dĕrūzīm-Bahāʾīm (Jerusalem: Mass, 1959).

Wainshal, Ziva, and Pelli, Dafna (eds.), Yĕrū_shalayim_ nĕtūnīm sṭaṭīsṭiyyīm (Jerusalem: Mĕkhōn Yĕrushalayim lĕ-Ḥeqer Israʾel, 1983).

Waschītz, Yōsef, ha-ʿAravīm bĕ-Eretz-Israʾel (Merḥavya: Sifriyyat Pōʿālīm, 1947).

Yalqūṭ ha-Pirsūmīm (Jerusalem: Government Printer, various years).

Yarōn, Qalman, and Grabelsky, Ōra (eds.), ha-Mifgash ha-ḥevratī-tarbūtī beyn Yĕhūdīm wa-ʿAravīm bĕ-ʿiqvōt simpōzyōn (Jerusalem: Association for Adult Education, 1968).

Yĕhōshuʿa, Jacob, ha-ʿEda ha-Mūslĕmīt bĕ-Israʾel (Jerusalem: Ministry for Religious Affairs, 1973).

(b) Articles

ʿAbbāsī, Maḥmūd, 'Hilkhey rūaḥ ḥadashīm bĕ-qerev ʿArviyyey Israʾel', Migwan, 53 (Nov. 1980), 41–4.

Abū ʿAṭsheh, Zaydān, 'Meḥaʾa neged ha-ʿAvōda: sṭūdenṭ Dĕrūzī masbīr ha-hatsbaʿa lĕ-RAQAḤ', Pī ha-Atōn (Jerusalem), 3 Mar. 1970, 2.

Abū Rukn, Sharīf, 'Shĕʾela shel zehūt', al-Hudà, Feb. 1976, 39–40.

Abū Ṭuʿma, Jalāl, '"Arviyyey Israʾel mitkahashīm lĕ-zīqatam ha-lĕʾūmīt', ha-Aretz, 26 May 1972, 12.

—— '"Arviyyey Israʾel mĕʿunyanīm bĕ-_shīllūv_', ha-Aretz, 22 Apr. 1982, 10.

Algazī, Yōsef, 'Pōʿālīm kaḥōl-lavan', ha-Aretz, 28 Mar. 1991, B1.

—— 'Ba-dere_kh_ lĕ-Ṭōrōnṭō', ha-Aretz, 5 July 1991, B4.

'Aloupḥ Hareven, Eḥad mi-kol _shīshsha_ Isrĕʾelīm wĕ-anaḥnū', Maʿarīv, 11 Dec. 1980, 5.

'Anaḥnū lōʾ jihād Islāmī', Kōteret Raʾ_shīt_, 277 (23 Mar. 1988), 20–3.

Argaman-Barneʿa, ʿAmalya, 'Yaḥasey _shĕkhenūt_ bi-_shĕkhūna_ mĕʿōrevet',

Yĕdīʿōt Aharōnōt, 20 Oct. 1982, 23.

Avīsar, Adar, and Marōn, Gideon, 'Intifāḍa zōḥelet lĕ-Ṭaiyyba', *Maʿarīv*, 4 Apr. 1990, D1.

Ayyalōn, ʿAmōs, 'Galīl shel ʿAravīm wĕ-Yĕhūdīm', *ha-Aretz*, 30 Nov. 1979, 2–3 Dec. 1979.

Azūlay, Ōrlī, 'Ṭerōr bĕ-shem Allāh', *Yĕdīʿōt Aharōnōt*, 6 Mar. 1981, Suppl., 5–7.

'Ba-migzar ha-ʿAravī: hanhaga ḥadasha', *Maʿarīv*, 3 Mar. 1989, B1.

Barqat, Ela, 'ha-Dĕrūzīm bĕ-Israʾel—shĕʾela shel zehūt', *ha-Aretz*, 8 Oct. 1976, 12–13.

Bar-Qōvets, Sīgal, 'Ḥayyey shīttūf', *Pī ha-Atōn*, Apr. 1991, 20–1.

Bar-Yōsef, Avīnōʿam, 'Kafr Qāsim: ha-kĕtōvet ʿal ha-qīr', *Maʿarīv*, 10 Mar. 1989, 4.

Bĕʾer, Yizhar, 'Naʿalayim reyqōt ba-ḥōl', *ha-Aretz*, 22 Mar. 1991, Suppl., 27, 30.

Ben, Alūf, 'ha-ʿAravīm ḥōzrīm el ha-qarqaʿ', *ha-Aretz*, 31 Aug. 1990, B5.

Ben-ʿAmmī, Naḥman, 'Siaḥ ʿal ʿAravīm', *Maʿarīv*, 15 July 1970, 19.

Ben-David, Yosef, 'Dĕfūsey hatsbaʿa mishtannīm bĕ-qerev Bedwiyyey ha-Negev', in J. M. Landau (ed.), *ha-Migzar ha-ʿAravī bĕ-Israʾel wĕ-ha-bĕḥīrōt la-Knesset, 1988* (Jerusalem: Mĕkhōn Yĕrūshalayim lĕ-Ḥeqer Israʾel, 1989), 85–114.

Bender, Erīk, ''Arviyyey artsĕkha wĕ-ʿArviyyey eretz aḥeret', *Pī ha-Atōn*, 28 Dec. 1977, 2.

Ben-Hillel, Sara, and Tsūr, Yĕhūda, 'ha-Yaʿad: mandaṭ me-ha-bōḥer ha-ʿAravī', *Ḥōtam*, 39 (23 Sept. 1988), 9–10.

Benqler, Rafī, 'ha-Dīlemma shel Noṣrat', *ʿAl ha-Mishmar*, 17 Oct. 1969, 5, 8.

Bishāra, ʿAzmī, 'ha-Ḥevra ha-ʿAravīt bĕ-Israʾel—mi-nĕqūdat rĕʾūt aheret', *Mĕdina, Mimshal we-Yĕḥasīm Beynlĕʾūmiyyīm*, 32 (Spring 1990), 81–6.

Bīzman, Aharōn, and Amīr, Yĕhūda, 'Dīmmūyīm lĕʾūmiyyīm hadadiyyīm shel Yĕhūdīm wa-ʿAravīm bĕ-Israʾel', *Mĕgammōt*, 28/1 (June 1983), 100–5.

Brodnitz, M. M., and Chemansky, Daniel, 'Teʿūs ha-kĕfar ha-ʿAravī bĕ-Israʾel', *Rivʿōn lĕ-Khalkala*, 128 (Apr. 1986), 533–46.

Cohen, Raʿanan, 'Ma she-lō naʿaseh ha-yōm yiqsheh lĕtaqqen mahar', *Davar*, 16 Nov. 1989, 5.

Cohen, Yaʿaqōv, 'ha-Bĕḥīrōt la-histadrūt bĕ-qerev ha-ʿAravīm', *Leqeṭ Yĕdīʿōt*, 28 (Apr.–Dec. 1969), 3–8.

Dāhir, Kāmil, 'ha-Rĕshīma ha-Mitqaddemet ḥayya wĕ-qayyemet w-fĕʿīla mĕʾōd', *ʿAl ha-Mishmar*, 14 June 1987, 8.

Danzig, Hillel, 'Dĕrūsha gīsha ḥadasha el ha-mīʿūṭ ha-ʿAravī', *Davar*, 9 Feb. 1971, 7, 10.

Dar, Yōʾel, 'Maʿarekhet ha-bĕḥīrōt ba-migzar ha-ʿAravī wĕ-ha-Dĕrūzī',

Davar, 21 June 1981, 7.

Darāwshe, ʿAbd al-Wahhāb, 'Mishqal ḥasar taqdīm', *Pōlīṭīqa*, 21 (June 1988), 22–3.

Darwīsh, Samīr, 'Lihyōt ʿAravī bĕ-Israʾel: maddūʿa hidlaqtī et massūʾat yōm ha-ʿatsmaʾūt', *ha-Aretz*, 17 June 1986, 14.

Dayyan, Aryeh, 'Sīʿat yaḥīd', *Kol ha-ʿĪr*, 2 Dec. 1988, 35–8.

—— 'ha-Sahar he-ḥadash', *Kol ha-ʿĪr*, 19 Jan. 1990, 29–31.

—— '"Ōlīm ʿaleyhem', *Kol ha-ʿĪr*, 9 Mar. 1990, 41–4.

—— 'ha-Mĕnahel qaraʾ lō wĕ-amar, mitstaʿer, illūts taqtsīvīʾ', *ha-Aretz*, 21 Dec. 1990, Suppl., 9, 11.

Diskin, Avraham, 'Heybeṭīm staṭīsṭiyyīm shel ha-hatsbaʿa ba-migzar ha-ʿAravī', in J. M. Landau (ed.), *ha-Migzar ha-ʿAravī bĕ-Israʾel wĕ-ha-bĕḥīrōt la-Knesset, 1988* (Jerusalem: Mĕkhon Yĕrushalayim lĕ-Ḥeqer Israʾel, 1989), 22–33.

'Doaḥ ha-qeren lĕ-fittūaḥ tekhnōlōgī ba-ḥinnūkh ha-ʿAravī', *ha-Aretz*, 1 Dec. 1986, 6.

'Dōqṭōr Cohen wĕ-ʿArviyyey Israʾel', *ha-Aretz*, 3 Aug. 1990, B3.

Dōr, Mōshe, 'ha-Sifrūt ha-ʿAravīt ha-tsōmaḥat ba-aretz', *Maʿarīv*, 18 Feb. 1972, 34.

Dōtan, Amnōn, 'Lĕʾan mitqaddemet ha-Rĕshīma ha-Mitqaddemet', *ʿAl ha-Mishmar*, 21 Sept. 1984, 11.

Elʿad, Elī, 'RAQAḤ nivlĕma ba-rĕḥōv ha-ʿAravīʾ', *ha-Aretz*, 31 Oct. 1969, 17.

—— 'ha-Aḥūza ha-ʿAravīt ʿavra lĕ-Allōn: hadīfat RAQAḤ ba-bĕḥīrōt neḥshevet kĕ-hatslaḥatōʾ', *ha-Aretz*, 7 Nov. 1969, 10.

—— 'ha-ʿArabīsṭīm ʿayefīm: haznaḥa ba-tīppūl ba-rĕḥōv ha-ʿAravī w-va-nōʿar', *ha-Aretz*, 30 Jan. 1970, 17.

—— 'Sṭūdenṭīm ʿAraviyyīm Isrĕʾeliyyīm mĕsayyʿīm li-fĕʿūlōt Fatḥ bĕ-qampūsīm bĕ-Artsōt ha-Bĕrit', *ha-Aretz*, 10 Apr. 1970, 12.

—— 'Mered ha-tsĕʿīrīm bĕ-Bāqa al-Gharbiyya', *ha-Aretz*, 18 Oct. 1970.

Elqayyam, Avīṭal, 'Heder qĕtsat aher', *Pī ha-Atōn*, 31/4 (Jan. 1989), 7.

Eyal, Elī, 'ha-Mered ha-shaqeṭ shel ha-tsĕʿīrīm ha-ʿAraviyyīm', *Maʿarīv*, 22 Jan. 1971, Suppl., 19–21.

—— 'Gam ha-Bedwīm ratsīm la-Knesset', *Maʿarīv*, 17 Aug. 1973, 18.

Eylōn, Giōra, 'Lĕ-mi ikhpat she-hithallef yōʿets rōʾsh ha-memshala lĕ-ʿinyĕney ʿAravīm', *Yĕdīʿōt Aḥarōnōt*, 16 Nov. 1990, 23–4.

Fabian, Naḥman, 'Hevley teʿūs ba-kĕfar ha-ʿAravī', *ha-Aretz*, 19 Aug. 1970, 5.

—— 'Noṣrat—ha-maʿōz shel RAQAḤ: mitqarĕvīm la-bĕḥīrōt', *ha-Aretz*, 20 Nov. 1970, 17.

—— '"Aravīm ka-ḥaverīm ba-ʿAvōda', *ha-Aretz*, 3 June 1973, 14.

Fallāḥ, Salmān, 'Beʿayōt yĕsōd ba-ḥinnūkh ha-Dĕrūzī bĕ-Israʾel', *Ha-Mizraḥ he-Ḥadash*, 32/125–8 (1989), 115–28.

Fawwāz, Kamāl, 'Dĕrūzīm wa-ʿAravīm ba-qampūs', *Pī ha-Atōn*, 10 Feb. 1970.

Förshner, Ḥaggay, 'ha-Merkaz yamlīts wĕ-yĕʾashsher', *Davar*, 22 Sept. 1991, 14.

Galīlī, Līlī, 'Seqer hashwaʾatī shel ḥōqer bĕ-ūnīversīṭat Ḥeyfa', *ha-Aretz*, 23 Dec. 1985, 2.

Ghānim, Asʿad, and Osetski-Lazar, Sara, 'Qaw yarōq, qawīm adūmmīm, ʿArviyyey Israʾel nōkhaḥ ha-intifāḍa', *Sĕqīrōt ʿal ʿArviyyey Israʾel*, 3 (May 1990), 1–23.

Gilbar, Gad, 'Mĕgammōt ba-hitpattĕḥūt ha-demōgrafīt shel ʿArviyyey Eretz Israʾel, 1870–1948', *Cathedra*, 45 (Sept. 1987), 43–56.

Gilbōʿa, ʿAmōs, 'ha-Im higgīʿa ha-intifāḍa lĕ-ʿArviyyey Israʾel', *Maʿarīv*, 8 June 1989, B3.

—— 'Lōʾ lĕhaṭmīn et ha-rōʾsh ba-ḥōl', *Maʿarīv*, 15 Dec. 1989, 4.

—— 'Eyn ʿArviyyey Israʾel; yesh Palesṭīnīm', *Maʿarīv*, 25 May 1990, B1.

—— 'Taʿasūqa la-ʿAravīm', *Maʿarīv*, 1 June 1990, E4.

—— 'Ṭaiyyba—ʿīr kĕ-mashal', *Maʿarīv*, 22 June 1990, E4.

Ginat, Joseph, 'Dĕfūsey hatsbaʿa wĕ-hitnahagūt pōlīṭīt ba-migzar ha-ʿAravī', in J. M. Landau (ed.), *ha-Migzar ha-ʿAravī bĕ-Israʾel wĕ-ha-bĕḥīrōt la-Knesset, 1988* (Jerusalem: Mĕkhōn Yĕrushalayim lĕ-Ḥeqer Israʾel, 1989), 3–21.

Greilshammer, Īlan, 'RAQAḤ wĕ-ha-bĕḥīrōt la-Knesset ha-12', in J. M. Landau (ed.), *ha-Migzar ha-ʿAravī bĕ-Israʾel wĕ-ha-bĕḥīrōt la-Knesset, 1988* (Jerusalem: Mĕkhōn Yĕrūshalayim lĕ-Ḥeqer Israʾel, 1989), 50–62.

Gūndar, Ūd, 'Gan yĕladīm ba-ḥatsar ha-misgad', *ha-Aretz*, 9 Jan. 1991, B2.

Guṭmann, Emanuel, 'ha-Bĕḥīrōt la-Knesset ha-shĕvīʿīt', *Gesher*, 15/61 (Dec. 1969), 15–21.

Guṭmann, Ūrī, 'Gīllūyey badlanūt lĕ-ʾūmīt bĕ-qerev ha-ḥūgīm ha-radīqaliyyīm shel ʿArviyyey Israʾel bi-shĕnōt ha-shivʿīm wĕ-ha-shĕmōnīm', MA thesis, Hebrew University of Jerusalem, 1990.

al-Ḥaj, Mājid, 'ha-Ḥamūla ha-ʿAravīt bĕ-Israʾel', *Migwan*, 54 (Dec. 1980), 33–6.

—— 'ha-Hashlakhōt ha-pōlīṭiyyōt wĕ-ha-ḥevratiyyōt shel ha-mifgashīm ha-Palesṭiniyyīm mi-shĕney ʿevrey ha-qaw ha-yarōq', in Arnon Soffer (ed.), *ʿEsrīm shana lĕ-milḥemet sheshet ha-yamīm* = *ʿIyyūnīm bĕ-Ḥeqer ha-Mizraḥ ha-Tīkhōn*, NS 7 (June 1987), 20–89.

—— 'Bĕḥīrōt ba-rĕḥōv ha-ʿAravī bĕ-tsel ha-intifāḍa', in J. M. Landau (ed.), *ha-Migzar ha-ʿAravī bĕ-Israʾel wĕ-ha-bĕḥīrōt la-Knesset, 1988* (Jerusalem: Mĕkhōn Yĕrūshalayim lĕ-Ḥeqer Israʾel, 1989), 35–49.

—— 'Aqademaʾīm bĕ-tsawārōn kaḥōl', *Pōlīṭiqa*, 29 (Nov. 1989), 24–7.

Ḥalabī, Rafīq, 'Anaḥnū ha-yĕlīdīm', *Kōteret Ra'shīt*, 3 (15 Dec. 1982), 22–3.

Ḥamāyisī, Rāsim, 'Tĕnūʿat meḥa'a mi-sūg ḥadash', *Davar*, 3 May 1989, 7.

Ḥasīd, Etty, 'Īdīliya bĕ-Ṭīra', *ha-Aretz*, 21 Dec. 1990, Suppl., 17.

Ḥavaqqūq, Yaʿaqōv, 'Mishpaḥat ha-jihād—ha-maḥteret ba-Mĕshūllash', *ha-Aretz*, 3 June 1981, Suppl.

Ḥaydar, ʿAzīz, 'ha-ʿAvōda ha-ʿAravīt', *Pōlīṭīqa*, 21 (July 1988), 24–7.

Hōn, Sha'ūl, 'Hafīkhat ḥatser bĕ-Qalansuwa', *Maʿarīv*, 17 Feb. 1974, 7.

ʿInbar, Avīṭal, '"Im ha-gav la-qīr', *Dĕvar ha-Shavūʿa*, 32 (11 Aug. 1989), 9–12.

Isrĕ'elī, ʿAmīhūd, 'Ifyūney ha-mī'ūṭīm bĕ-Isra'el bi-shĕnōt ha-80', *Natīv*, 2/3 (May 1989), 17–26.

Kahanā, Nūrīt, 'Raq vīlōn mafrīd beyn mishpaḥa lĕ-mishpaḥa', *ha-Aretz*, 16 Oct. 1989, 11.

——— 'Hitpaṭṭer mazkal ha-dōr ha-tsaʿīr ba-Miflaga ha-Demōqraṭīt ha-ʿAravīt bi-gĕlal tĕmīkhata bĕ-Ṣaddām', *ha-Aretz*, 24 Aug. 1990, A3.

——— Shĕlīsh mi-bĕney ha-ʿeda ha-Yĕvanīt hīggĕrū min ha-aretz me-az pĕrōts ha-intifāḍa', *ha-Aretz*, 26 Dec. 1990, A5.

Kahbā, Sufyān, 'Ma yeytse la-ʿAravīm me-ha-ʿaliyya?', *ha-Aretz*, 7 Dec. 1990, B3.

Kamāl, Zakī, '"Ōd ʿelbōn la-Dĕrūzīm', *ha-Aretz*, 3 Jan. 1991, B8.

Karmel, Ḥezī, 'ha-Qōl ha-ʿAravī ba-bĕḥīrōt: kōḥa shel RAQAḤ gadel meʿaṭ', *Maʿarīv*, 30 Oct. 1969, 11.

Kaspī, Aryeh, 'Mĕgayyĕrīm et qaw ha-ʿōnī', *ha-Aretz*, 1 Dec. 1989, Suppl., 9.

Kaspīt, Ben, 'Khōmeynīzm ʿeser daqqōt mi-Tel-Avīv', *Maʿarīv*, 14 Sept. 1990, Suppl., 6–10.

Katz, Yōram, 'Maʿarekhet ha-bĕḥīrōt la-histadrūt ba-migzar ha-ʿAravī/ha-Dĕrūzī', offprint (Tel-Aviv: Mifleget ha-ʿAvōda ha-Isrĕ'elīt, 1989).

Khūrī, Tawfīq, 'ha-Mahpakh ba-migzar ha-ʿAravī', *Migwan*, 62 (Aug. 1981), 40–2.

Klinov, Ruth, 'Yĕhūdīm wa-ʿAravīm bĕ-kōaḥ ha-ʿavōda ha-Isrĕ'elī: sakhar wĕ-ramat haskala', *Rivʿōn lĕ-Khalkala*, 145 (Aug. 1990), 130–44.

Knaʿan, Ḥavīv, '57% me-ḥavrey RAQAḤ hem pōʿalīm', *ha-Aretz*, 21 Feb. 1969, 16.

——— 'ha-Aderet ha-adūmma shel ha-lĕ'ūmanūt ha-ʿAravīt', *ha-Aretz*, 26 Oct. 1969, 11.

Knōller, Yĕhūdīt, 'Tsarōt ḥadashōt bĕ-mivney ha-qevaʿ', *ha-Aretz*, 3 Dec. 1990, B3.

'Kol shilṭey ha-histadrūt be-yishshūvīm ʿAraviyyīm w-vĕ-yishshūvīm mĕʿōravīm yihyū bi-shĕtey ha-safōt', *ha-Aretz*, 30 Jan. 1989, 3.

Kressel, Gideon, 'ha-Histaggĕlūt ha-eqōlōgīt wĕ-ha-tarbūtīt shel Bedwīm mitʿayyĕrīm bĕ-merkaz ha-aretz', in Aharon Layish (ed.), *ha-ʿAravīm bĕ-Isra'el: rĕtsīfūt w-tĕmūra* (Jerusalem: Magnes Press, 1981), 140–67.

Landau, J. M., 'Nīkkūr w-mĕtaḥīm ba-hitnahagūt ha-pōlīṭīt', in Aharon Layish (ed.), *ha-ʿAravīm bĕ-Israʾel: rĕtsīfūt w-tĕmūra* (Jerusalem: Magnes Press, 1981), 197–212.

Lavīʾ, Tsvī, 'ha-Bedwīm baʾīm ha-ʿīra—naṯshū ōhel lĕ-maʿan ḥavīla', *Maʿarīv*, 16 June 1970, 16.

Layish, Aharon, 'ha-Irgūn ha-ʿadatī shel ha-Mūslĕmīm', in Aharon Layish (ed.), *ha-ʿAravīm bĕ-Israʾel: rĕtsīfūt w-tĕmūra* (Jerusalem: Magnes Press, 1981), 123–9.

Levi, Gideon, 'Kĕ-shetaqīmū mĕdīna demōqraṭīt—ṭalpĕnū', *ha-Aretz*, 1 June 1990, Suppl., 13–14.

Levin, Mike, 'Tĕfīsōt qitsōniyyōt qibbĕlū legītīmatsiyya', *ha-Ūnīversīṭa* (Jerusalem), 5 (Winter 1991), 18–21.

Mālik, Ibrāhīm, 'ha-Tĕnūʿa ha-Islāmīt bĕ-Israʾel—beyn ha-dĕveqūt ba-mĕqōrōt lĕ-maḥaseh ha-pragmaṭīzm', *Sĕqīrōt ʿal ʿArviyyey Israʾel*, 4 (Aug. 1990), 1–14.

Manṣūr, ʿAtallāh, 'Radīqalīzatsiyya ba-rĕḥōv ha-ʿAravī', *ha-Aretz*, 9 Mar. 1978, 10.

—— 'Maḥteret Mūslĕmīt ba-Mĕshūllash', *ha-Aretz*, 27 Feb. 1981, 15.

—— 'ha-Meyrūts aḥarey ha-qōl ha-ʿAravī', *ha-Aretz*, 2 June 1981, 12.

—— 'Histaggĕrūtam shel ʿArviyyey Israʾel', *ha-Aretz*, 18 Oct. 1982, 7–8.

—— 'Milḥemet ha-tĕnūʿa ha-Islāmīt ba-ḥillōniyyūt', *ha-Aretz*, 5 May 1983.

—— 'Miflaga lĕʾūmīt la-ʿAravīm', *ha-Aretz*, 30 July 1984, 9.

—— 'Eyn hakkara memshaltīt ba-ʿeda ha-Mūslĕmīt', *ha-Aretz*, 8 Sept. 1985, 9.

—— 'ʿAravīm, Palesṭīnaʾīm, Kĕnaʿanīm', *ha-Aretz*, 12 Jan. 1986, 9.

—— 'Memshelet Peres—sīkkūm', *ha-Aretz*, 19 Oct. 1986, 3.

—— 'Raq la-ʿAravīm ikh pat me-ʿAravīm', *ha-Aretz*, 2 Nov. 1986, 9.

—— 'Zĕqenīm baʿaley hash paʾa', *ha-Aretz*, 21 Apr. 1987, 13.

—— 'Mī mĕnahel et Vaʿadat ha-Maʿaqav ha-ʿElyōna', *ha-Aretz*, 20 Mar. 1988, 11.

—— 'Lōʾ mizdahīm ʿim ha-mĕdīna', *ha-Aretz*, 19 June 1988, 11.

—— 'Meḥaʾa neged ha-ʿAvōda', *ha-Aretz*, 18 Sept. 1989, 11.

—— '60% me-ha-sṭūdenṭīm ha-ʿAraviyyīm ba-aretz lamĕdū ha-shana miqtsōʿōt reyʾaliyyīm', *ha-Aretz*, 22 Sept. 1989, A6.

—— 'Daf ḥadash ba-Galīl', *ha-Aretz*, 5 Oct. 1989, 11.

—— 'Mikhlalōt lĕ-hakhsharat anshey dat Mūslĕmiyyīm yippatĕḥū bĕ-Bāqa al-Gharbiyya w-vĕ-Umm al-Faḥm', *ha-Aretz*, 10 Oct. 1989, 3.

—— 'Livnōt et ha-bayit tĕḥīlla', *ha-Aretz*, 1 Aug. 1990, 22.

—— 'Mĕnūddīm ba-histadrūt', *ha-Aretz*, 6 Aug. 1990, B3.

—— 'Mibĕʿad la-rĕʿala', *ha-Aretz*, 19 Aug. 1990, B3.

—— 'Ḥayyīm ʿal ha-tsava"', *ha-Aretz*, 26 Nov. 1990, B3.

—— 'ḤADASH kĕdey lishmōr yashan', *ha-Aretz*, 23 Dec. 1990, B3.

—— 'ha-Taqqanōt ha-ḥadashōt yaqellu ʿal rīshshūy mivnīm ba-migzar ha-

214   *Select Bibliography*

ʿAravī', *ha-Aretz*, 2 Jan. 1991, A5.

Manṣūr, ʿAtallāh, 'Meʾōt Dĕrūzīm hitʾassĕfū bĕ-Kafr Yāṣīf bĕ-mehaʾa ʿal hadaḥat Rafīq Ḥalabī mi-"Mebbaṭ"', *ha-Aretz*, 6 Jan. 1991, A7.

—— 'Vatīqey al-Arḍ heqīmū gūf hadash ʿim ʿeqrōnōt zehīm', *ha-Aretz*, 10 Jan. 1991, A5.

—— 'Bĕney ha-kĕfar mĕʾargĕnīm hafganat tĕmīkha bĕ-ʿemdatʿIrāq', *ha-Aretz*, 11 Jan. 1991, A3.

—— 'Kĕvar lōʾ kavōd gadōl', *ha-Aretz*, 4 Mar. 1991, B3.

—— 'Raʾshey ha-rĕshūyōt ha-ʿAraviyyōt yafgīnū bĕ-mehaʾa ʿal qīppūḥan', *ha-Aretz*, 7 Mar. 1991, A5.

Margalit, Dan, 'ha-Shūttaf mistalleq me-ha-ʿisqa', *ha-Aretz*, 9 Feb. 1988, 13.

Maṣalḥa, Salmān, 'Anashīm bĕ-tōkh millīm', *Pōlīṭīqa*, 21 (June 1988), 44–50.

Maṣālḥa, ʿUmar, ''Arviyyey Israʾel bi-Mĕdīnat Israʾel', in Adam Dōrōn (ed.), *Mĕdīnat Israʾel wĕ-Eretz Israʾel* (Tsōfīt, Beyt Berl, 1988), 315–25.

Mashʾūr, Luṭfī, 'Palestīnaʾī, ʿAravī, Isrĕʾelī', *ha-Aretz* 26 Oct. 1990, B2.

Mayer, Thomas, 'ha-Tsĕʾīrīm ha-Mūslĕmiyyīm bĕ-Israʾel', *ha-Mizraḥ he-Ḥadash*, 32/125–8 (1989), 10–20.

Maymōn, Shōsh, 'Nimʾas lī lĕmasher et ha-kĕʾev shellī', *Yĕdīʿōt Aharōnōt*, 28 Oct. 1988, Suppl., 12–13.

Mĕnaḥem, Q., 'Hefqerūt "demōqrāṭīt"', *Davar*, 26 Oct. 1969, 7.

Mendler, Nīlī, 'Talmīdīm ʿAraviyyīm mi-Noṣrat matslīḥīm ba-bagrūt yōter mi-talmīdeyha ha-Yĕhūdiyyīm', *ha-Aretz*, 7 Feb. 1990, A5.

—— 'Dōaḥ lĕ-sar ha-ḥinnūkh: ha-Aḥīm ha-Mūslĕmiyyīm mishtallĕṭīm ʿal mōsĕdōt ḥinnūkh ba-migzar ha-ʿAravī wĕ-gōrmīm lĕ-haqtsana', *ha-Aretz*, 28 Dec. 1990, 1.

Mīʿārī, Maḥmūd, 'Beʿayat ha-zehūt beyn ha-maskīlīm ha-ʿAraviyyīm bĕ-Israʾel', in Alouph Hareven (ed.), *Ehad mi-kol shīshsha Isrĕʾelīm* (Jerusalem: Van Leer Institute, 1981), 170–4.

Misgav, Ḥayyīm, 'Ezraḥīm mĕnūkkarīm', *ha-Aretz*, 12 Mar. 1991, B4.

Mishʿal, Nissīm, 'RAQAḤ hitslīḥa litsōr lĕ-ʿatsma tadmīt shel miflaga ʿAravīt', *ha-Tsōfeh*, 23 June 1972, Suppl., 2.

Moreh, Shmuel, 'ha-Sifrūt ba-safa ha-ʿAravīt bi-Mĕdīnat Israʾel', *ha-Mizraḥ he-Ḥadash*, 9/33–4 (1958), 26–38.

Muʿallim, Mazzal, 'Noṣrat—mĕnassīm lĕhatstsīl et ha-dū-qiyyūm', *Maʿarīv*, 25 May 1990, B2.

Mūsà, Diyāb Maḥmūd, 'Shĕʿat heshbōn ha-nefesh lĕ-ʿArviyyey Israʾel', *ha-Aretz*, 27 Oct. 1990, 9.

Nāshif, Hāshim, 'Hishtallĕvūt ha-ōkhlūṣiyya bĕ-Mizraḥ Yĕrūshalayim bĕ-misgeret ha-bīttūaḥ ha-lĕʾūmī', *Bīttūaḥ Lĕʾūmī*, 2 (Dec. 1971), 95–9.

Nĕhōraʾī, Yaʾīr, 'Eretz Israʾel ha-shĕlema, tsad beyt', *Yĕrūshalayim*, 19 Jan. 1990, 8–10.

Ōlīva, Yĕhūda, 'ha-Dĕrūzīm bĕ-Isra'el—be'ayat zehūt 'atsmīt wĕ-hishtayyĕkhūt pōlīṭīt', *Mĕdīna w-Mimshal*, 2/1 (1972), 98–109.

Oppenheimer, Yōnatan, 'ha-Dĕrūzīm be-Isra'el ka-'Aravīm w-khĕ-lo' 'Aravīm', *Maḥabarot lĕ-Meḥqar w-lĕ-Viqqoret*, 3 (Dec. 1979), 41–58.

Ōsetskī, Sara, and Ghānim, As'ad, 'Nittūaḥ tōtse'ōt ha-bĕḥīrōt la-histadrūt ba-migzar ha-'Aravī', *Sĕqīrōt 'al 'Arviyyey Isra'el*, 1 (18 Mar. 1990), 1–18.

Peled, Matityahū, 'Ma'amad ha-mī'ūṭ ha-'Aravī bĕ-Isra'el', *Ma'arīv*, 1 Aug. 1975, 20.

Peleg, Avraham, 'ha-Im atta mūkhan lĕhityadded 'im Aravī?', *Ma'arīv*, 3 Sept. 1971, 16.

Peres, Yochanan, and Davis, Nira, ''Al zehūtō ha-lĕ'ūmīt shel ha-'Aravī ha-Isrĕ'elī', *ha-Mizraḥ he-Ḥadash*, 18/1–2 (1968), 6–13.

Perī, Smadar, '38 reshūyōt 'Araviyyōt—90 milyōn sheqel gera'ōn', *Yĕdī'ōt Aharōnōt*, 27 Feb. 1990, 7.

Qanāzi', George, 'Be'ayat ha-zehūt ba-sifrūt shel 'Arviyyey Isra'el', in Alouph Hareven (ed.), *Eḥad mi-kol shishsha Isrĕ'elīm* (Jerusalem: Van Leer Institute, 1981), 149–69.

—— 'Yĕsōdōt idey'ōlōgiyyīm ba-sifrūt ha-'Aravīt bĕ-Isra'el', *ha-Mizraḥ he-Ḥadash*, 32/125–8 (1989), 129–38.

Qayman, Charles, 'Aḥarey ha-asōn: ha-'Aravīm bi-Mĕdīnat Isra'el 1948–1950', *Maḥbarōt lĕ-Meḥqar w-lĕ-vikkōret*, 10 (10 Dec. 1984).

Qeydar, Yōkhī, and Qisṭer, Yōsef, 'Ma kō'ev la-sṭūdenṭīm ha-Dĕrūzīm mi-Dāliyat al-Karmil', *Mar'ōt*, 20 Apr. 1971, 3.

Qōl, Mōshe, 'Pĕraqīm mi-yōman mĕdīnī', *Tĕmūrōt*, 9 (June 1976), 3–4.

Rabīnōvīts, Danī, 'Ḥalōm shel shĕnayim 'al tsela' ha-har', *ha-Aretz*, 9 Aug. 1991, B2.

Reiter, Itzhak, 'ha-Miflaga ha-Demōqraṭīt ha-'Aravīt w-mĕqōma ba-ōryenṭatsiyya shel 'Arviyyey Isra'el', in J. M. Landau (ed.), *ha-Migzar ha-'Aravī bĕ-Isra'el wĕ-ha-bĕḥīrōt la-Knesset, 1988* (Jerusalem: Mĕkhōn Yĕrūshalayim lĕ-Ḥeqer Isra'el, 1989), 63–84.

Rekhess, Elie, 'ha-'Aravīm bĕ-Isra'el wĕ-'Arviyyey ha-Shĕṭaḥīm: zīqqa pōlīṭīt wĕ-sōlīdariyyūt lĕ'ūmit 1967–1988', *ha-Mizraḥ he-Ḥadash*, 32/125–8 (1989), 165–91.

Rimāl, S., 'La-Dĕrūzīm dĕrūshim merkĕzey ḥinnūkh tīkhōn', *ha-Aretz*, 4 Sept. 1970, 17.

Ringel-Hofman, Ariela, 'ha-Intifāḍa zōḥelet la-Galīl', *Yĕdī'ōt Aharōnōt*, 28 July 1989, Suppl., 8–11.

—— 'ha-Islām kĕvar kān', *Yĕdī'ōt Aharōnōt*, 2 Mar. 1990, Suppl., 18–20.

—— 'Bĕ-Noṣrat 'Illīt mĕdabbĕrīm 'al kĕvīsh 'ōqef Noṣrat', *Yĕdī'ōt Aharōnōt*, 9 Oct. 1990, 12–13.

Rōn, Lī'at, 'Mūkhan lalekhet 'al arba', raq tĕnū lī liḥyōt', *Ma'arīv*, 28 Aug. 1991, C3.

Rosenblum, Dōrōn, 'Ma beyn RAQAḤ lĕ-MAQĪ', *Davar*, 2 Oct. 1969.

Rosenblum, 'Īrīt, 'Kenes ḥeyrum s̲h̲el ha-ʿeda ha-Dĕrūzīt hitrīʿa neged ha-kavana lĕhas̲h̲'ōt et Rafīq Ḥalabī', *ha-Aretz*, 9 Dec. 1990, A4.

Rosenfeld, Henry, 'ha-Pōʿel ha-ʿAravī ha-navvad', *Dū-S̲h̲avūʿōn ha-Ūnīversīṭa* (Jerusalem), 8 (8 Feb. 1970), 1, 4.

—— 'S̲h̲innūy, maḥasōmīm lĕ-s̲h̲īnnūy wĕ-niggūdīm ba-mis̲h̲paḥa ha-kafrīt', in Aharon Layish (ed.), *ha-ʿAravīm bĕ-Israʾel: rĕtsīfūt w-tĕmūra* (Jerusalem: Magnes Press, 1981), 76–103.

Rubinstein, Amnon, '"Arviyyey Israʾel: gīs̲h̲a mĕtsīʾūtīt', *Kalkala wĕ-Ḥevra*, June 1966, 29–31.

Rubinstein, Danī, 'ha-Ballōnīm matsīgīm et ha-hōweh he-ḥas̲h̲ūk̲h̲', *Davar*, 30 Nov. 1972, 7.

—— 'Simḥat ha-gĕvūra wĕ-ha-tsĕlīḥa', *Davar*, 24 Mar. 1974, 7.

—— 'Kĕvar lōʾ mak̲h̲nīsīm ōrḥīm', *ha-Aretz*, 7 Sept. 1990, B5.

—— 'Noṣrat liqrāt tĕlat-qiyyūm', *ha-Aretz*, 29 Nov. 1990, 2.

—— '"Ittōn Isrĕʾelī mĕʾōd', *ha-Aretz*, 4 Jan. 1991, 13–14.

—— 'Lōʾ lĕ-s̲h̲erūt lĕʾūmī', *ha-Aretz*, 10 Jan. 1991, B1.

—— 'Jihād lĕ-ḥillōnīm', *ha-Aretz*, 4 Mar. 1991, B3.

Ṣarṣūr, Saʿd, 'Ḥinnūk̲h̲ ʿAravī bi-mĕdīnah Yĕhūdīt', in Alouph Hareven (ed.), *Eḥad mi-kol s̲h̲ishsha Isrĕʾelīm: Yaḥasey gōmĕlīn beyn ha-mīʿūṭ ha-ʿAravī wĕ-ha-rōv ha-Yĕhūdī bĕ-Israʾel* (Jerusalem: Van Leer Institute, 1981), 113–31.

Schiff, Zeʾev, 'Dĕrūzīm s̲h̲enaflū bĕ-s̲h̲ūrōt Tsahal', *ha-Aretz*, 28 May 1970, 15.

—— 'Pĕʿūlōt ha-s̲h̲īn-beyt ba-ūnīversīṭaʾōt', *ha-Aretz*, 22 Jan. 1971, 9.

Schmelz, ʿUziel, 'ha-Mivneh ha-demōgrafī s̲h̲el ha-ʿAravīm wĕ-ha-Dĕrūzīm bĕ-Israʾel', *ha-Mizraḥ he-Ḥadas̲h̲*, 28/111–12 (1979), 244–54.

—— 'ha-Tifrōset ha-merḥavīt s̲h̲el ha-ʿAravīm wĕ-ha-Dĕrūzīm bĕ-Israʾel w-mĕʾafyĕney yis̲h̲shūveyhem', *ha-Mizraḥ he-Ḥadas̲h̲*, 29/113–16 (1980), 100–13.

—— 'Kōaḥ ha-ʿavōda', in Aharon Layish (ed.), *ha-ʿAravīm bĕ-Israʾel: rĕtsīfūt w-tĕmūra* (Jerusalem: Magnes Press, 1981), 46–75.

—— 'ha-Tĕnūʿa ha-ṭivʿīt wĕ-gīddūl ha-ōk̲h̲lūsiyya', in Aharon Layish (ed.), *ha-ʿAravīm bĕ-Israʾel: rĕtsīfūt w-tĕmūra* (Jerusalem: Magnes Press, 1981), 11–45.

Seligson, M. A., and Caspi, Dan, 'Iyyūm, motsaʾ ʿadatī wĕ-haskala—sōvlanūt kĕlapey ha-ḥerūyōt ha-ezraḥiyyōt s̲h̲el ha-mīʿūṭ ha-ʿAravī bĕ-Israʾel', *Kīwwūnīm*, 15 (May 1982), 37–53.

S̲h̲ābi, Avīva, 'Memshala ba-derek̲h̲', *Yĕdīʿōt Aḥarōnōt*, 25 Dec. 1987, Suppl., 6, 28.

—— 'Puṭṭar bi-gĕlal s̲h̲īr', *Yĕdīʿōt Aḥarōnōt*, 8 June 1990, Suppl., 49–50.

—— 'Me-ʿōleh lĕ-ʿōleh asōnenū ʿōleh', *Yĕdīʿōt Aḥarōnōt*, 23 Nov. 1990, 6–7.

Shaḥar, Rōn, 'Dū-qiyyūm bĕ-avīrat haqtsana', *ha-Aretz*, 3 Jan. 1991, B4.

Shapira, Bōʿaz, 'ha-Intifāda ha-riʾshōna', *ha-Aretz*, 29 Mar. 1991, B7.

Shĕḥōrī, Īlan, "Arviyyey Yāfō 1981: hitʾargĕnūt lĕʾūmanīt', *ha-Aretz*, 28 May 1981, 11.

Shībī, Ḥayyīm, 'Sarbanīm ba-dam', *Yĕdīʿōt Aḥarōnōt*, 18 May 1990, Suppl., 18.

Shīdlōwsky, Binyamīn, 'Tĕmūrōt bĕ-fīttūaḥ ha-kĕfar ha-ʿAravī bĕ-Israʾel', *ha-Mizraḥ he-Ḥadash*, 15/57–8 (1965), 25–37.

Shōḥaṭ, Nīr, 'ha-Hagīga ha-mĕshūttefet li-khĕvōd shĕnat ha-lashōn ha-ʿIvrīt wĕ-ha-lashōn ha-ʿAravīt', *Mifgash*, 13–14 (Summer–Autumn 1990), 108–21.

'Sīḥa bĕ-veyt Abū Nimr', *Kōteret Raʾshīt*, 277 (23 Mar. 1988), 18.

Smooha, Sammy, "Aravīm wĕ-Yĕhūdīm bĕ-Israʾel—yaḥasey mīʿūṭ wĕ-rōv', *Mĕgammōt*, 22 (Sept. 1976), 397–423.

—— 'Mĕdīniyyūt qayyemet wĕ-alṭernaṭīvīt kĕlappey ha-ʿAravīm bĕ-Israʾel', *Mĕgammōt*, 26/1 (Sept. 1980), 7–36.

—— 'Hashwaʾa beyn ha-Palesṭīnīm ba-Shĕṭaḥīm w-vĕ-Israʾel kĕ-mivḥan lĕ-tezat ha-sīppūaḥ ha-zōḥel ha-lōʾ-hafīkh', in Arnon Soffer (ed.), *ʿEsrīm shana lĕ-milḥemet sheshet ha-yamīm = ʿIyyūnīm bĕ-Ḥeqer ha-Mizraḥ ha-tīkhōn*, NS 7 (June 1987), 37–56.

Snīr, Rĕʾūven, 'Petsaʿ eḥad mi-pĕtsaʿav—ha-sifrūt ha-ʿAravīt ha-Palesṭīnīt bĕ-Israʾel', *Alpayim*, 2 (1990), 244–68.

Soffer, Arnon, 'Yĕḥasīm mishtannīm shel rōv w-mīʿūṭ w-vittūyam ha-merḥavī—ha-miqreh shel ʿArviyyey Israʾel', *Ōfaqīm bĕ-Geyʾografiya*, 9–10 (1984), 69–80.

—— "Arviyyey Israʾel, mi-kĕfar lĕ-meṭrōpōlīn w-ma halʾa?', *ha-Mizraḥ he-Ḥadash*, 32/125–8 (1989), 97–105.

Sṭendel, Ōrī, 'Mĕgammōt ha-hatsbaʿa la-Knesset ha-ʿasīrīt bĕ-qerev ʿArviyyey Israʾel', *ha-Mizraḥ he-Ḥadash*, 30/117–20 (1981), 138–48.

—— 'Zĕkhūt ha-shōnī shel ʿArviyyey Israʾel—heybeṭīm mishpaṭiyyīm', *ha-Mizraḥ he-Ḥadash*, 32/125–8 (1989), 192–207.

Sufyān, Kahbā, 'Sīsmat ha-shiwyōn nōtĕra kĕ-shehayta', *ha-Aretz*, 10 Oct. 1990, 47.

Ṭal, Yeraḥ, 'Mōkhĕrīm et ha-kĕnesiyya', *ha-Aretz*, 24 Dec. 1990, B3.

—— 'ha-Dĕrūzīm mūflīm lamrōt ha-sherūt ha-tsĕvaʾī', *ha-Aretz*, 26 Dec. 1990, A2.

—— 'ha-Paʿar yigdal, ha-tsĕfīfūt tigbar', *ha-Aretz*, 2 Jan. 1991, B3.

Thōn, Ūrī, 'ha-Ḥinnūkh ba-ʿeda ha-Dĕrūzīt', *ha-Aretz*, 14 Aug. 1990, 17.

Toledano, Sh., "Arviyyey Israel: haʿarakhōt shenitbaddū', *ha-Aretz*, 4 Sept. 1981, 14.

—— 'Mashmaʿūt ha-hatsbaʿa ha-ʿAravīt', *ha-Aretz*, 7 Sept. 1981, 9.

Tsimḥōnī, Daphne, 'ha-Maʿarakh ha-pōlīṭī shel ha-Nōtsrīm bĕ-Israʾel', *ha-Mizraḥ he-Ḥadash*, 32/125–8 (1989), 139–64.

Ṭūbī, Tawfīq, 'Liqrāt ha-bĕḥīrōt la-rĕshūyōt ha-mĕqōmiyyōt', *ʿAraḵhīm*, 69 (Feb. 1982), 12–35.

Winter, Michael, 'Beʿayōt yĕsōd bĕ-maʿareḵhet ha-ḥinnūḵh', in Aharon Layish (ed.), *ha-ʿAravīm be-Israʾel: rĕtsīfūt w-tĕmūra* (Jerusalem: Magnes Press, 1981), 168–79.

'Yaḥasey Yĕhūdīm wa-ʿAravīm bĕ-Yĕrūshalayim', *Dappey Meydaʿ* (Jerusalem), 1970, 21–6.

Yĕrūshalmī, Shalōm, 'Nigrarīm la-qalpey', *Kol ha-ʿĪr*, 17 Nov. 1989, 14–16.

Yinon, Avraham, 'Kamma nōsʾey mōqed ba-sifrūt shel ʿArviyyey Israʾel', *ha-Mizraḥ he-Ḥadash*, 15/57–8 (1965), 57–84.

Zaḵh, Natan, "Al reqaʿ tsaʿaqat ha-yamīm ha-ṭĕrūfīm', *Pōlīṭīqa*, 21 (June 1988), 51–6.

Zayd, Qāsim, 'Hasīrū et ha-tawīt', *ha-Aretz*, 25 July 1971, B4.

3. Other Languages

(a) Books

Arian, Alan (ed.), *The Elections in Israel—1969* (Jerusalem: Academic Press, 1972).

Arian, Asher (ed.), *The Elections in Israel—1973* (Jerusalem: Academic Press, 1975).

—— (ed.), *The Elections in Israel—1977* (Jerusalem: Academic Press, 1980).

—— and Shamir, M. (eds.), *Elections in Israel—1984* (New Brunswick, NJ: Transaction Books, 1986).

Ansprenger, Franz, *Juden und Araber in Einem Land* (Munich: Kaiser Verlag, 1978).

Ashkenassi, Abraham, *Opinion Trends among Jerusalem Palestinians* (Jerusalem: Leonard Davis Institute for International Relations, 1990).

Barkovskiy, L. A., *Arabskoye nasyelyeniye Izrailya* (Moscow: Nauka Press, 1988).

Ben-Dor, Gabriel, *The Druzes in Israel: A Political Study* (Jerusalem: Magnes Press, 1979).

Ben-Porat, Yoram, *The Arab Labor Force in Israel* (Jerusalem: Falk Institute for Economic Research, 1966).

Bensimon, D., and Errera, E., *Israël et ses populations* (Paris: Éditions Complexes, 1977).

Betts, R. B., *The Druze* (New Haven, Conn.: Yale University Press, 1988).

Blanc, Haim, *The Arabic Dialect of the Negev Bedouin* (Jerusalem: Israel Academy of Sciences and Humanities, 1970).

Caplan, Gerald, *Arab and Jew in Jerusalem* (Cambridge, Mass.: Harvard University Press, 1980).

Caspi, Dan, Diskin, Abraham, and Gutmann, Emanuel (eds.), *The Roots of Begin's Success: The 1981 Israeli Elections* (London: Croom Helm, and New York: St Martin's Press, 1984).

Cohen, Abner, *Arab Border-Villages in Israel* (Manchester: Manchester University Press, 1965).

Cohen, Erik, *Integration vs. Separation in the Planning of a Mixed Jewish–Arab City in Israel* (Jerusalem: Levy Eshkol Institute, 1973).

Czudnowski, Moshe, M., and Landau, Jacob M., *The Israeli Communist Party and the Elections for the Fifth Knesset, 1961* (Stanford, Calif.: Hoover Institution, 1965).

Ecumenical Theological Research Fraternity in Israel, *Christians in Israel and the Yom Kippur War* (Jerusalem: n.d. [1974]).

Eisenstadt, S. N., and Peres, Y., *Some Problems of Educating a National Minority* (Jerusalem: Hebrew University, 1968).

Elazar, Daniel J., and Sandler, Shmuel (eds.), *Israel's Odd Couple: The 1984 Knesset Elections and the National Unity Government* (Detroit: Wayne State University Press, 1990).

Freedman, Robert, O. (ed.), *Israel in the Begin Era* (New York: Praeger, 1982).

Ginat, Joseph, *Women in Muslim Rural Society: Status and Role in Family and Community* (New Brunswick, NJ: Transaction Books, 1982).

Greilshammer, Alain, *Les Communistes israéliens* (Paris: Fondation Nationale des Sciences Politiques, 1978).

Haidar, Aziz, *The Arab Population in the Israeli Economy* (Tel-Aviv: International Centre for Peace in the Middle East, 1990).

al-Haj, Majid, *Social Change and Family Processes: Arab Communities in Shefar-A'm* (Boulder, Colo., and London: Westview Press, 1987).

—— and Rosenfeld, Henry, *Arab Local Government in Israel* (Tel-Aviv: International Centre for Peace in the Middle East, 1988).

Harari, Yechiel, *The Arabs in Israel 1973: Statistics and Facts* (Givat Haviva: Centre for Arab and Afro-Asian Studies, 1974).

—— *The Arabs in Israel 1975–1976* (Givat Haviva: Arab and Afro-Asian Monograph Studies, 1977).

Hofman, John, et al., *Arab–Jewish Relations in Israel* (Bristol, Ind.: Wyndham Hall Press, 1988).

Jeraisi, Sami, *Reflections on Problems of Arab Youth* (Givat Haviva: Centre for Arab and Afro-Asian Studies, n.d.).

Kanaana, Sharif, *Channels of Communication and Mutual Images between the West Bank and Areas in Israel* (Bir-Zeit: Bir-Zeit University Publications, 1976).

—— *Socio-Cultural and Psychological Adjustment of the Arab Minority in Israel* (San Francisco: R and E Research Associates, 1976).

Karasova, T. A., *Blok Maarakh v partiyno-politichyeskiy sistyeme Izrailya* (Moscow: Nauka Press, 1983).

Kark, Ruth (ed.), *The Land that Became Israel: Studies in Historical Geography* (Jerusalem: Magnes Press, 1989).

Krajzman, Maurice, *La Minorité arabe en Israël* (Brussels: Centre National des Hautes Etudes Juives, 1968).

Kretzmer, David, *The Legal Status of the Arab in Israel* (Tel-Aviv: International Centre for Peace in the Middle East, 1987).

Landau, Jacob M., *The Arabs in Israel: A Political Study* (London: Oxford University Press, 1969).

—— *The Arabs and the Histadrut* (Tel-Aviv: Department of Higher Education—Histadrut, 1976).

—— *The Politics of Pan-Islam: Ideology and Organization* (Oxford: Oxford University Press, 1990).

—— Özbudun, Ergun, and Tachau, Frank, (eds.), *Electoral Politics in the Middle East: Issues, Voters and Élites* (London: Croom Helm, and Stanford, Calif.: Hoover Institution Press, 1980).

Lehman-Wilzig, Sam, *Stiff-Necked People, Bottle-Necked System: The Evaluation of Roots of Israeli Public Protest, 1946–1986* (Bloomington, Ind.: Indiana University Press, 1991), ch. 4.

Lustick, Ian, *Arabs in the Jewish State: Israel's Control of A National Minority* (Austin, Tex.: University of Texas Press, 1980).

McLaurin, R. D. (ed.), *The Political Role of Minority Groups in the Middle East* (New York: Praeger, 1979).

Maʿoz, Moshe (ed.), *Palestinian Arab Politics* (Jerusalem: Truman Institute Studies, 1975).

Marʿi, S. Kh., *Arab Education in Israel* (Syracuse, NY: Syracuse University Press, 1978).

Marx, Emanuel, *Bedouin of the Negev* (Manchester: Manchester University Press, 1967).

Penniman, Howard R. (ed.), *Israel at the Polls: The Knesset Elections of 1977* (Washington, DC: American Enterprise Institute for Public Policy Research, 1979).

Ramras-Rauch, Gila, *The Arab in Israeli Literature* (Bloomington, Ind.: Indiana University Press, 1989).

Rekhess, Elie, *A Survey of Israeli Arab Graduates from Institutions of Higher Learning in Israel (1961–1971)* (Tel-Aviv: Tel-Aviv University and the American Jewish Committee, 1974).

Relations Between Ethnic Majority and Minority (Tel-Aviv: International Centre for Peace in the Middle East, 1987).

Sayegh, Fayez A., *Discrimination in Education against the Arabs in Israel* (Beirut: Research Center, Palestine Liberation Organization, 1966).

Schweitzer, C. C., and Nemitz, M. (eds.), *Krisenherd Nah-Ost: Analysen–Wertungen–Dokumente* (Cologne: Markus Verlag, 1973).

Semyonov, Moshe, and Lewin-Esptein, Noah, *Hewers of Wood and Drawers of Water* (Ithaca, NY: ILP Press, 1987).

Simon, R. J., *Continuity and Change: A Study of Two Ethnic Communities in Israel* (Cambridge: Cambridge University Press, 1978).

Smooha, Sammy, *The Orientation and Politicization of the Arab Minority in Israel* (Haifa: Institute of Middle Eastern Studies, 1984).

—— *Arabs and Jews in Israel*, i (Boulder, Colo.: Westview Press, 1989).

Statistical Abstract of Israel, various years.

Stock, Ernest, *From Conflict to Understanding: Relations between Jews and Arabs in Israel since 1948* (New York: Institute of Human Relations Press, 1968).

Tessler, Mark, *Arabs in Israel* (Hanover, NH: American Universities Field Staff, 1980).

Toledano, Sh., *Jewish–Arab Relations during the Yom Kippur War* (Jerusalem: Martin Buber Education Centre, 1974).

Weigert, Gideon, *Israel's Presence in East Jerusalem* (Jerusalem: 1973).

Wild, Stefan, *Ghassan Kanafani: The Life of a Palestinian* (Wiesbaden: Harrassowitz, 1975).

Zureik, E. T., *The Palestinians in Israel: A Study in Internal Colonialism* (London: Routledge and Kegan Paul, 1979).

Zogby, James J., *Perspectives on Palestinian Arabs and Israeli Jews* (Wilmette, Ill.: Medina Press, 1977).

(b) Articles and Unpublished Studies

Abu-Gosh, Subhi, 'The Election Campaign in the Arab Sector', in Alan Arian (ed.), *The Elections in Israel—1969* (Jerusalem: Academic Press, 1972), 239–52.

'All We Want Is to Be Treated as Equals', *Jerusalem Post*, 26 June 1987, 5.

Anne, Joyce, 'Interview with Tawfiq Zayyad', *American Arab Affairs*, 25 (Summer 1988), 48–54.

Angst, Doris, 'Arabs in Israel: In Search of Identity', *Swiss Review of World Affairs* (Zurich), 33/1 (Apr. 1983), 14–19.

Arian, Asher, 'Voting Behaviour: Israel', in J. M. Landau, E. Özbudun, and Frank Tachau (eds.), *Electoral Politics in the Middle East: Issues, Voters and Elites* (London: Croom Helm, 1980), 173–84.

—— 'The 1988 Israeli Elections—Questions of Identity', *Jerusalem Letter/ Viewpoints*, 83 (15 Jan. 1989), 1–6.

El-Asmar, Fauzi, 'The Portrayal of Arabs in Hebrew Children's Literature', *Journal of Palestine Studies*, 16/1 (Autumn 1986), 81–94.

Baransi, Saleh, 'All This Time We Were Alone', *Merip Reports*, 96 (May 1981), 16–23.

Bayadsi, Mahmud, 'The Arab Local Authorities: Achievements and Problems', *New Outlook* (Tel-Aviv), 18/160 (Oct.–Nov. 1975), 58–61.

Be'er, Yizhar, 'Empty Shoes in the Sand: Israel's Arabs Take Stock', *New Outlook*, 34/314–15 (April–May 1991), 31–3.

Beinin, Joel, 'From Land Day to Equality Day', *Middle East Report*,

Jan.–Feb. 1988, 24–7.

Ben-Adi, H., 'Doctors to the Bedouin', *Jerusalem Post Magazine*, 17 July 1970, 5.

Ben-David, Joseph, 'The Negev Bedouin: From Nomadism to Agriculture', in Ruth Kark (ed.), *The Land That Became Israel: Studies in Historical Geography* (Jerusalem: Magnes Press, 1989), 181–95.

Ben-Dor, Gabriel, 'Electoral Politics and Ethnic Polarization: Israeli Arabs in the 1977 Elections', in Asher Arian (ed.), *The Elections in Israel— 1977* (Jerusalem: Academic Press, 1980), 171–85.

Brinner, William M., 'The Arabs of Israel: The Past Twenty Years', *Middle East Review*, 20/1 (Fall 1987), 13–21.

Coone, Tim, 'Strangers in the State', *Middle East*, 67 (May 1980), 36–8.

Darawshe, Abdel Wahab, 'The Intifada and Israeli Arabs', *New Outlook*, 32/297–8 (Nov.–Dec. 1989), 30–1.

Dunsky, Marda, 'A New Reality Sparks New Fears', *Jerusalem Post*, 10 Mar. 1989, Suppl., 9.

Franchon, Alain, 'La Mort lente des chrétiens de Jérusalem', *Le Monde*, 25 Dec. 1990, 1, 4.

Frankel, Oz, 'Living with Fundamentalism', *Jerusalem Post*, 10 Mar. 1989, 9.

Friedler, Ya'acov, 'Israeli Arabs Are Strongly Committed to Democracy', *Jerusalem Post*, 1 June 1986, 4.

Frisch, Hillel, 'Between Instrumentalism and Separation: The Arab Vote in the 1984 Knesset Elections', in Daniel J. Elazar and Shmuel Sandler (eds.), *Israel's Odd Couple: The 1984 Knesset Elections and the National Unity Government* (Detroit: Wayne State University Press, 1990), 119–34.

García, Sandra Anderson, 'Israeli Arabs: Partners in Pluralism or Ticking Time Bomb?', *Ethnicity*, 7 (1980), 15–26.

Geffner, Ellen, 'An Israeli Arab View of Israel', *Jewish Social Studies*, 36/2 (Apr. 1974), 134–41.

Ginat, Joseph, 'Israeli Arabs: Some Recent Social and Political Trends', *Asian and African Studies*, 23/2–3 (Nov. 1989), 183–204.

Goell, Yosef, 'Demolition Disorders', *Jerusalem Post*, 20 Dec. 1985, 5–6.

—— 'Histadrut's Failure in the Arab Sector', *Jerusalem Post*, 30 Jan. 1987, 16.

—— 'True Unions', *Jerusalem Post*, 6 Feb. 1987, 10.

Gradstein, Linda, 'Just a Little In-Between', *Jerusalem Post*, 15 July 1987, 5.

Graham-Brown, Sarah, 'The Poetry of Survival', *Middle East*, 122 (Dec. 1984), 43–4.

Gutmann, Emanuel, 'Parliamentary Elites: Israel', in J. M. Landau, E. Özbudun, and Frank Tachau (eds.), *Electoral Politics in the Middle East: Issues, Voters and Elites* (London: Croom Helm, 1980), 273–97.

Haddad, Suhaila, McLaurin, R. D., and Nakhleh, Emile A., 'Minorities in Containment: The Arabs of Israel', in R. D. McLaurin (ed.), *The Political Role of Minority Groups in the Middle East* (New York: Praeger, 1979), 76–108.

al-Haj, Majid, 'Standing on the Green Line', *Israeli Democracy*, Winter 1988, 39–41.

—— and Rosenfeld, Henry, 'The Emergence of an Indigenous Political Framework in Israel: The National Committee of Chairmen of Arab Local Authorities', *Asian and African Studies*, 23/2–3 (Nov. 1989), 205–44.

Hofman, John E., 'Social Identity and the Readiness for Social Relations between Jews and Arabs in Israel', *Human Relations*, 35/9 (1982), 727–41.

'Israel: Erfolg der Kommunisten bei Gewerkschaftswahlen', *Informations Bulletin: Materialen und Dokumente kommunistischer und Arbeiterparteien*, 19 (1969), 950–1.

Israeli, R., 'Arabs in Israel: The Surge of a New Identity', *Plural Societies*, 11/4 (Winter 1980), 21–9.

Kaye, Helen, 'Beit Hagefen's 25 Years of Activity', *Jerusalem Post*, 18 Jan. 1991, 11.

Kenan, Amos, 'Communication between Jewish and Arab Writers', *New Outlook*, 14/120 (Jan.–Feb. 1971), 19–21.

Khleif, Baheej, *et al.*, 'The Arab–Israeli Encounter', *Sociologia Internationalis*, 9 (1971), 167–78.

Kislev, Ran, 'Land Expropriation: History of Oppression', *New Outlook*, 19/169 (Sept.–Oct. 1976), 23–32.

Kohansky, Mendel, 'An Israeli Arab's Coexistence', *Jerusalem Post Magazine*, 17 July 1970, 16.

Kraus, Vered, 'The Opportunity Structure of Young Israeli Arabs', in John Hofman *et al.*, *Arab–Jewish Relations in Israel* (Bristol, Ind.: Wyndham Hall Press, 1988), 67–91.

Landau, Jacob M., 'A Note on the Leadership of the Israeli Arabs', *Il Politico* (Pavia), 27/3 (1962), 625–35.

—— 'The Arab Vote', in Alan Arian (ed.), *The Elections in Israel—1969* (Jerusalem: Academic Press, 1972), 253–63.

—— 'Electoral Issues: Israel', in J. M. Landau, E. Özbudun, and Frank Tachau (eds.), *Electoral Politics in the Middle East: Issues, Voters and Elites* (London: Croom Helm, 1980), 69–91.

—— 'The Arab Vote', in D. Caspi, A. Diskin, and E. Gutmann (eds.), *The Roots of Begin's Success: The 1981 Israeli Elections* (London: Croom Helm, 1984), 169–89.

—— 'Hebrew and Arabic in the State of Israel: Political Aspects of the Language Issue', *International Journal of the Sociology of Language*, 67 (1987), 117–33.

Lennon, David, 'Israel's Unwilling Arabs', *Middle East International*, 120 (14 Mar. 1990), 7–8.

Lustick, Ian, 'Zionism and the State of Israel: Regime Objectives of the Arab Minority in the First Years of Statehood', *Middle Eastern Studies*, 16/1 (Jan. 1980), 127–46.

—— 'Israel's Arab Minority in the Begin Era', in Robert O. Freedman (ed.), *Israel in the Begin Era* (New York: Praeger, 1982), 121–50.

—— 'Creeping Binationalism within the Green Line', *New Outlook*, 31/283 (July 1988), 14–19.

Makhoul, Nejwa, 'Changes in the Employment Structure of Arabs in Israel', *Journal of Palestine Studies*, 11/3 (Spring 1982), 77–102.

Mar'i, Sami, 'Policy and Counter-Policy: The Status of Arab Education in Israel', in *Relations between Ethnic Majority and Minority* (Tel-Aviv: International Centre for Peace in the Middle East, 1987), 35–41.

Mar'i, Sami Khalil, 'Sources of Conflict in Arab–Jewish Relations in Israel', in John E. Hofman *et al.*, *Arab–Jewish Relations in Israel* (Bristol, Ind.: Wyndham Hall Press, 1988), 1–20.

—— and Levi, Avraham M., 'Modernization or Minority Status', *Journal of Cross-Cultural Psychology*, 10/3 (Sept. 1979), 375–89.

Mi'ari, Mahmoud, 'Traditionalism and Political Identity of Arabs in Israel', *Journal of Asian and African Studies*, 22/1–2 (1987), 33–44.

Moreh, Shmuel, 'Arabic Literature in Israel', *Middle Eastern Studies*, 3/3 (Apr. 1967), 283–94.

Moriel, Liora, 'Negev Bedouin: Don't Separate Us from Other Israeli Arabs', *Jerusalem Post*, 25 Oct. 1985, 3.

Nakhleh, E. A., 'Post-Israeli Election Polarizations and Changes', *Middle East Insight*, 3/6 (1984), 18–25.

Nakhleh, Khalil, 'Cultural Determinants of Palestinian Collective Identity: The Case of the Arabs in Israel', *New Outlook*, 18/160 (Oct.–Nov. 1975), 31–40.

'New Centre in Triangle', *Middle East*, 109 (Nov. 1983), 12.

Ochsenwald, W. L., 'Arab Muslims and the Palestine Problem', *Muslim World*, 56/4 (1976), 287–96.

'The Other Israelis: A MOMENT Interview', *Moment*, 7/4 (Apr. 1982), 11–17.

Peres, Yochanan, 'Modernization and Nationalism in the Identity of the Israeli Arabs', *Middle East Journal*, 24/4 (Autumn 1970), 479–92.

Peretz, Don, 'Israeli Jews and Arabs in the Ethnic Numbers Game', *Ethnicity*, 8 (1981), 233–55.

—— and Sammy Smooha, 'Israel's Tenth Knesset Elections—Ethnic Upsurgence and Decline of Ideology', *Middle East Journal*, 35/4 (Autumn 1981), 506–26.

Petreanu, Dan, 'Pragmatic Fighter for Arab Rights', *Jerusalem Post*, 20

May 1988, 6.

Regev, Avner, 'Israeli Arabs and Islam', *Israeli Democracy*, Spring 1991, 30–1.

Reiter, Yitzhak, 'Forming their Identity', *Israeli Democrary*, Fall 1989, 31–4.

Rekhess, Elie, 'Israeli Arab Intelligentsia', *Jerusalem Quarterly*, 11 (Spring 1979), 51–69.

—— 'Israeli Arabs and the Arabs of the West Bank and Gaza: Political Affinity and National Solidarity', *Asian and African Studies*, 23/2–3 (Nov. 1989), 119–54.

Robins, Edward, 'Attitudes, Stereotypes and Prejudices among Arabs and Jews in Israel', *New Outlook*, 15/136 (Nov.–Dec. 1972), 36–48.

Robins, Edward Alan, 'Pluralism in Israel: Relations between Arabs and Jews', Ph.D. dissertation, Tulane University, 1972.

Romann, Michael, 'Jews and Arabs in Jerusalem', *Jerusalem Quarterly*, 19 (Spring 1981), 23–46.

Rosenberg, Bernard, 'The Arabs of Israel', *Dissent*, 27 (Spring 1980), 161–71.

Rouhana, Nadim, 'Collective Identity and Arab Voting Patterns', in A. Arian and M. Shamir (eds.), *Elections in Israel—1984* (New Brunswick, NJ: Transaction Books, 1986), 121–49.

Rubinstein, Eliakim, 'The Lesser Parties', in Howard R. Penniman (ed.), *Israel at the Polls: The Knesset Elections of 1977* (Washington, DC: American Enterprise Institute for Public Policy Research, 1979), 193–5.

Rudge, .David, 'Close Encounters of Another Kind', *Jerusalem Post Magazine*, 20 Oct. 1988, 8.

Schölch, Alexander, 'Die Beziehungen den Palestinensern in Israel und auf dem Westufer seit 1967', *Orient*, 24/3 (Sept. 1983), 422–7.

Seliktar, Ofira, 'National Integration of a Minority in an Acute Conflict Situation: The Case of Israeli Arabs', *Plural Societies*, 12/3–4 (Autumn–Winter 1981), 25–40.

—— 'The Arabs in Israel: Some Observations on the Psychology of the System of Controls', *Journal of Conflict Resolution*, 28/2 (June 1984), 247–69.

Shamir, Michal, and Sullivan, John L., 'Jews and Arabs in Israel', *Journal of Conflict Resolution*, 29/2 (June 1985), 283–305.

Shokeid, Moshe, 'Strategy and Change in the Arab Vote: Observations in a Mixed City', in Asher Arian (ed.), *The Elections in Israel—1973* (Jerusalem: Academic Press, 1975), 145–66.

Slater, Julia, 'Palestinians in Israel: Who Are They?', *Middle East International*, 329 (8 July 1988), 16–17.

Smooha, Sammy, 'Control of Minorities in Israel and Northern Ireland',

Comparative Studies in History and Society, 22/2 (Apr. 1980), 256–80.

Smooha, Sammy, 'Jewish and Arab Ethnocentrism in Israel', *Ethnic and Racial Studies*, 10/1 (Jan. 1987), 1–26.

—— 'A Typology of Jewish Orientations toward the Arab Minority in Israel', *Asian and African Studies*, 23/2–3 (Nov. 1989), 155–82.

—— and Hofman, John E., 'Some Problems of Arab–Jewish Coexistence in Israel', *Middle East Review*, 9/2 (Winter 1976–7), 5–14.

—— and Peretz, Don, 'The Arabs in Israel', *Journal of Conflict Resolution*, 26/3 (Sept. 1982), 451–84.

Soffer, Arnon, 'Geographical Aspects of Change within the Arab Communities in Northern Israel', *Middle Eastern Studies*, 19/2 (Apr. 1983), 213–43.

Stendel, Ori, 'The Rise of New Political Currents in the Arab Sector in Israel, 1948–1974', in Moshe Ma'oz (ed.), *Palestinian Arab Politics* (Jerusalem: Truman Institute Studies, 1975), pp. 107–44.

Stock, Ernest, 'Israel—A Jewish Polity with a Multi-Ethnic Population', *Patterns of Prejudice* (Washington, DC), 15/4 (1981), 34–41.

Talhami, Ghada, 'Islamic Fundamentalism and the Palestinians', *Muslim World*, 78/3–4 (July–Oct. 1988), 173–88.

Tekiner, Roselle, 'On the Inequality of Israel's Citizens', *Without Prejudice*, 1/1 (Fall 1987), 48–57.

Tessler, Mark A., 'Israel's Arabs and the Palestinian Problem', *Middle East Journal*, 31/3 (Summer 1977), 313–29.

—— 'The Identity of Religious Minorities in Non-Secular States: Jews in Tunisia and Morocco and Arabs in Israel', *Comparative Studies in History and Society*, 20/3 (July 1978), 359–73.

—— 'Secularism and Nationalism in the Israeli–Palestinian Conflict', *UFSI Reports*, 9 (1982), Asia, pp. 1–12.

Toledano, Sh., 'Israel's Arabs—A Unique National Minority', *International Problems* (Tel-Aviv), 12/23 (June 1973), 39–43.

Tsimhoni, Daphne, 'Continuity and Change in Communal Autonomy: The Christian Communal Organization in Jerusalem 1948–80', *Middle Eastern Studies*, 22/3 (July 1986), 398–417.

Watad, Muhammad, 'Co-Existence', *New Outlook*, 13/117 (Sept.–Oct. 1970), 68–73.

Weigert, Gideon, 'Arab–Jewish Economic Cooperation in Israel', *Die Welt des Islams*, NS 8/4 (1963), 243–51.

—— 'Arabische Jugend in Ost-Jerusalem', in C. C. Schweitzer and M. Nemitz (eds.), *Krisenherd Nah-Ost: Analysen–Wertungen–Dokumente* (Cologne: Markus Verlag, 1973), 93–100.

'What Future for the Palestine Arabs?', *War and Peace* (New York), 10/6 (June–July 1970), 3–11.

Yishai, Yael, 'Challenge Groups in Israeli Politics', *Middle East Journal*,

35/4 (Autumn 1981), 544–56.

Zureik, Elia, 'Transformations of Clan Structure among the Arabs in Israel: From Peasantry to Proletariat', *Journal of Palestine Studies*, 6/1 (Autumn 1976), 39–66.

—— 'Crime, Justice and Underdevelopment: The Palestinians under Israeli Control', *International Journal of Middle East Studies*, 20/4 (Nov. 1988), 411–42.

INDEX

Frequently occurring terms, such as Arab minority, Arabs, Israel, Israelis, Middle East, or Palestine, have not been included. The definite article has not been considered in the alphabetical sequence.